W9-AJQ-121

Johnny Depp

A MODERN REBEL

Johnny Depp

A MODERN REBEL
Revised and Updated

Brian J. Robb

PLEXUS, LONDON

Text copyright © 1995, 2004, 2006 by Brian J. Robb
Copyright © 2004, 2006 by Plexus Publishing Limited
Published by Plexus Publishing Limited
25 Mallinson Road
London SW11 1BW
www.plexusbooks.com
First printing 2006

British Library Cataloguing in Publication Data
Robb, Brian J.
  Johnny Depp : a modern rebel. - 3rd ed.
  1. Depp, Johnny 2. Motion picture actors and
  actresses - United States - Biography
  I. Title
  791.4'3028'092

ISBN–10: 0–85965–385–4
ISBN–13: 978–0–85965–385-5

Cover design by Brian Flynn
Book design by Phil Smee
Printed in Spain by Bookprint S.L., Barcelona

Acknowledgements
A book such as this cannot be completed – especially
within the time – without the help, patience and
support of a lot of people.
   My love and thanks to my wife Brigid and son
Cameron for their patience with my working hours
and constant support.
   Gratitude is due to my team of speedy US
researchers, George Fergus and John Lavaille
(particularly for *21 Jump Street* material and tapes);
John Riley at BFI Information and Library services;
Mike Wingate at C&A Video in Edinburgh for access to
Depp movies and *The Searchers* for turning up some
of the early, more obscure stuff. For their assistance
thanks are due to Holly Millea of *Premiere*, whose
interview with Depp was invaluable; Tracey Jacobs,
Depp's agent at ICM and Simon Chambers of the
Storm model agency were also helpful.
   Other organisations and individuals who helped out
along the way (in ways too various to mention) were:
the Directors Guild of America; the American Film
Institute; Michelle Sewell; Buena Vista (at Cannes);
Simone Bendicaine (Cannes); Tracey Mosh and Pat
Kingsley at PMK; Kim Langley at Disney; Berlin Film
Festival; Cannes Film Festival; Edinburgh Film Festival;
the National Film Theatre (Terry Staples' programme
notes); at Scot-FM – Kirsty Stuart, Chris Mann, Iain
Agnew and Fiona Reid (*Scotland on Sunday*); Lara
Williamson (*Sky Magazine)*; Paul Cockburn; Wes
Craven; Bob Carmichael; everyone at *The Central
Times*, as well as everyone at the various film
production, distributors and publicists offices.
   I'd like to thank those who maintain the following
Internet sites for their (often unsung) research efforts:
Phil's Winona Ryder Page (Phil Anglin); Pathfinder
(Time/Warner); Yahoo Internet Search; the Cardiff
Movie Database and Demon Internet Services.
   I would like to thank the following magazines and
newspapers for their coverage of Johnny Depp over
the years: *Film Review; The List; Vox; GQ; Sky
Magazine; Esquire; Attitude; Entertainment Weekly;
Sight and Sound; Empire; Premiere* (US, UK and
French editions); *Village Voice; Film Threat; Fangoria;
Cinefantastique; Starlog; Interview; Vogue; American
Film; Time Out; What's On In London; The Face;
Rolling Stone; Hello!; Monthly Film Bulletin; Time;
TOTP Magazine; Movieline; Variety; New Yorker; TV
Guide; New Statesman and Society; Film Monthly;
Fear; Film Comment; Scotland on Sunday; The
Guardian; The Daily Record; The Mail on Sunday;
The Daily Mail; Sunday Telegraph; The Scotsman; The
Herald; Today; The Sunday Times; The Independent;
The Evening Standard; The Daily Telegraph; The
Edinburgh Evening News; The Sunday Express; The
Spectator; The Hampstead and Highgate Express; The
New York Times; The Observer* and *The Daily Express.*
   Grateful thanks to the following: All Action Pictures;
Robin Kennedy/All Action Pictures; Dean Cummings/
All Action Pictures; Alpha Photographic Press Agency;
Richard Chumbury/Alpha photographic Press Agency;
British Film Institute Stills Library; Brad Feirce/Katz
Pictures/Eyes; Karen Hardy/Katz Pictures/Outline Press;
People in Pictures; E.J. Comp/Retna; Philip Saltonstall/
Retna; Ronald Grant Archive; Range Everett; Andrew
Murray/Sygma; Sunset Boulevard/Sygma; Ron
Galella/Sygma; Alex Bailey/Sygma; Eric Robert/Sygma;
Alan Lewis/Sygma; Frank Trapper/Corbis Sygma; Eric
Gaillard/Reuters/Corbis; Lucy Nicholson/Reuters/
Corbis; Lisa O'Connor/ZUMA/Corbis; John
Spellman/Retna Ltd; Armando Gallo/Retna Ltd.
   Film stills courtesy of Twentieth Century Fox;
Paramount Pictures; Touchstone/Buena Vista
International/Disney; MGM; TriStar Pictures; Castles
Burning in association with MCA Pay TV programming
Inc; Hemdale Film Corporation; Stephen J Cannell
Productions Inc; Imagine Entertainment; New Line
Cinema; Constellation/UGC/Hachette Premiere; New
Line Productions for American Zoetrope; Cinefilm;
Majestic Films International; United International
Pictures; Pathé Distribution Ltd; Working Title; El Mar
Pictures; Miramax; Walt Disney Pictures; Columbia
Pictures Corporation.
   Finally, thanks to my publishers Sandra Wake and
Terry Porter, and to Nicky Adamson for her role as
editor, and special thanks to Phil Smee both for his
patience and creativity in designing this book.

Contents

INTRODUCTION

A Modern Rebel

Johnny Depp used to be a Hollywood outsider. Once seen by some as a modern rebel in the James Dean mode, Depp has grown-up considerably over the past decade. Now in his forties, he has left behind his rabble-rousing, hotel-wrecking, paparazzi-baiting tearaway image, and replaced it with that of a loving partner to French singer Vanessa Paradis and father to his two children, Lily-Rose and Jack.

It has been a most unexpected turnaround. He once avoided Hollywood blockbuster movies and pursued a relentlessly uncommercial series of roles, but having children has given Depp licence to take part in family-fare like *Pirates of the Caribbean*, its sequels and Tim Burton's *Charlie and the Chocolate Factory*. At the same time he's still pursuing his single-minded quest to play strange characters in strange ways, as shown by his Earl of Rochester in *The Libertine* or his as yet unrealised plan to play the totally paralysed Jean-Dominique Bauby in *The Diving Bell and the Butterfly*. With two critically-acclaimed, genuine blockbusters under his belt in *Sleepy Hollow* and *Pirates of the Caribbean*, Johnny Depp has been able to carve out a new life for himself in France with Paradis and his children, away from the press and the pressures of Hollywood which had so weighed on him previously.

Willing to pick and choose his roles, from the fulfilling and arty (*The Man Who Cried, Before Night Falls, Chocolat*) to the bank-balance boosting mainstream (*The Astronaut's Wife, Secret Window*), Depp is usually the best thing about any film he appears in. He can make a bad movie worth watching and he can bring something totally unique to a good project.

In 1995, Johnny Depp was a big star, an A-list name who'd made millions of dollars without ever starring in a genuinely successful box office movie. His image adorned the bedroom walls of millions of teenage girls the world over, but he continued to rail against the commodification of his image as he had done since his days as a teen heart-throb TV star on *21 Jump Street*. He turned down the lead role in countless mainstream success stories – *Speed, Legends of the Fall, Thelma & Louise, Robin Hood: Prince of Thieves* – in favour of quirkier fare like *Ed Wood, Don Juan DeMarco* and *Benny & Joon*.

In 2003, Depp surprised many by becoming an even bigger star, seemingly enjoying a second wind in his career via his unlikely scene-stealing turn as addled pirate captain Jack Sparrow in *Pirates of the Caribbean*. 'I only wanted to be in a movie that my kids could see,' said Depp of the choice. 'It was mentioned that they were considering a movie based on the *Pirates of the Caribbean* ride, and I said I was in. There was no screenplay, no director, nothing. For some unknown reason, I just said I was in.'

Depp found, in a movie he explicitly did for his kids, a way to combine the quirkiness of the off-kilter characters he'd played in the past (to limited commercial success) like Edward Scissorhands, Ed Wood, Sam in *Benny & Joon*, and even Raoul Duke in *Fear and Loathing in Las Vegas,* with a successful, mainstream movie. He'd pulled off the same trick as Ichabod Crane in *Sleepy Hollow* and as Agent Sands in *Once Upon A Time In Mexico*, but it was Jack Sparrow who stayed in the minds of audiences, kids and adults alike. 'I had never experienced that before,' Depp said. 'And it's been fun to visit Hollywood and talk to studios as a bankable actor for a change.'

Depp's personal life has seen equally dramatic changes over the past ten years. As his relationship with Kate Moss crumbled in the mid-to-late-1990s – over the issue of having children – Depp took up with French singer Vanessa Paradis. 'I pretty much fell in love with Vanessa the moment I set eyes on her,' claimed Depp. 'As a person, I was pretty much a lost cause at that time in my life. She turned all that around for me with her incredible tenderness and understanding.'

The pair rapidly had a family, with two kids, Lily-Rose and Jack, and bought houses in rural France, Paris and Los Angeles. The man who'd never settle down, who rented property rather then bought, was now happily playing the role of doting father and 'husband' (Paradis and Depp are not married, but both consider themselves to be husband-and-wife anyway).

'I love our house in the country,' said Depp of his new idyll. 'I can walk to the nearby village and have a coffee and no one pays any notice. I'm just another dad with my daughter on my knee. The time I've spent in France with Vanessa has solidified my belief that I can keep a major distance from Hollywood and still keep in the game. Acting is my living, but I don't want to live it. Living in France is the first time I can honestly say I feel at home.' It's an outcome any Johnny Depp fan leaving a cinema screening of *Nick of Time* in 1995 would have been very surprised by.

The one common factor to all that Depp does, on screen and off, is surprise. It's as if he keeps himself interested, in himself and in his career, by constantly surprising himself by his choices, in life and in movies. 'There's a drive in me that won't allow me to do certain things that are easy,' he admitted. 'I can weigh all the options, but there's always one thing that goes: "Johnny: this is the one." And it's always the most difficult – it's always the one that will cause the most trouble…'

While he may be bankable and a critical success, Johnny Depp has done it all on his own terms by tackling the roles he wants to play in his own unique way. 'All the amazing people that I've worked with – Marlon Brando, Al Pacino, Dustin Hoffman,' Depp said, 'have told me consistently: don't compromise. Do your work, and if what you're giving is not what they want, you have to be prepared to walk away.'

It is that combination of surprise and uncompromising desire to fight for his own uniquely skewed vision that has brought Johnny Depp to the pinnacle of his career – complete with a Screen Actors Guild award and Oscar nomination for

Pirates of the Caribbean. He shows no sign that this mainstream acclaim will in anyway deflect him from playing the Hollywood game his way. 'I've been around long enough to know that one week, you're on the exclusive list of guys who can open a movie,' said Depp, 'and then the next week, you're off the list. It's been a fun ride, and I'm enjoying it for all it's worth.'

This is the story of that rollercoaster ride, from Owensboro, Kentucky in 1963 to France in 2006 and beyond…

At the start of his career, Johnny Depp was not the obvious Hollywood heartthrob – with tattoos and spiked up hair he referred to himself as a 'catacomb dweller'.

CHAPTER ONE

Slow Burn

WHENEVER Johnny Depp expanded his repertoire of offbeat and oddball film characters, journalists writing magazine profiles would ask the actor about his childhood.

'I just didn't fit in anywhere,' Depp said of his childhood, filtering his real life into his 'reel' life through the misfit characters he played. In particular, his role in 1994 as Ed Wood seemed to have special echoes for him. 'Like him I also grew up feeling like an obtuse piece of machinery. It was the same feeling I had about Edward Scissorhands.'

Depp seemed to feel the need to reinvent his childhood in the light of each part he played, layering his fading memories with a fictional history created for his own screen roles. This was something more than just giving the journalists the copy they'd come to expect, the story they'd already written in their heads. It is, in fact, the first clue to the possibility that the Johnny Depp once paraded for public consumption – the wild living, wild loving, ever young rebel – was just another fictional creation by one of the world's most talented actors.

Born John Christopher Depp II in Owensboro, Kentucky, on June 9th 1963, Johnny Depp was the youngest of four children, with two older sisters, Debbie and Christi, and an older brother, Dan; two of the children from his mother's first marriage. His father, John Depp senior, was a public servant in Owensboro, working as a city engineer. His mother, Betty Sue, worked as a waitress in a local coffee house. 'Years and years I watched her wait tables. I'd count her change at the end of the night,' said Depp of his mother, the parent who made the most impact on him. 'She cursed like a sailor, played cards and smoked cigarettes.' The family were typical working class Americans, benefiting from the explosion in cheap tract housing first developed in the 1950s. They lived in a suburban town, had suburban lives and dreamed suburban dreams. It was the 1960s and post-war promises had come good. The American dream was realisable. If you worked nine to five, you could have the house and the car and the family, just like on the postcards and in the magazines. So it was for the Depp family.

All except for little Johnny. He felt a higher calling. His maternal grandfather was a full-blooded Cherokee, giving Depp the sharp cheekbones and sculptured visage that was to grace a thousand magazine covers the world over as he grew to maturity in the public gaze. Depp's family genes also meant he was part German and part Irish. As a youngster, he wanted to be true to his Indian heritage, playing a version of Cowboys and Indians, in which his Indian refused to die, no matter how many times his childhood friend Sal Jenco fired off his cap gun.

This fiercely independent spirit seemed to spill over into a larger problem with rules, regulations and authority figures that was to stay with Depp all his life, and was to be the source of many later conflicts. Try as they might, John and Betty Sue couldn't get young Johnny to play the nice suburban game. On one early occasion, Johnny was suspended from school for exposing his buttocks to a teacher as an act of defiance when ordered to do some mundane task.

'I was a weird kid,' Depp freely admitted. 'I wanted to be Bruce Lee, I wanted to be on a SWAT team. When I was five, I think I wanted to be Daniel Boone.' Depp kept lizards as pets, attempting to train them to follow his directions by tapping them on their heads. His earliest recalled childhood memory of his oldest Cherokee relative is also a little startling. 'My great-grandmother's toenails. I don't know why, but I can just remember seeing them. They were like cashews. She was about 102 when she died, and I was just a kid.'

As Depp grew up his interests changed. Music was a constant, though, and one of his first musical obsessions was with the band Kiss, for whom performance and image were almost as important as the music. His major real-life hero was stunt motorcyclist Evel Knievel, who in the 1970s was wowing audiences the world over with his feats of daring, jumping over rows of vehicles on his especially designed star spangled Chopper bike. It wasn't all pop culture that occupied space in Depp's imagination. For a while he had an obsession with Vincent Van Gogh, with the artist's life and struggle, as much as his works of art.

Young Johnny Depp's constant problem was equating his imaginative life with the dreary suburban surroundings in which he grew up, stifled and dissuaded from expressing his creative drives. When he was seven the family moved from Kentucky to Florida, to the working class town of Miramar, just outside Miami. 'Miramar was like Endora, the town in *What's Eating Gilbert Grape?*,' he said. 'It had two identical grocery stores opposite each other and nothing much ever happened there.' The family lived in a motel for about a year, until his father found work again as a public works official. Staying in the motel was an early taste of the lifestyle that Depp was to live later in his life, never owning a home, but merely renting short term or staying in a succession of hotels.

It was another family member – not his parents – who finally allowed young Johnny to realise fully the life that was building up for him in his imagination. 'My uncle was a preacher and he had this gospel group,' Depp told director John Waters in *Interview* magazine. 'He did the whole bit where he stood up at the podium and held his arms out crying, and said, "Come on, run up, and be saved." And people would come up to his feet – that whole weird idol thing.'

Sitting in the audience at many of his uncle's sessions, the young Depp saw the art of performance up close. He learned how to capture and hold the attention of an audience. He saw the tricks and techniques his preacher uncle used to convince

Johnny Depp in Private Resort, a teen sex comedy made in 1985
which is usually left off his official career resume.

13

his followers of the truth of what he said, of the importance of what he revealed, of the accuracy of the artifice he employed. An interest in music was already developing in the young man, and he yearned to get up on stage and try it all out for himself. After all, being a rock and roll star seemed to beat being a gas station attendant, the fate that Depp feared awaited him if he played by the rules and successfully worked his way through the school system, as his parents wished.

'My cousins had a gospel group and they came down and played gospel songs, and that was the first time I ever saw an electric guitar,' said Depp of his preacher uncle. 'I got obsessed with the electric guitar, so my Mom bought me one from them for $25. I was about twelve years old. Then I locked myself in a room for a year and taught myself how to play, learned off records, and then I started playing in little garage bands. The first group I was ever in was called Flame. Then I was in The Kids. They were the ones who moved to Hollywood.'

Johnny Depp was not slow in developing a distinctive image for his band. 'At first we'd wear T-shirts that said Flame on them. At thirteen I was wearing plain T-shirts. Then I used to steal my Mom's clothing. She had all these crushed velvet shirts with French-cut sleeves. And, like, seersucker bell bottoms. I dreamed of having platforms, but couldn't find any,' he confided to Waters.

Away from music, Depp's school career was not going according to his parents' plans. 'I'd been in high school three years, and I may have just walked in yesterday. I had, like, eight credits. I was in my third year of high school and I didn't want to be there. I was bored out of my mind and I hated it.'

'I hung around with bad crowds,' Depp said in a 1988 interview. 'We used to break and enter places. We'd break into the school and destroy a room or something. I used to steal things from stores.'

Later in his career, Depp found himself being asked for an autograph by one of his former teachers. He was outraged. 'I mean, what was I supposed to say? He'd failed me. I remember one time this teacher yelled at me so heavily in front of the entire class. He didn't have any time for me then, and now, all of a sudden, he wants my autograph? *They* all thought I was going to end up a drug addict, in jail.'

His teachers probably had good reason to worry about Depp's future. By his own account, his teenage years were not exactly innocent: 'I started smoking at twelve, lost my virginity at thirteen and did every kind of drug there was by fourteen. Pretty much any drug you can name, I've done it...I wouldn't say I was bad or malicious, I was just curious,' he admitted. 'I certainly had my little experiences with drugs. Eventually, you see where that's headed and you get out.'

The young man showed enough foresight to realise that his textbook teen rebellion was not the answer to his problems. He might escape the job at the gas station, but he'd end up in and out of jail instead. Depp claimed to have given up hard drugs at fourteen, although he could never lose his taste for tobacco and alcohol. It was a much more traumatic incident in his early life that turned Depp around, from just another tearaway teen, to a focused young man who developed goals for himself, then relentlessly pursued them to success.

Depp's parents, John and Betty Sue, divorced when he was fifteen. It was the second time Betty Sue had suffered a failed marriage. As the youngest, Johnny was the last kid to leave home. 'I can remember my parents fighting and us kids wondering who was going to go with whom if they got divorced,' recalls Depp of this traumatic period.

He went to live with his mother, whose name he had tattooed on his left arm, enclosed in a heart. On his right bicep was an Indian Chief's head, encapsulating his affinity with the Cherokee nation. Depp developed an interest in tattoos and self-scarring at about the age of twelve, just before his parents split up. Self-mutilation has been recognised for some time as a manifestation of emotional turmoil, particularly in the young. 'I remember carving my initials on my arm,' he said, 'and I've scarred myself from time to time since then. In a way your body is a journal and the scars are sort of entries in it.'

Despite the emotional shake up brought about by his parents' break up, Depp was to remain resolutely loyal to both of them. 'These are the most important people in my life. You know, I would die for these people. If someone were to harm my family or a friend or somebody I love – I would eat them. I might end up in jail for 500 years – but I would eat them.'

He didn't escape the split without emotional scars, but came to rely on his brother Dan and sister Christi for support. 'My father left [with other sister Debbie] and my mother was deeply hurt and sick physically and emotionally. That's a very traumatic thing for a family to go through, so we all pulled together and did the best we could.' The splitting apart of the family at a time of life when many young people suffer emotional confusion, resulted in young Depp becoming deeply insecure. He already regarded himself as an outsider, having failed in education and gathered a reputation for being an oddball. The failure of his parents' marriage was a further push for Depp to define himself. His hang ups from this period were to resurface in his choice of career roles and in his inability to commit in his personal relationships.

Depp's best friend in Florida was Sal Jenco, later to be a co-star in the TV series *21 Jump Street*, as well as the inspiration for Iggy Pop's character in *Dead Man*, and manager of Depp's infamous Sunset Strip Hollywood night-club, The Viper Room. Shortly before he left high school, Depp moved out of the house he was sharing with his mother to live with Sal in the back of a car. Sal had nowhere else to live and Depp didn't want his friend to feel abandoned. More importantly, it was a way of escaping his parents and the trauma of their split, and to begin making a life for himself, even if it was pretty sordid. The 1967 Impala which Depp now called home had back seats filled with empty beer cans, and the two boys lived by eating submarine sandwiches filched from the local 7-Eleven store.

Depp finally gave up the uneven struggle with academic achievement and authority and dropped out of high school in 1979, plunging straight away into a rock and roll career with his band, The Kids. They started on the bottom rung, doing cover songs and warming up the audience for other, bigger bands, but Depp had bigger ambitions in mind. The Kids started to develop their own material, which sounded 'a bit like U2 maybe mixed with the Sex Pistols'. The Kids were something of a local sensation in Florida, opening for a succession of bigger names such as the B52s and Talking Heads.

'I played rock'n'roll clubs in Florida,' recalls Depp of his rock music beginnings.

'I was underage, but they would let me come in the back door to play, and then I'd have to leave after the first set. That's how I made a living, at about $25 a night. At times we would make $2,100 – we used to make that for the entire group and the road crew, which is a lot.'

'We did a show with Iggy Pop when I was eighteen. After we did two shows I got really drunk, really drunk. I was at the bar after the club had closed. I was, I don't know, getting ready to puke or something. And I saw Iggy in skimpy little pants wandering around the club with a dog. And for some reason, and I don't know why – I started screaming at him. I started screaming and yelling at him "Fuck you!" I don't know why, because I always idolised him. And he walked over to me and just looked at me, and I thought he was gonna hit me. And he said "You little turd." And he walked away.' Depp was to be reunited with Iggy Pop on the set of his film *Cry Baby*, and they discussed the incident. According to Depp, he said 'I was probably in the same condition as you, maybe worse.'

By 1983, Depp was enjoying modest local success as a musician. However, the twenty-year-old had a new adventure he was about to embark upon: marriage. Lori Ann Allison, a 25-year-old musician, was the sister of one of his co-musicians in The Kids. They hooked up, got married very quickly and drifted around trying to talk themselves into a record deal. When it became clear it was never going to happen, the strain started to show.

'You know, I was married when I was twenty. It was a strong bond with someone, but I can't necessarily say I was in love. That's something that comes around once, man, maybe twice if you're lucky. And I don't know that I experienced that, let's say, before I turned 30,' reflected Depp on his first marriage. It wasn't the only romantic experience the young Depp had enjoyed. 'I remember being in seventh grade and I was one of the kids that was considered a burnout. I had the most intense crush on this very popular girl. I pined for this girl, like beyond Romeo and Juliet. Shocking. I just chewed my tongue up for her. Eighth grade comes along, we hang out a little at those parties where you end up making out. So we did that and I just couldn't have been happier. Then she goes for the football guy, and leaves me just dangling in the breeze.

'Years later, after I dropped out of high school, I'm playing a club. I'm on-stage and I look out and I'm like, "Fuck, it's her!" So I finished the set and I go directly to the bar where she's sitting and I walk up to her and it's that face, man – incredible. And I went, "It's so nice to see you!" And I look at her and she's 250 pounds! She is a mammoth, but her face is still the same. I went, "Oh my, nice to see you – how many kids do you have?" And she had four kids – what fitting payback for fucking breaking my heart when I was a little kid.'

Depp grew to regard his time with Lori Ann Allison as part of the process of growing up, of moving from his suburban background to the opportunity laden town of Hollywood. 'I guess I have very traditional kinds of sensibilities about that kind of stuff – you know, a man and a woman sharing their life together and having a baby, whatever – and I think for a while I was trying to right the wrongs of my parents because they split up when I was a kid, so I thought I could do it differently – make things work. I had the right intentions, but the wrong timing – and the wrong person. But I don't regret it; I had fun and I learned a lot.' More succinctly,

Depp said: 'It wasn't working out, so we took care of it.'

Before finally ending his relationship with Lori Ann Allison, she, Depp and The Kids made a final break with Florida. They relocated to Los Angeles, in a last ditch, all-out bid for rock and roll fame. 'Don Ray, a guy who booked all the bands at the Palace in Hollywood, thought we should come out,' Depp explained. 'He wanted to manage us, so he pitched me some money, and we saved up some money and we drove out there.'

Getting work in Hollywood wasn't as easy as The Kids felt it might have been. 'It was horrible,' admitted Depp to Waters in *Interview*. 'There were so many bands it was impossible to make any money. So we all got side jobs. We used to sell ads over the telephone. Telemarketing. We got $100 a week. We had to rip people off. We'd tell them they'd been chosen by so-and-so in their area to receive a grandfather clock. They would order $500 worth of these fucking things and we would send them a cheap grandfather clock. It was horrible.'

Depp also made some money by selling personalised pens to companies over the phone. 'My first acting job,' is how Depp viewed this first real paid occupation. It was cut short when he finally moved over to film acting. 'I was working a day job selling ink pens over the phone and getting maybe $100 a week, and I thought "What have I got to lose?". After all, it was clear that Depp really wasn't cut out to be a salesman. 'The last couple of times I did it, I just said "Listen, you don't want this stuff, man."'

Things with The Kids were bubbling along, but the band were going nowhere. Having made the trip to LA, they found themselves repeating what they'd been doing in Florida, opening for larger bands, but not being taken seriously themselves. 'We did good shows in LA. We played with the Bus Boys and Billy Idol,' claimed Depp. But there didn't seem to be a pop career awaiting Johnny Depp and Lori Ann Allison, so the partnership was dissolved through a divorce, made final in 1985 when Depp was just 22. Depp suffered deep guilt; he felt he was repeating the scenario he'd lived through when his own parents had split up, only seven years earlier. The failure of the relationship was the last nail in the coffin of his failed music career. It was time for a new direction.

Johnny's split with Lori Ann was reasonably amicable, and when she started dating actor Nicolas Cage, nephew of film director and producer Francis Ford Coppola, Depp and Cage became friends. Cage suggested he try out acting, and put Depp in touch with his agent. As a result, Johnny Depp found himself called to an audition for his first film, a low budget horror movie entitled *A Nightmare on Elm Street* (1984).

Film director Wes Craven had been working in the low budget independent horror film sector since the early 1970s when he had a controversial success with *The Last House on the Left* (1972), a revenge tale loosely based on Ingmar Bergman's *The Virgin Spring*. Craven was preparing a film based on a bundle of newspaper cuttings he'd kept about a series of bizarre deaths which seemed to be related through the victims' nightmares. He'd come up with the idea for the razor-fingered, burn-scarred villain, Freddy Krueger, a role to be played by actor Robert Englund. All he needed now was a group of charismatic teens to be stalked by the fedora wearing monster. Heather Langenkamp was cast as the heroine, Nancy – the only one who escapes Freddy's clutches by the film's climax. The part of her boyfriend in *A Nightmare on Elm Street* was the role for which Depp found himself auditioning. Before the audition, Depp had managed to persuade a friend to stay up with him for two nights running, coaching him on the lines.

The description of the character in the script bore little relation to Depp. 'I was just not what Wes had written for the story,' Depp explained later. 'He had written the part of a big, blond, beach jock, football player guy. And I was sort of emaciated, with old hairspray and spiky hair, earrings, a little catacomb dweller. Then five hours later that agent called me and said, "You're an actor."'

There may have been other reasons why Depp was cast in the role. Wes Craven's daughter had an interest in the young Depp, a fact that can hardly have harmed his chances. Even this early, the would-be rocker found himself trading on his good looks to find fame and fortune through his movie roles. Craven had his daughter and her friends check out the competition, and from all the auditioning actors they settled on Depp. 'He had a quiet charisma that none of the other actors had,' Craven confirmed, from his own perspective as director. 'Johnny really had that sort of James Dean attraction. He just had a very powerful, yet very subtle personality. My teenage daughter and her friends were at the reading, and they absolutely flipped over him. He's got real sex appeal for women.'

Depp found himself on his first movie set playing Glen Lantz, who fails to stay awake and thus fend off the attentions of dream villain Freddy Krueger. He falls asleep lying on his bed – allowing Krueger to wreak havoc as the bed swallows and destroys Glen, spitting him out in a stream of blood. The filming of Depp's first death scene was quite a stretch, both for the neophyte actor and his experienced director. Craven filmed in a rotating set to achieve the desired seamless effect. The director and his cameraman were strapped into a pair of Datsun B-210 car seats, mounted on one wall of the specially constructed revolving room, along with the camera rig. Depp then performed his scene. The entire room rotated, with 110 gallons of blood substitute (water mixed with starch and colouring agents) pumping out of the bed, and appearing in the finished film to climb up the walls.

'I love this stuff,' Depp told *Fangoria* magazine who reported on the filming of the terror tale. 'The kid falls asleep and it's all over, he's sucked right into the bed and spit out as blood. His bloody body rises straight out and then topples over, too. I heard somebody talk about having a dummy shot out of the bed, but I said "Hey, I want to do this! It'll be fun! Lemme do it!"' It was also reported that a TV version was shot with a skeleton being ejected from the bed, rather than the corpse. None of these extra scenes found their way into any of the released versions of the film, just the 100 gallons of blood.

It wasn't just his obvious acting ability that made Depp stand out on the set of the film. 'Everybody on *A Nightmare on Elm Street* was so freaked out, going "Jesus, the kid's got tattoos!"' Depp recalled a decade later. 'Then tattoos became a huge trend. It's funny because people in ten years are going to be depressed about some of the scratches they got on their bodies.'

Shooting for the low budget New Line film finished in July 1984, with an October 1984 premiere set for the movie. However, writer and director Craven had

a dispute with producer Robert Shaye over the ending. Shaye wanted a clear sequel hook to allow further films to be made, while Craven wanted the film to stand on its own. Craven lost the battle, and remained in conflict with Shaye and New Line Cinema on and off for ten years, through all the following sequels, right up to his own *Wes Craven's New Nightmare* (1994), touted as the final Freddy film.

Depp made $1,200 a week for his six weeks work on *A Nightmare on Elm Street*. It was his first taste of the money that can attach itself to show business successes. ''Never had I seen anything like that. It was amazing to me that someone wanted to pay me that much money, which was just union scale.' Depp wasn't expecting instant fame and a host of offers to come to his door as a result of playing the part of Glen Lantz. He was, after all, now known as the dispensable kid eaten by a bed. 'I got sucked into the bed. What kind of reviews can you get opposite Freddy Krueger? "Johnny Depp was good as the boy who died"?' However, the film itself did get some good coverage, mainly for director Craven, and Langenkamp as Freddy's vanquisher.

For his part, Craven was happy to see what happened to many of the principals, Depp among them, who made their debuts in his film. 'Everyone has gone on to

Johnny Depp's first role was in A Nightmare on Elm Street, as the heroine's boyfriend and one of Freddy Krueger's first dream victims.

19

better things and I'm very gratified by that,' he said.

'I just kept working and I did a few more things here and there,' said Depp of his post-*Nightmare* opportunities, 'and I studied at the Loft Studio.' It was clear from his decision to take acting classes that Depp now saw more future in acting than as a musician. The Kids broke up following Depp's change of career, not least because he also started playing in another rock band, called Rock City Angels. His fellow band members in The Kids were not pleased. 'They were mad,' commented Depp philosophically. 'They probably still hate me.'

Johnny Depp's next two films are generally omitted from his official film resumé, as they consisted of the traditional early roles which the star would rather remain unseen by his current fans. The first was a sex comedy entitled *Private Resort* (1985). The film was shot in Florida which enabled Depp to return to his home turf. Written by Gordon Mitchell and directed by George Bowers, *Private Resort* is an example of the early 1980s teen sex comedy, a limited genre which quickly ran out of steam. Johnny Depp plays Jack, a young would-be stud spending four days at a holiday complex in Miami with his buddy Ben, played by Rob Morrow – a young actor later to feature to much greater effect in *Quiz Show* (1994) and on TV in *Northern Exposure*. From the opening shots of barely bikini-clad women around a swimming pool, it is clear that this pre-AIDS awareness comedy is an early prototype for *Baywatch.* To Jack and Ben, the private resort of the title is 'the promised land'.

No sooner have the hapless pair arrived than they are caught up in all sorts of standard farcical goings on involving a jewel thief known only as The Maestro (Hector Elizondo), an agitated hotel security guard, a menagerie of women and a bully called Curt (played by comedian Andrew Dice Clay – who has the 'Dice' missing from his billing).

Private Resort climaxes in a chase which the director and writer obviously hoped would be riotously funny, including all the principals running hell for leather after Depp and Morrow. (Morrow in drag – Depp would have to wait until 1994 when he made *Ed Wood.*) Even with occasional attempts to ape routines hijacked from the Three Stooges and the Marx Brothers, *Private Resort* has little to recommend it, except the sight of a naked Johnny Depp fifteen minutes into the film, for some the only attraction.

The second movie Depp likes to leave off his filmography was made the following year for cable TV. *Slow Burn* (1986) is a sub-Hitchcockian thriller, co-starring Eric Roberts (brother of the rather more famous Julia) and Beverly D'Angelo. Produced by Joel Schumacher and directed by Matthew Chapman, *Slow Burn* was based on an Arthur Lyons novel entitled *Castles Burning*. Set among the rich and famous of Palm Springs, the film attempted to evoke the spirit and atmosphere of 1940s *film noir*, an intention ruined by shooting the whole thing in the bright Californian sunshine! Eric Roberts' deadpan delivery of the hokey voice over doesn't improve matters either.

Depp – with a sillier haircut than those he sported in *A Nightmare on Elm Street* and *Private Resort* – plays Donnie, the son of millionaire Dan Hedaya (later to co-star opposite Depp again in *Benny & Joon*). Eric Roberts is Jacob Asch, a gadget obsessed private eye who was once a journalist, hired by artist Gerald

McMurtry to find his ex-wife (played by D'Angelo) who is now married to Hedaya. His investigations uncover the standard web of deceit which leads to Depp's spoilt rich kid character being kidnapped and then gruesomely dismembered. Playing Depp's conspiratorial girlfriend Pam Draper in *Slow Burn* was Emily Longstreth, who also played Rob Morrow's waitress girlfriend Patti in *Private Resort*. Longstreth and Depp were very good friends at the time and enjoyed the opportunity to work together again.

Although better than most TV attempts at this genre, *Slow Burn* is a limited exercise in recreating a lost genre of film. It also features a performance from Depp where the young actor is clearly treading water, given the limited and unchallenging role he'd landed. His high school kid character, though, is a precursor of his later part in the TV series *21 Jump Street*.

Depp has little to say about *Slow Burn* and *Private Resort*. 'I made some shitty movies when I was first starting out, but I'm not embarrassed by them, especially as I didn't think I was going to be an actor – I was just trying to make some money. I was still a musician. When I first started out I was just given the opportunity, and there was no other way to make that kind of money. Apart from crime. I couldn't believe how much they were paying me,' he readily admitted.

Slow Burn was to be Johnny Depp's last major movie appearance for some years; his acting apprenticeship continued in a regular TV role. All that the young actor had been through in his life so far had prepared him for the teen school kid roles he'd played. Playing Glen in *A Nightmare on Elm Street,* Jack in *Private Resort* and Donnie in *Slow Burn* came naturally as they all featured aspects of Depp's real life personality – he was playing his own age within his own experience of reality. That was all to change with his later film roles. His background would play a part in determining his choice of roles and would have a profound effect on his off screen life. 'His childhood informs who he is, but his choice of roles is where he wants to live as an artist,' said his *Arizona Dream* and *Don Juan DeMarco* co-star Faye Dunaway. 'Whatever has happened to Johnny Depp, this is what he in his own uniqueness made of it.'

With his band gone and his work on *A Nightmare on Elm Street* gaining the young actor good notices, Johnny Depp was beginning to think he could take to acting, despite his low opinion of *Slow Burn* and *Private Resort*. The money was good and he found the work easy enough – as for the prospects, he just had to look around Los Angeles to see the evidence of what could happen if you made it big in the movie business.

It didn't happen immediately, however. Lack of experience caught up with him and Depp had great trouble getting any new work for over a year. 'No one was knocking down my door with scripts,' he said. He was considering abandoning the enterprise altogether, until a film called *Platoon* came along and gave him the creative and professional boost he needed.

Platoon began in the real-life experience of writer and director Oliver Stone. As a Vietnam veteran, Stone had returned to an America that didn't know how to welcome its soldiers back. There was no victory to celebrate, only half-hearted compromise and the ignominy of defeat – so the country ignored them instead.

The film didn't get made when Stone first wrote the screenplay. 'I think it was too harsh a look at the war – too grim and realistic. It was rejected everywhere,' recalled Stone. Unable to get finance or backing from any American studio or independent producer, Stone ended up with the backing of British producers and European money to make *Platoon* – perceived by many before production as an anti-American film.

Charlie Sheen starred in the film as a nineteen-year-old 'grunt' named Chris Taylor, a volunteer American soldier sent out to Vietnam, only to find himself caught up in the battle between two officers: the 'evil' Barnes (Tom Berenger) and the 'good' Elias (Willem Dafoe). Concentrating on the effect of the war on American soldiers, rather than the rights and wrongs of America's presence in South-East Asia, *Platoon*'s eventual success was to unleash a horde of copycat Vietnam films into cinemas the world over.

'I went to read for Oliver Stone, and Oliver scared the shit out of me!' recalled Depp. 'I read for him and he said, "OK, I need you for ten weeks in the jungle." It was a great experience.' Two and a half months in the Philippines might have sounded like a holiday to Depp, but he didn't reckon on the tough training course director Stone had in mind for his cast. He didn't just want people to be acting the parts of soldiers, he wanted his young actors to become soldiers.

The 30 actors, from Hollywood, New York, Texas, Tennessee and the Philippines, didn't know what had hit them during their thirteen days of hard, no-slack, field training. 'I set up a training programme that was intentionally difficult and physically demanding,' explained Dale Dye, a Vietnam veteran who worked with Stone. 'I believe that the only way a man can portray the rigours of jungle combat is to get a taste of it.' Dye also turned up in the movie, playing Captain Harris – as did Oliver Stone, having promoted himself to the rank of Major.

A 60-mile ride from Manila into the bush kicked off the beginning of Johnny Depp's training to be an infantryman. Wearing baggy fatigues and jungle boots, the young actor was issued with a dog tag, rifle, bayonet, poncho, flashlights and red night filters, water canteens and other infantry gear. Out in the jungle, the days merged into one another. The field training called for Depp to kip down with another actor in two man fox holes, which they'd dug themselves – by hand. For Depp's first experience of filming abroad, he was perhaps expecting plush trailers and cordon bleu cooking. Instead he had a rations tin, with plastic wrapped slices of meat, cold hot dogs and tubs of what he could only describe as 'bean something or other'. The pre-cooked hamburgers were a definite treat. Each day was filled with classes on the M-16 rifle and squad radio procedures, intermingled with classes on scene study and character analysis, led by Oliver Stone.

Depp quickly had to get used to the 100-degree temperatures, the drenching humidity, the dirt, the swarms of red ants and the sheer exhaustion of it all. He'd heard the saying that 'War is hell.' His experience on *Platoon* persuaded the young actor that training for it, even just for a movie, was a close second. Depp would have felt even worse if he knew at this point that much of his work as the character Lerner, the unit's translator, was going to end up on the cutting room floor, giving him a minimal presence in the finished film.

When filming began, role call for the cast was a cheery 5am – except for Tom

Berenger, who had to get up about two hours earlier to allow the make-up department to put on the facial scar his character sports throughout the movie. Filming progressed at a brisk pace, but not without incident. With only 54 days committed to the jungle filming, Stone knew he couldn't push for more time and had to simply get the shots he needed in the time available. 'During the shoot,' wrote Stone, 'four or five production people are fired, and there are the usual fights, raging line-producer battles, several broken limbs, one near-fatal viper bite, hordes of insects, early monsoon rains, and too many scary moments in helicopters.'

Although the work of getting the script committed to celluloid proceeded well, the twelve-hour days, six-day weeks and constant jungle humidity took their toll on the cast and crew, Depp among them. Everyone involved in the filming of *Platoon* was struck down at one stage with an unidentified fever bug, with half the crew not showing up for night filming on the 42nd day of the shoot. But by compromising on some of the shots he wanted, Oliver Stone was able to wrap production of *Platoon* at five in the morning on the 54th day of filming in the jungle.

It was in the editing that Johnny Depp's performance as the translator Lerner was to suffer the most. Stone seems to have regretted some of the decisions he took in editing the picture, feeling that the process of editing is an inevitable compromise which dilutes the intention of the original script and can marginalise the work of the performers.

Platoon became the highest grossing film of the month during its February 1987 release in the United States, evidence of the general change in attitude to the Vietnam war among the American public. Over the weekend ending 1 February, the film grossed $8.1 million ticket sales in fewer than 600 cinemas nationwide. Not bad, for a Vietnam war film no studio wanted to make. Orion, distributing the film in the United States, had originally released the film in just six cinemas in December 1986 in New York, Los Angeles and Toronto, allowing anticipation to build due to word of mouth. The slow roll-out release also provoked many column inches in newspapers, using the film as a hook to discuss many of the unresolved issues of America's role in the Vietnam war.

The critics talked up *Platoon*'s Oscar prospects with their rave reviews for the film. After all the controversy stirred up, Oliver Stone walked off with four Oscars for Best Picture, Best Director, Best Sound and Best Editing. The Vietnam war was over at last for him. He had other controversies to tackle in his future film-making career.

In 1987 Depp's romantic life blossomed once again. He met and began dating an attractive, young, would-be actress named Sherilyn Fenn. She was seventeen, while Depp was now 23. Although his ex-wife had been five years older than Depp, his future relationships from this point on were all to be with women significantly younger than himself.

The on-off relationship with Fenn, who is now better known for her 1990 sex-bomb role as Audrey Horne in David Lynch's bizarre TV soap *Twin Peaks*, ran through to about 1988, mid-way into his run as Hanson on *21 Jump Street*. 'Neither of us was famous then,' is the only remark Depp makes these days on the two-year liaison.

Depp was clear about what he felt about these early relationships, but wasn't happy with the image left in many people's minds by the reporting of his private life in the teen magazines, who constantly wanted to know who he was sleeping with. 'I don't regret any of them. I had a good time,' he said of his early relationships. 'Most of what's been written about me has been completely false. People have created an image that has absolutely nothing to do with me, and they have the power to sell it, to shove it down the throats of people. I'm an old-fashioned guy who wants marriage and kids.'

Depp has painted a very rosy picture of his own behaviour during his time with Fenn, even though he was easily tempted by one night stands. 'I like to think that I'm very considerate of other people's feelings, and I was trained as a small child to always try my best at everything. I think I'm a mixture of romantic and realist. I'm a realist about some stuff, but I also wholeheartedly believe that in a society where people get divorced every five minutes you can still stay married for 50 or 75 years. It's been done and it's beautiful. When I see a couple celebrating their 75th wedding anniversary, I just think that it's totally incredible.'

At the same time, Depp wanted licence to go his own way, regardless of others' feelings. His reluctance to commit to a relationship seems rooted in his parents' divorce. The young Depp didn't want to repeat the pattern established by his parents. He'd already failed at the marriage game once in his short life. He wasn't about to fall into that trap again. 'When I see someone who just follows their dream and succeeds, and just does basically what they want to do and doesn't have to answer to anyone, obviously not harming anyone, that's great,' he has said, clearly in defence of his own erratic personal behaviour.

Johnny Depp's first real taste of the big time came in 1987, when he secured the leading role in a new TV series entitled *21 Jump Street*. Originally titled *Jump Street Chapel*, after the building in which the detectives in the series were to be based, *21 Jump Street* came from the production stable of Stephen J. Cannell, who had been behind the successful adventure series *The A-Team*. The series was created by writer-producer Patrick Hasburgh. Hasburgh wanted Depp for the leading role of Tom Hanson, but Depp at first refused the part and wouldn't even look at the script, feeling that to come from a respected and well reviewed film like *Platoon* to an untried and untested new TV series was too big a gamble, even if the security of a series was attractive. So Depp didn't jump in head first to the part – he approached the prospect of featuring in a possibly long running TV series with his usual ambivalence.

'I got a call from my agents, who said "These people want you to come and read for this TV thing." And I said "No, no, no, no, no…" I didn't want to sign some big contract that would bind me for years. So they hired somebody else to do it, and they fired him after about a month, and then they called me again and said "Would you please come in and do it?" My agents said "The average span of a TV series is thirteen episodes, if that. One season." So I said OK.'

Committed to filming a pilot, the production company went ahead with another young actor – the now forgotten Jeff Yagher – in the role. After three weeks, Yagher was history, and Depp was back in the producers' minds. What had been shot of the pilot was enough to convince the then-rising Fox Network that *Jump Street Chapel* had series potential. They ordered more episodes and a change of name to *21 Jump Street*. The network and the producers agreed about the leading actor, though, and so they decided to seriously approach Depp once again, overcoming his reluctance to commit to a project that might eat up years of his life. Finally, with the disappointments of *Platoon* fresh in his mind, Depp chose security.

Series creator Patrick Hasburgh knew they had the right man for the role: 'If this were the 1950s, he'd move to Paris or hang out with Jack Kerouac.' Depp had the right kind of innate coolness and latent teen-appeal that the production needed to be a success. Now all the producers had to do was mould their star accordingly. 'What struck me about him when he auditioned is that he wasn't nervous,' said supervising producer Steve Beers. 'He was laid back. He had this presence. He's an unusual personality. He's also one of the nicest people I've ever worked with.'

The first step was to complete shooting on the originally abandoned first episode, introducing Johnny Depp as Tom Hanson, undercover high school cop. The pilot presents Hanson as a character with a problem. He's a second generation, twentysomething cop, whose fresh-faced looks make him appear barely fifteen – a fact the other cops in the precinct, and the bad guys he has to deal with on the street, never miss an opportunity on which to comment. The lack of respect, from cops and criminals alike, is getting Hanson down – he just wants to be a good cop, like his father was.

His superiors offer him a choice: desk duty or the chance to join an elite group of undercover cops who work out of an old, abandoned chapel. These cops all look young enough to infiltrate the local high schools to ferret out the teens who are there not to study but to sell drugs. Hanson chooses the chapel. For his new assignment, Hanson has to relearn what it is to be a teenager. His companions on the undercover crime fighting squad included Dustin Nguyen as H. T. Ioki, a Japanese-American; Holly Robinson as Judy Hoffs; and Peter DeLuise as Doug Penhall. In charge of this peculiar outfit was Frederic Forrest as hippie hangover Captain Richard Jenko, replaced after only seven episodes by Stephen Williams (who went on to find further success and notoriety as *The X-Files* Mr X, later in the 1990s). The series concept was based on a controversial, real life operation that had been in effect in Los Angeles since 1974. The youth anti-drug program had hit the headlines in 1986, the year before *21 Jump Street*, when one of the real undercover agents allegedly developed a romantic relationship with a seventeen-year-old high school student.

Depp found himself relocated to Vancouver in British Columbia, Canada to shoot the series. After a few months finding his feet, he also managed to persuade his mother Betty Sue and his step-father to move there and live with him. It wasn't to be the only reminder of his Florida days. His childhood friend Sal Jenco came up north to visit and so impressed the *21 Jump Street* production team with his party piece of filling his mouth with air and blowing it out like some strange looking fish, that he was cast as a semi-regular character, nick-named Blowfish.

Depp was not overly fond of the character he was playing on television. 'Hanson is not someone I'd want to have pizza with. I don't believe in having undercover cops in high school – it's spying. The only thing I have in common with

Tom Hanson is that we look alike.' He was being paid $45,000 per episode, but the isolation of the locations in Vancouver and the fifteen-hour filming days took their toll. Having friends in the cast – primarily among them Peter DeLuise (son of Dom DeLuise) – proved to be a lifeline. 'If Peter wasn't on the show I would have gone insane or jumped into the river. He's my saviour.'

Helping to overcome his loneliness and isolation, Depp persuaded Sherilyn Fenn to come to Vancouver with him. He even managed to get the aspiring actress a guest spot on the series' ninth episode entitled 'Blindsided'. Fenn played the daughter of a policeman who claims her father is abusing her. She tries to hire Hanson, who is undercover in the school with Penhall in their recurring guise of the drug dealing McQuaid brothers, to kill him for her. While her performance was not going to threaten Depp's rising stardom, it did show a glimmer of the promise she would later fulfil in *Twin Peaks* and her film career in the mid-1990s.

There was one aspect of *21 Jump Street's* success that Depp wasn't immediately prepared for: the adulation; but it was something he had to get used to quickly. Anticipating the deluge, the producers attempted to introduce Depp slowly to the world of the teen magazines. 'They had come to me in the beginning and said, "We want you to do these interviews and stuff for these magazines," and I said, "What magazines?" And they said, "*Sixteen! Teen Beat! Teen Dream! Teen Poop! Teen Piss! Teen Shit!*" ' Depp found himself having to toe the line in the early days of the series, posing for photographs clutching a gun, wearing his torn jeans and black t-shirts, looking moody for countless photographers. Then there were the daft questions about favourite colours and the labels slapped onto him by journalists seeking a shorthand way of getting Depp across to their audience. 'Those are things that are out of my control. It's very nice to be appreciated, but I'm not really comfortable with it. I've never liked being the centre of attention. It comes with the territory.'

Patrick Hasburgh felt that Depp coped remarkably well with what almost amounted to overnight stardom, when the series began airing in April 1987. 'Historically, when a show becomes really popular, actors turn into giant assholes, but not Johnny. He once lit his underwear on fire in the middle of the set, but that was because no-one had cleaned up his motor home in a long time. The show's success may prevent Johnny from taking feature offers, but he's being cool about it. Cooler than I'd be in his shoes. And if I were his age and looked like he does, I'd be dead by now. Girls follow him everywhere, screaming.'

'It's scary,' said Depp, finding himself the subject of millions of adolescents' fantasies. 'It's terrifying. People come up to you and start crying. Everybody compares everyone to James Dean these days. If you're lucky they mention Brando or DeNiro. They invite you to put on an instant image.'

In its regular prime time slot, *21 Jump Street* rapidly became the show most watched by young American females in the eighteen-34 age range. Depp soon found his fame eclipsing that of Michael J. Fox, at the height of his *Family Ties* days. The biggest indicator of his impact on the youthful audience watching the show were the fan letters.

'More than Michael J. Fox, more than Charlie Sheen, more than Rob Lowe –

Johnny Depp gets the greatest volume of mail of all our clients,' said a representative of Fan Handle, a Los Angeles based star mail handling service. 'I'd say 10,000-plus pieces a month. Of course, TV guys always get more than film guys.'

'I've gotten weird letters, suicide letters, girls threatening to jump if I don't get in touch with them,' admitted Depp of his fan mail. 'So you think, "This is bullshit," but then you think, "What if it's not?" Who wants to take that chance? I write them back, tell them to hang in there – if things are that bad they have to get better. But I'm not altogether stable myself, so who am I to give advice?' The letters ranged from the funny to the seriously worrying. 'Kids write to me and say they are having these problems or they want to commit suicide or something. It's scary. I have to say, "Listen, I'm just an actor, not a professional psychologist. If you need help, you should go and get it."'

The fame of *21 Jump Street* was phenomenal in the United States. The cast were mobbed on city tours such as the one they took to Chicago in August 1988. In scenes reminiscent of Beatlemania at its height, the actors were welcomed by crowds of screaming teenagers, men and women, desperate to get autographed photos of their idols, especially the reclusive Johnny Depp who was whisked to and from these appearances in huge limos, flanked by a pair of burly bodyguards. Depp featured on the cover of American teen magazines like *Tiger Beat* and *The Big Bopper*. He was voted one of *Rolling Stone* magazine's 'Hot faces of 1988' and tagged one of *US* magazine's 'Ten Sexiest Bachelors'.

Johnny Depp in Oliver Stone's Platoon. Much of his work as Lerner, the platoon's translator, ended up on the cutting room floor.

Depp didn't enjoy any of it, he found it difficult to cope with the idea that 'someone was selling this character called Johnny Depp.' He quickly became frustrated with the series and frustrated with the image of himself that was being sold. He put some of his feelings into words in the introduction to the book *Burton on Burton*, a series of interviews with *Edward Scissorhands* and *Ed Wood* director Tim Burton: 'Dumb-founded, lost, shoved down the gullets of America as a young Republican. TV Boy, heartthrob, teen idol, teen hunk. Plastered, postered, postured, patented, painted, plastic!!! Stapled to a box of cereal with wheels, doing 200 mph on a one-way collision course bound for Thermos and lunch box antiquity. Novelty boy, franchise boy.' It got to the stage where Depp could not bear to watch the show and he even gave up reading the scripts properly, simply learning his bits by rote. 'I'm afraid I started navel-gazing. I started thinking like, "There are 365 days in a year, but for 275 of those days, I'm saying someone else's words. And they're bad words. And I only get to say my own words for 90 days."'

His intial misgivings about getting locked into a TV series were proving well-founded and the security he'd sought in the TV role was beginning to feel like a trap. He had film ambitions he wanted to pursue, but his contract for *21 Jump Street* was holding him back. His success as Hanson had returned Depp's confidence to his pre-*Platoon* levels and now he wanted out: 'I'd signed up for six seasons and regretted it before a single episode aired. It was the first time I could pay my rent, but I'd see all these commercials about me. I felt like a box of cereal.'

Depp began to assert some of his power on the *21 Jump Street* set, refusing to do certain episodes if he had problems with the scripts, and trying to push the producers to make the show ever more meaningful by tackling issues ripped from the headlines of the newspapers. He secretly hoped that by being a pain in the ass he could force the producers to fire him – or in Hollywood speak 'release him from his contract', thus allowing him to get his movie career back on track.

'Sometimes there are things that I personally and morally don't agree with. Like one episode where my character had to set a cross alight. It was supposedly dealing with racism, but I don't think it worked – I had to light this cross and I found that pretty repulsive. In the end I did it, even though I didn't think the episode dealt with the issue correctly.' In another incident, Depp refused to appear in an episode where a high school student is murdered when he's wrongly suspected of being an informer, while the real informer stays quiet to keep in with the students. Depp felt the episode was morally dubious, and forfeited his $45,000 for the episode, when his role was given to Richard Greico's Booker character. 'I was very concerned from the beginning that *Jump Street* would never be preachy or point the finger. I'm not a good-guy role model. Hanson's pretty gung-ho about his job.'

Creator Patrick Hasburgh suggested that Depp's own background fed into the character he was playing on the series. 'He's a kid who has often experienced the same problems we're dealing with on the show.' But towards the end of his fourth season with the show, Depp felt the producers were out of touch with who he was. 'They wanted me to do a public service announcement that said: "Hi, I'm Johnny Depp, and listen; stay in school and graduate, because it means the world to me and you," and all this stuff. And I thought, well, I've been working for these people for four years. Don't they know I'm a drop-out? How can I tell people to stay in school. Then they said: "Oh, yes – we forgot."'

Depp did participate in some of the public service announcements that ran in relation to issue-based episodes of *21 Jump Street*, but he took a much more active role in their production, writing and directing, as well as featuring in mini-promos relating to AIDS, pornography or racism. It was his first behind-the-camera experience. Depp went on to direct two public service style announcements for a child-abuse helpline service for American TV and got involved in the American Make A Wish Foundation. 'It helps cancer patients or people who aren't going to live a long time. They write in and say: "It's my dream to meet Johnny Depp," or someone, and we meet up with them. It can be heartbreaking, but you meet a lot of very sweet people. I wouldn't trade that in for the world. Ego, money, career – you can take it all so seriously. But faced with a kid who's dying, it all means nothing.' Depp maintained his links with the foundation, accompanying an eleven-year-old girl on a set visit when he was making *Ed Wood.* He also started making his own short films. At this early stage he was harbouring an ambition to star in a movie version of Jack Kerouac's *On The Road*, an ambition he was still pursuing ten years later in the mid-1990s. He hoped it would be a way of broadening an image which he felt had become impossibly restricting, as well as being an opportunity to indulge his interest in the Beat poets.

Increasingly frustrated with the limited, repetitive nature of the role of Tom Hanson, Depp began suggesting ludicrous changes to his dialogue and when they were refused, he'd simply change them anyway during recording, fully aware that the speed of TV production didn't allow much leeway for constant re-takes. Lines like 'This is a great place, Doug' became 'Nice digs, Doug, you dog, dig 'em,' after Depp had finished with them. In his ever more desperate campaign to get himself fired from the show, Depp would put forward plainly ridiculous suggestions for his character development that were never going to get past the series' story editors and producers. One of them involved the discovery that his character was obsessed with peanut butter, and would be caught by the other characters smearing it over his naked body. The producers passed on Depp's ideas, but didn't fire him either. 'For the last two years of the show I didn't know what my character's name was,' claimed Depp. They may have rejected his ideas, but a producer on *21 Jump Street* had some sympathy for his stance: 'I don't always agree with him, but I can see where he's coming from. He fights hard for what he believes in, and he has a tendency to fight for other people as well.'

Depp countered this argument with one of his own – any difficulties on his part were only because he was pursuing a vision for the show. 'My feeling is that the show needs to go deeper into certain issues, like racism and gang violence. In television there are strict boundaries, so there's only so much you can do, but the only way to change something is to fight it.' Depp put forward other ideas for his character in an *Interview* magazine chat with John Waters in 1990. 'I think they should make the character start to lose his mind. Because, you know, the hazards of being a policeman can make you go crazy. I think he should go completely insane. They should really break the boundaries that there are in television. They should put him in an asylum.'

An episode based on a variation of this idea did turn up late in the run of *21 Jump Street*, in which Depp's Tom Hanson goes undercover into a juveniles' asylum to investigate alleged abuses by the staff against the residents. Hanson's faked illness and drug addiction is so convincing to the staff that they lock him away, and refuse to believe his delusions about being an undercover cop. More episodes like that and Depp might have stayed with *21 Jump Street* a bit longer. 'I learned a lot of lessons from *21 Jump Street*,' Depp said of the experience when it was all over, 'and it was very good for me in many ways. It fed me and put me on the map, so I can't really complain. But when you're doing a series like that there's really no creative controls – the word creative doesn't really exist in their vocabulary. So I said to myself that the first chance that I got, I was going to do exactly what I wanted to do and not compromise. Since then I've been lucky enough to do the films I've wanted to do and to work with the directors I've wanted to work with.'

The biggest legacy of his days as 'TV Boy' was his status as a teen pin-up idol, a constant focus for the teen magazines, even after the series ended. 'Whenever a young actor comes out they have to pin him with some sort of label, so they call him "bad boy" or they use that horrible word "rebel". It's all so played out and stupid. I just like to do roles which are kind of interesting and cool. When I started I got a lot of scripts where I would carry a gun, kiss a girl and walk around a corner and pose, things like that. That's why I liked *Cry Baby* – it made fun of the teen idol stuff, the screaming girls.'

The labelling he suffered this early in his career fuelled Depp's determination to make sure that each and every film he did was different from the last. His reason for some of the oddball choices of roles he was to make later can be traced to his reaction against the teen idol tag that was applied to him.

The teen rebel image was something Depp may have wanted to shake off, but his behaviour off *21 Jump Street*'s Vancouver set suggested he'd taken the persona a little too much to heart. In the first of a series of arrests and brushes with the law that were to recur throughout his career, Depp found himself under lock and key in Vancouver in 1989. Very late one night Depp tried to visit some friends at their hotel. It was one where Depp himself had stayed during his initial arrival in the city, so he was known by the staff there. However, a security guard on the door was determined not to let the actor in.

'He had a boner for me,' said Depp, characteristically scathing of authority. 'He had a wild hair up his ass, and he got real mouthy with me, saying: "I know who you are, but you can't come up here unless you are a guest." The mistake he eventually made was to put his hands on me. I pushed him back, and then we sort of wrestled around a bit, and I ended up spittin' in his face.' The police were called and weren't interested in hearing Depp's story. He was locked up for the night in Vancouver's central police station, fingerprinted and posed for mug shots. Depp's only interest in the whole event was in trying to obtain copies of the police photographs. Depp admitted responsibility and the charges were dropped. 'I've got a bit of a temper,' he was willing to concede. It wasn't the last time that Depp's fiery temperament was going to get him into trouble.

During his days on *21 Jump Street*, Depp's lack of commitment to his

TV Boy – Depp felt increasingly constrained by the creative limitations of 21 Jump Street, and by the teen-idol image created for him.

relationship with Sherilyn Fenn finally took its toll. She had returned to Los Angeles, and although Depp would also head south at weekends, staying in the Chateau Marmont hotel on Sunset Strip, the distance became too much for the relationship to bear. Depp's continued dalliances with other women were also a prime factor.

In 1989, the actor was linked with actress Jennifer Grey, who had partnered Patrick Swayze in the hit movie *Dirty Dancing*, but was known for little else. Depp was reportedly engaged to both Fenn and Grey at different times (although 'engagement' is usually a journalistic exaggeration for a relationship that appears to be more than a one-night stand), as well as being spotted out and about with a variety of others. His romantic notoriety prompted the short-lived popularity of a bumper sticker which read: 'Honk, if you haven't been engaged to Johnny Depp.'

Yet, despite the manifest failures of his romantic adventures, Depp still claimed to be in awe of the magic of marriage and saw it as the ultimate achievement to aim for: 'I want to get married, have kids, a couple of goldfish, lawnmower, asphalt driveway, eat doughnuts in the morning.' But he couldn't escape his expressed desire to also remain footloose and fancy free, either. 'I'm interested in doing what I'm doing right now and not really planning anything for tomorrow.

Depp's personal insecurity seemed to have struck again. His two relationships had collapsed, even though both had apparently reached the stage of

The cast of 21 Jump Street, undercover cops working in a high school setting.

engagements. He felt trapped by his romances, trapped in his TV role, constantly worried that he was missing out on something else, losing film parts because of his restrictive contract, losing women because he was tied to a long-term relationship. His constant need to move on, from *Platoon* to *21 Jump Street* to something else, anything else; from Fenn to Grey to someone new and fresh, was a reminder of his childhood days, his separated family and his own divorce. Depp's fear of failure, both professional and personal, drove his career and life forward in a constant search for the new and different, at the expense of stability and consolidation. The eternal adolescent refused, Peter Pan-like, to grow up.

His ICM agent Tracey Jacobs saw his unusual film choices as deliberate decisions on Depp's part. 'He made a choice when he came out of the television series to take a left turn as opposed to a right. "I have taken the road less well travelled and that has made all the difference." That would be the quote I would use to describe him in general.'

CHAPTER TWO

Cry Baby

THE 'road less travelled' that Johnny Depp set out upon in his second chance at the movies saw him actively pursue those roles that stars such as Tom Cruise would not even consider. The chance for Depp to work with director John Waters was exactly what the newly determined and single-minded actor was looking for.

Maverick film-maker John Waters has over the years crossed from beyond-the-pale independent American film in the 1970s to mainstream Hollywood features in the 1990s, while still maintaining his dark, radical edge. Working with Waters was Johnny Depp's return to the cinema, and both the role and the director were to set a pattern that Depp would attempt to maintain for most of his screen career.

Waters found himself dubbed the 'Pope of Trash' by William S. Burroughs, author of the controversial *Naked Lunch*. Between 1964 and 1967, the young Waters dabbled in 8mm and 16mm shorts. Waters' rise to notoriety came in 1972, when he launched an overweight (at 300 pounds) transvestite named Harris Glenn Milstead (screen name Divine) to celluloid immortality by having him eat freshly produced dog excrement in *Pink Flamingos*. 'He didn't think it was going to hurt his career,' said Waters. 'At that point he didn't think he was going to have a career. When he did it, he did it like a pro. He spat it out, brushed his teeth and then got on with his life. *Variety* said it was the most disgusting caper in film history. It was a pretty crazy thing for us to do, but not that crazy. I didn't think we'd still be talking about it 25 years later!'

Born just outside Baltimore, in 1946, Waters spent his childhood creating car pile ups with his toy cars and getting turned on by the wicked queen in Walt Disney's *Cinderella*. Attending a local Catholic school only helped to meld Waters' warped personality further. The Catholics say you can't do anything, so you want to do everything.' Which is exactly what Waters set out to do in 1960s America. Expelled from New York University for smoking pot, Waters spent his time going to the movies and renewed his childhood acquaintance with Glenn Milstead.

By the time he reached his third amateur film in 1968, Waters' sensibility was more or less formed. *Eat Your Makeup* featured a group of kidnapped young models forced to model themselves to death in front of their friends. Waters moved up to features, churning out wacky enterprises like *Mondo Trasho* (1969), *Multiple*

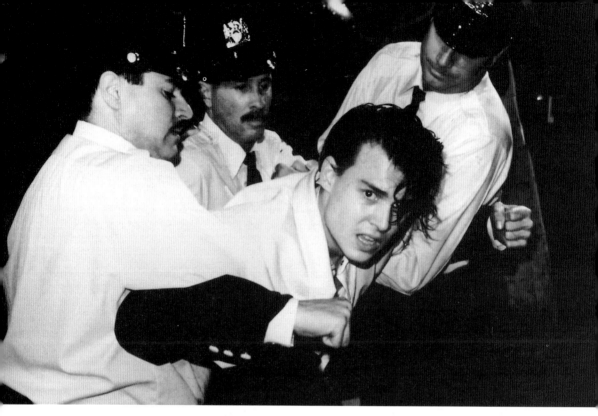

Maniacs (1970) and the infamous *Pink Flamingos* (1972). With a growing gang of regular contributors, known as The Dreamland Group, Waters supported himself and his guerrilla film-makers through welfare money and shoplifting.

The *Variety* response to *Pink Flamingos* ("surely one of the most vile, stupid and repulsive films ever made") did nothing to harm Waters' growing reputation as American cinema's shockmeister. Two more 1970s films, *Female Trouble* (1974) and *Desperate Living* (1977) were the final fling of unadulterated Waters. As he entered the 1980s with *Polyester* (1981, complete with Odorama and a scratch and sniff card), Waters was mellowing his material and reaching out to a wider audience. His battles to raise funds for his films and to have them accepted by Hollywood studios came to an end with 1988's *Hairspray*, a camp, colourful spoof of 1950s teenagers. While some of his hardcore fans thought Waters had sold out, he went on to secure his Hollywood acceptance with a further 1950s spoof, *Cry Baby* (1990). Enter Johnny Depp, who saw the film as a chance to escape from the monotony of more *21 Jump Street*. Waters conceived of *Cry Baby* as the ultimate juvenile delinquent love story, a tale to be set before the onset of sex, drugs and rock'n'roll in the late 1950s. Waters chose his home city of Baltimore as the setting and 1954 as the year.

The central character of this pre-rock'n'roll Romeo and Juliet was to be Wade Walker, the son of executed criminals, a tough, good-looking teenager from the wrong side of the tracks, known to all as Cry Baby. He falls in love with Allison Vernon-Williams, a beautiful, rich, 'square' girl, whose raging hormones combine with the evil influence of rockabilly music to drive her into a nightmare world of gang warfare and hoodlum passion. Allison's crowd of squares face off against the

Life imitating art – Depp as Cry Baby Wade Walker is jailed. In real life, Depp had a few brushes with the law and spent several nights behind bars.

delinquent gang led by Cry Baby in a take off of early Elvis movies filtered through other 1950s 'Juvenile Delinquent' films such as *High School Confidential* and *Rock Around the Clock*.

Naturally, Waters' 1950s teen satire had to be a rock'n'roll musical, so he devised a series of set pieces that would allow for a couple of wonderful, colourful, camp musical numbers. 'It's a spoof,' said Waters, 'a kind of joke on the really wild, untamed youth movies from the early 1950s – except it's the reverse of those movies because the bad guys are who you root for and the good guys are the villains.'

With the death of Glenn 'Divine' Milstead in 1988, two weeks after the premiere of *Hairspray*, John Waters had lost his leading lady. 'When Divine died there was just no question about having a man dress up as a woman in my films again. There's just no point… Divine was the best.' Johnny Depp once again escaped having to don woman's clothing in a film role, thanks to Waters' decision. '*Cry Baby* was going to be my first "boy" movie,' said Waters. 'It made sense to me, because I always wanted to make a movie about this whole era.'

Waters maintained a file of actors and actresses whom he'd like to work with and, upon completing each new script, he turned to it to try out casting ideas. 'More than anything, I need actors who can take a step back and laugh at

Cry Baby director John Waters always felt Depp looked good in prison fatigues, but Depp wasn't so keen when he was jailed in 1994 after trashing his hotel room at The Mark.

themselves good-naturedly.' When it came to casting the lead character for *Cry Baby*, Waters decided to take a look at what was going on in the contemporary teen world. Who were the teen pin-ups of the late 1980s? 'I went out and bought about twenty teen magazines, which was really mortifying. I found myself hiding them under my jacket. When I got home and started looking through them, Johnny Depp was on the cover of almost every one of them.'

Waters was pleased to discover that Depp seemed to have the essential attitude about himself and his image to make working together a fruitful experience. 'Johnny hated being a teen idol, and I told him the best way to get rid of an image, any image, is to make fun of it. I think he was brave to take this part because, first off, he told me that it was the most peculiar script he had ever seen, and by portraying Cry Baby, he's right out there, making fun of himself.'

For Depp's part, he couldn't have been more pleased that Waters' script arrived when it did. '*Cry Baby* came along at a good time for me,' the actor recalled. 'I had been looking at film ideas for a while and was getting disillusioned. Most of what I read was flat, just schlock. I was sent so many scripts which just echoed what I was doing on *Jump Street*, and I wanted something that would be totally different. John first sent me a letter and then we talked a bit and met, and then he gave me a script. I was so excited because not only was it really funny, but it made fun of all those clichés and sensitive hero roles I had been reading for so long.'

For *Cry Baby*, John Waters had the backing of a major studio, Universal, and Imagine Films, a production company co-owned by Brian Grazer and Ron Howard, ex-*Happy Days* star turned director. Grazer had taken the decision to back *Cry Baby* on the basis of seeing only one previous Waters film. 'The only movie of John's I ever saw was *Hairspray*,' Grazer admitted, 'and I loved it. I thought it had the highest hipness quotient of any movie I'd ever seen. And the *Cry Baby* script totally captivated me because it was a slick 1990s *West Side Story*.' Waters recalled the first meeting between the suits from Imagine Entertainment and his proposed star, 'Johnny came into this lovely Hollywood office in complete rags. In the middle of the meeting he looked at me and gave a sneer. At that moment I realised he would do just fine. He understood the whole plot of the film.'

Moving up the scale in Hollywood came as something of a shock to John Waters. His budget jumped dramatically, but so did the length of time it took to shoot his films. Previously his work had been made on the run, with scenes being shot quickly, without fuss, before moving onto the next one. Now, on *Cry Baby*, he had a huge Hollywood crew to deal with. 'They gave me $8 million to make a movie, not $10,000. While we were making *Cry Baby* it would amaze me, though. I'd look out and see this enormous crew and think "I gave all these people jobs from these ridiculous ideas, somehow, and produced employment." For teamsters!'

'Car scenes are a drag, they take the longest to film,' complained Waters. 'For the chicken race (the movie's climax), I had to sit in the car for a week. One whole week, every day. They only actually drove a short distance, and we had to get up to speed, to make it with this big camera trucking 30 people around and mikes and everything. Then cut. And you had to drive all the way around and start over again to get the next ten seconds of film. In both cars. So it took forever, and they were on top of the car, singing…'

Accusations that Waters had sold out with *Cry Baby* began as soon as the project was underway. But he was unrepentant: 'Each time there's a little backlash from people who say "Oh, we like it better when it was this or that," people who want Johnny Depp to eat shit. But if it was like that it would never reach any more people. If you make it for the people who've seen your other movies, that's like those bad left-wing magazines, preaching to the converted. The only challenge left for me is to make a Hollywood hit with my sense of humour intact, which *Cry Baby* certainly has. There are some people who hate the fact that I've made a Hollywood movie, but for me this is getting the last laugh, really. That's the ultimate subversive thing to do.'

Waters did feature some of his regular players in *Cry Baby* including Mink Stole and Ricki Lake, who'd appeared in *Hairspray*. Waters had always found bizarre juxtapositions of casting in his films, and *Cry Baby* was no exception. Alongside seventeen year old newcomer Amy Locane, who played *Cry Baby*'s girlfriend, Waters signed up rising Hollywood actor Willem Dafoe (Depp's *Platoon* co-star), ex-porn 'actress' Traci Lords and heiress and one-time hostage/freedom fighter Patty Hearst. Also in the cast was Iggy Pop, reunited with Depp for the first time

Rebel, Rebel – Cry Baby allowed Depp to spoof his 21 Jump Street teen-idol image.

since the actor's days with The Kids.

Depp was clear about his reasons for accepting the part, and it went straight to the centre of his frustration with the role he was playing on *21 Jump Street*. 'One of the main reasons for doing the movie was because it would be contradictory to what everyone sees me as, or what I've been labelled as by some fuckhead with a tie.' He enjoyed his time working on the film, particularly because he was actively encouraged to contribute to the creation of the role. 'For someone who writes and directs, someone who is basically the entire creative force, the real surprise is how open John is to ideas and suggestions,' said Depp of his director. 'He was real accessible, not distant or brooding. He'd listen to ideas about adding or taking out lines. If I was having a problem with something he'd rehearse with me. I mean, he'd actually get out there with me. No other director I've worked with has stood there and danced for me, to help me understand a step.'

Rachel Talalay was another regular collaborator with Waters, beginning on *Polyester*, before developing her career as a producer of the *Nightmare on Elm Street* series of films, which gave Johnny Depp his first acting break. She'd returned to produce Waters' *Hairspray* and *Cry Baby*. She would later feature Depp in a cameo

A menagerie of misfits – the Drapes from Cry Baby, including teen rebel Depp, second from the right.

in her directorial debut *Freddy's Dead: The Final Nightmare* and go on to direct the cult film developed from the British comic book character *Tank Girl* (1995). She worked closely with Waters on the set during the shooting of *Cry Baby*, and observed his working practices, seeing how he got the performance he wanted from his leading man. 'I saw him work with Johnny Depp in the fight scene in *Cry Baby*; he wanted Johnny to be really heroic, so instead of just telling him that he wanted him to be like Erroll Flynn or something, he ran up and sang 'Ride of the Valkyries' to him. Johnny just looked at him, and the next thing we knew, Johnny was this hero coming down the hill. That was a remarkable John Waters moment. Afterwards, Johnny had a glow on his face and he said: "That's the only time I've been directed like that!".'

With eleven musical numbers in *Cry Baby*, Depp found his teen band background came in handy, although he didn't actually get the chance to sing the vocals for the film himself. Los Angeles based singer and songwriter James Intveld was brought in by the production to provide the vocals and instrumentation for Depp's character. Depp's musical knowledge did however prove useful in another area. He was heavily involved with the film's musical supervisors in the choice of vintage guitars, amplifiers and other accessories for the band numbers.

The film allowed John Waters to achieve one of his childhood ambitions. 'The biggest high with *Cry Baby* was that it was an official selection for the Cannes Film Festival. The midnight screening was completely sold out. Standing ovation. They loved it. Standing at the top of that red carpet and turning around with eight million paparazzi, with Ricki Lake and Rachel Talalay, my producer, was a huge high to me. That was a fantasy I wanted since I was fourteen. So *Cry Baby* was a good experience for me in the long run. Out of all my movies it was probably the happiest on the set. There were some problems, but I think that people had a lot of fun working on it. Nobody hated each other when it was over, or anything.'

During the filming, Depp and Waters developed a close friendship and the two would keep in touch in later years. 'I think Johnny obviously has a temper,' said Waters of the young actor's sometimes hot-headed outbursts and reckless actions. One incident saw Depp almost destroy the good looks his movie career was trading on. In an echo of some of his reckless childhood activities, Depp had blown on a naked flame with a mouthful of gasoline, an action he understatedly described in retrospect as 'a really ridiculous thing'. Depp's face ignited and only the quick moves of a friend saved the actor from becoming a burn casualty and a headline grabbing story. With Depp's habit of scarring his body and his brushes with people in authority, particularly uniformed cops and security guards, Waters sometimes saw him as a timebomb waiting to explode.

Waters' film was widely welcomed by critics the world over, although it did better box office in foreign territories (mainly Europe and Australia) than it did in America. 'In Australia *Cry Baby* did great, but *Cry Baby* did better than any of my other movies in Europe. In Paris, they loved it. It got rave reviews, because they loved the film genre it made fun of. They have Johnny Halliday – who is Cry Baby,' said Waters. 'But here [America], the kids who didn't know that genre thought it was corny. They didn't get the joke. Young kids here never saw those Elvis movies. In Paris they did. They revere that kind of American juvenile delinquent movie.' The

film received a certain amount of criticism simply because Waters had produced a Hollywood movie, albeit one with his offbeat sense of humour and eye for the bizarre and disgusting still intact. 'The meanest reviews were from people who'd championed me in the beginning when no-one else would,' said Waters. 'They went into it not liking the fact that I'd made a movie for Universal, I think. The funny thing is, the people who said they wished *Cry Baby* was more like *Pink Flamingos*, hated *Pink Flamingos*.'

Rolling Stone was willing to give Waters the benefit of the doubt. Peter Travers wrote: 'Waters' bad taste is unassailable. The subversive comic thrust of *Cry Baby* shows he simply had to find new ways to channel his baser instincts. The wizard of odd still runs amok.' *Variety,* scourge of Waters' earlier *Pink Flamingos*, strongly supported *Cry Baby*, claiming his 'mischievous satire of the teen exploitation genre is entertaining as a rude joyride through another era, full of great clothes and hairdos. Depp is great as the delinquent juve, delivering the melodramatic lines with straight-faced conviction, and putting some Elvis-like snap and wiggle into his moves.' Depp's performance as the tortured tear-away came under other critics' scrutiny. *Sight and Sound* highlighted the casting of 'a bona fide teen idol (Johnny Depp)' in the lead role. *The Independent's* Adam Mars-Jones was slightly worried that Waters had cleaned up his act, by not getting Depp as down and dirty as he did Divine. 'The acting of the principals, Johnny Depp and Amy Locane, is assured enough. Waters

Director John Waters (second from left) coaches Johnny Depp as he prepares to spoof his own image in Cry Baby.

may make Johnny Depp, currently a top teen idol in the States, crawl through sewers half-naked to escape from prison, but his underwear is only cosmetically smirched and the sequence is innocent of gloating.' *Empire* magazine was enthusiastic: 'Glowing with period kitsch and beautifully hammed up by both the principals (Depp and Locane)...*Cry Baby* has real jokes and an infectious head of steam.'

Depp finally had the movie success he'd been looking for – and into the bargain, much to his great satisfaction, the film had at last managed to destroy the teen idol image he'd been stuck with for almost four years. He still had to return to *21 Jump Street* for one more season, before finally departing the show and taking the plunge into movies full time, courtesy of another maverick film director, Tim Burton. First, though, there was another new development in his private life.

Winona Horowitz was born on October 29th 1971 and named after the town Winona, Minnesota. Her parents – Michael and Cindy Horowitz – soon moved to Mendochino, California and pursued the 1960s hippie lifestyle. Winona's godfather was, after all, LSD guru Timothy Leary. A year later the family were in Petaluma, California, where Winona grew up and still calls home. It was when their daughter took up acting at the age of twelve that Michael and Cindy Horowitz had to get used to having a daughter now named Winona Ryder, her new surname 'borrowed' from rocker Mitch Ryder. Spotted by an LA casting director on an audition tape for the movie *Desert Bloom*, Ryder made her first film *Lucas* in 1986, at the age of fifteen. She quickly developed a dark, death-obsessed movie persona in films like Tim Burton's *Beetlejuice* (1988) and Michael Lehman's *Heathers* (1989).

The rising TV idol and the teen starlet were a movie match made in heaven. Johnny Depp and Winona Ryder first met at the premiere of her film *Great Balls of Fire* (1989) in which she played the teenage bride of Jerry Lee Lewis (played by a mis-cast Dennis Quaid). Their eyes met in the lobby, and according to both it was love at first sight: 'It was a classic glance,' said Depp, 'like the zoom in *West Side Story*, and everything else gets foggy.' Adds Ryder: 'It wasn't a long moment, but it was suspended.' The pair weren't introduced properly, however, until a couple of months later, when a mutual friend brought them together. 'My friend Josh introduced us. When I met Winona, and we fell in love, it was absolutely like nothing ever before – ever. We just started hanging out, and we've been hanging out ever since. I love her more than anything in the whole world,' gushed Depp at the time.

'I never really had a boyfriend before,' Winona Ryder confided to *Premiere* magazine in 1989. She quickly discovered she shared much in common with Johnny Depp, not least a mutual obsession with J. D. Salinger's *The Catcher in the Rye*. Jack Kerouac was another mutual obsession. Their interest in first editions of the works of Beat writers was easily fuelled by regular visits to Winona's father's counter culture book store.

The intense and unstable romance between the two started six months before Depp was due to begin making the movie *Edward Scissorhands*. They met up during Depp's weekend stays at the Chateau Marmont hotel during his final few months on *21 Jump Street*. Ryder later characterised the early days of their relationship as 'embarrassingly dramatic'. Their affair was quickly taken up by the tabloids and the teen magazines. He was 26, she was seventeen, but they were both the biggest stars of their generation – the fact that they were 'getting engaged' was headline news.

Depp had been down this path before, pursuing and getting involved with a much younger woman. His previous engagements to starlets like Fenn and Grey, as well as his infidelity, didn't seem to worry Ryder. 'People assume it bothers me that he's been engaged before, but it really doesn't. We have a connection on a deeper level. We have the same colouring, but we're from very different backgrounds, so we're interested in each other the whole time.'

Depp was so involved in this relationship that he felt the need to set the record straight on his previous liaisons, so widely reported in the press as 'engagements'. 'I've never been one of those guys who goes out and screws everything that's in front of him. When you're growing up you go through a series of misjudgements. Not bad choices, but wrong choices…you know, people make mistakes. I was really young for the longest time. My relationships weren't as heavy as people think they were. I don't know what it is, possibly I was trying to rectify my family's situation or I was just madly in love. There's been nothing throughout my 27 years that has been comparable to the feeling I have with Winona. Whatever I've been through before, it hasn't been this long. It wasn't like "Hi, nice to meet you, here's a ring". It was about five months before we got engaged.'

This was a different relationship for Depp. It was the nearest he was to come actually to getting married, his often expressed wish, but a situation his previous behaviour was unlikely to bring about. 'I want to get married,' said Ryder. 'I've got that feeling that this is right, this is it. But I don't want to do it just so I can say I did it. I want to have, like, a honeymoon and the whole shebang. We're going to get married as soon as we have time and we're not working.' But by the middle of 1991, the marriage plans were put on hold; the official reason given was that the couple could not find a suitable gap in their respective working schedules.

Depp was well used to press attention, from his *21 Jump Street* days, but for Winona Ryder it was all new. 'We don't feel like royalty,' she said. 'We read in the papers when they make that comparison and it makes us giggle. It makes us self-conscious in a way that neither of us enjoys. It's uncomfortable to be watched all the time or to have people eavesdropping on your conversations in a restaurant. Then they make things up about you which is even worse. I've really been exposed to the tabloids this year.'

Depp felt that their relationship helped both of them to cope with the success they were beginning to enjoy and the press attention that came with it. 'People don't realise, but this big jump in success can be a shock. I've gone from selling pens over the telephone to where I get paid a lot of money to make films. Sometimes I don't think I'll ever get used to it. Nothing really prepares you for this, but having Winona to share it with is a big help. She knows exactly what I'm going through, because she's going through the same thing. I think because we are in love we do feel happy with each other's success. We are getting used to being a celebrity couple, although sometimes people just want to know a bit too much about you.'

As the relationship developed Depp added to his tattoo collection by having Winona Forever tattooed on his arm. 'You can't lose a tattoo down a drain' was Depp's excuse for not opting for a more conventional engagement ring. 'I love Winona. I'm going to love her forever. Putting her on my arm solidified it. Tattoos are permanent. There was a bit of pain involved, but kind of enjoyable pain, like an electrical stimulation.' Ryder was rather taken aback by Depp's physical marking of their relationship. Continuing his habit since childhood of recording significant events as marks on his body, Depp's tattoo was simply a more extreme way of signalling how serious this romance was for him. 'I'd never seen anyone get a tattoo before,' said Ryder, 'so I guess I was pretty squeamish. I sort of was in shock. I kept thinking it was going to wash off or something. I couldn't believe it was real. I mean, it's a big thing, because it's so permanent.' Permanence seemed to be what Depp was seeking in this relationship. 'There's something inside of me that she knows really well that no one else knows or will ever know,' said Depp of Ryder. 'Life is trial and error, but when you find the one who is really it, there is just no mistaking it.'

It was during his three year on-off romance with Winona Ryder that Johnny Depp developed his hatred for the press. All actors have a love-hate relationship with journalists. Most are willing to use the press to build their careers and push their films when it suits them, but when their private or professional lives take a turn for the worse, the press are the last people actors want to see. Even when things are going well, being asked the same questions 10,000 times is, at the least, irritating. It was this aspect that seemed to get to Depp, more than any other. 'I'll be in the john of some bar and some stranger will come up and say, "So, are you and Winona still together?" At the urinal, for Christ's sake!'

One incident in particular drew the unwanted attention of the press to the celebrity couple. Ryder was due to star in Francis Ford Coppola's *The Godfather Part III* as the daughter of the Corleone family. She flew to Rome to take the part, but never left her hotel room, as she came down with a respiratory infection and a high fever. Told by her doctor she couldn't work, Ryder reluctantly withdrew from the film and returned to Petaluma to stay with her parents.

The press, however, were quick to attribute different motivations to Ryder's change of heart, placing boyfriend Johnny Depp centre frame. He was due to start work on his first major mainstream film role in *Edward Scissorhands*, and wanted Ryder to play the part of Edward's cheerleader girlfriend Kim Boggs. Unfortunately, the filming schedules of *The Godfather Part III* and *Edward Scissorhands* overlapped: Ryder couldn't do both. According to some sections of the press, Depp even flew to Rome himself, to collect Ryder and make sure she returned with him to co-star in his movie.

'I was told by my doctor I couldn't work,' claimed Ryder. 'I don't know why nobody believed it. The truth was so simple.' Depp claims he flew out to Rome to hold Ryder's hand and field her phone calls, mainly from *The Godfather*'s producers. It was fortuitous that she recovered in time to take part in the filming of *Edward Scissorhands*.

'Maybe people thought that Johnny was influencing me,' said Ryder, 'but he wasn't. He was just taking care of me, ordering room service, sticking his fingers down my throat, helping me throw up.' She credited Depp as a stabilising influence that got her through her *Godfather* troubles. 'Johnny and I have always been able to hang out together and separate ourselves from the unreality of the acting business. After the *Godfather* thing, I had nothing left in my system. I was a wreck

in every sense of the word and I just needed to rest and do nothing.'

Before embarking on *Edward Scissorhands* with Johnny Depp, Ryder was simply focused on making sure their relationship worked out. 'He is an amazing person whom I have an enormous amount of respect for and very deep feelings for,' she said of Depp. 'It's not a possessive, weird little Hollywood promenade.'

Edward Scissorhands began as a cry from the heart in the mind of a young boy called Tim Burton. Isolated as a child, Burton expressed his inability to communicate with those around him in a sketch – of a boy like himself, with a shock of wild, out of control black, straggly hair, and deadly scissor blades in place of fingers. It was an image reminiscent of the classic German children's story *Struwelpeiter*. His childhood imagination was driven by watching old horror movies on TV and drawing cartoons, many of which were dark or gruesome in nature.

Burton's first feature film came in 1985 with the quirky *Pee Wee's Big Adventure*, starring Paul Rubens as the child-like Pee Wee Herman in search of his lost bicycle. He followed this with the macabre comedy *Beetlejuice* (1988) which starred Michael Keaton as the title character, a demon who haunts the afterlives of a couple (Geena Davis and Alec Baldwin) killed in a car crash. Winona Ryder co-starred as their daughter Lydia Deetz and the object of Beetlejuice's affections. The $13 million film was the surprise hit of 1988. It grossed over $73 million and was hailed by critic Pauline Kael as 'a comedy classic'.

Burton had gathered a cult following from making very personal idiosyncratic productions, such as the five minute short *Vincent* (1982), the quirky *Pee Wee's Big Adventure* (1985) and surprise success *Beetlejuice* (1988). It was these films that convinced Warner Brothers that Burton was the man to helm their 1989 big budget blockbuster version of *Batman*. Burton ran into controversy almost right away with *Batman* in his casting of comic actor and *Beetlejuice* star Michael Keaton in the lead role of the caped crusader. Very different from the camp 1960s TV series which had starred Adam West, this Batman was a far darker vision and became the biggest grossing film of its year. Burton returned to the fold in 1992 for *Batman Returns*, an even more warped sequel which was just as successful. In between bat movies, Tim Burton turned his attention to *Edward Scissorhands* and the image that had haunted him from his childhood. Burton still had the drawing of the scissor-fingered figure, and he used it as the basis for a tale of love and despair set in a fantasy suburbia, not unlike the real life world of 1950s America in which he'd grown up.

Burton had read Caroline Thompson's novel *First Born* and, introduced to her through their agent, was sure he'd found the right collaborator for his project. She had been commissioned by Burton during pre-production of *Beetlejuice* to come up with a script for *Edward Scissorhands*.

'The idea actually came from a drawing I did a long time ago,' Burton explains. 'It was linked to a character who wants to touch, but can't, who was both creative and destructive – those sort of contradictions can create an ambivalence. It is a very teenage thing that had to do with relationships. I just felt I couldn't communicate.' 'Tim had the image of this character,' said Caroline Thompson of her unusual scripting assignment. 'He said he didn't know what to do with it, but the minute he described it and said the name *Edward Scissorhands*, I knew what to do. It was Tim

The role of Edward Scissorhands was the first to allow Depp to bring his love of silent movie acting to a modern role.

who came up with the image of the guy with the hedge clipper hands and I came up with everything that had to do with them.

Originally the idea was to produce *Edward Scissorhands* as a musical comedy and Thompson even wrote a song for it entitled 'I Can't Handle It'. The idea was scrapped in a subsequent revision, although most of the rest of the script remained remarkably similar to the early drafts. The story turned out to be another variation on Burton's obsession with the Frankenstein theme. Edward is the unfinished creation of an inventor (Vincent Price), who doubles up as his father, in echoes of Disney's Pinocchio. Before Edward is completed and given proper hands, the inventor dies. Sometime later, he's discovered by dedicated Avon Lady Peg Boggs (Dianne Wiest) making an out of the way call to the inventor's castle. There she discovers Edward and takes him home to live with her family in a weird, off-the-wall pastel coloured vision of suburbia. He becomes an object of fascination for the neighbours, whom he wins over at first with his hedge trimming and hairdressing skills, before they turn against him.

'The film is not autobiographical,' insists Burton. 'That's why I felt lucky to have Johnny, because he brought to it a lot of themes that are nearer his life which, when I started to talk to him, I liked very much. I could look at him and draw upon his world.' 'That character was the closest to me,' said Depp of *Edward Scissorhands*. 'Edward had a lot more dialogue in the script. But I personally felt that he was a little boy in the brain. A really small child.'

Johnny Depp wasn't the first automatic choice for the role. His most recent film had been *Cry Baby*, made in the slot between seasons of *21 Jump Street*. He was far from being a box-office draw, and it was a box-office draw that 20th Century Fox – the studio who backed Burton's vision – wanted for the lead in this quirky and possibly risky film. 'I was given a list of five people who were considered box office, and three of them were Tom Cruise,' admits Burton of the casting process. 'He certainly wasn't my ideal, but I talked to him. He was interesting, but I think it worked out for the best. A lot of questions came up – I don't really recall the specifics – but at the end of the meeting I said to him, "It's nice to have a lot of questions about the character, but you either do it, or your don't do it".'

Tom Cruise didn't do it – although he had been keen to play the role. He was just worried about his box office features being covered up in make-up and scars and had requested Burton that the ending of the film be changed so that Edward's features could revert to normal. The *LA Times* even reported that Cruise finally opted out of the film due to his fear of the characters 'lack of virility', not a consideration that would ever put Johnny Depp off a role.

'I was glad Johnny did it,' said Burton of his eventual star. 'I can't think of anybody else who would have done it for me that way. I didn't really know him. I hadn't seen that TV show he'd been in, but I must've seen a picture of him somewhere.'

Depp was trying hard to get out of his contract for *21 Jump Street*, having had his taste for movie making reawakened by his experiences with John Waters on the set of *Cry Baby*. 'When I first read *Edward Scissorhands*,' he said, 'I realised that it was something that was only going to come around once, that I would never see it again.' Receiving the script for *Edward Scissorhands* seemed to be a godsend – a way out of TV hell and a challenging and unique movie role to boot. 'I felt so

attached to this story,' wrote Depp in his introduction to Mark Salisbury's compilation of interviews with Tim Burton, *Burton on Burton*. 'Then reality set in. I was TV boy. No director in his right mind would hire me to play this character. I had done nothing workwise to show that I could handle this kind of role. How could I convince the director that I was Edward, that I knew him inside and out?'

A meeting was quickly arranged between Depp and Burton to discuss the possibility of him playing the role. Depp prepared by watching Burton's previous films: *Beetlejuice, Batman* and *Pee Wee's Big Adventure*. Having seen the films, Depp had even less confidence that he would win the role and tried to back out of the meeting. It was only with firm guidance from his ICM agent Tracey Jacobs that Depp and Burton finally came face-to-face in the coffee shop of the Bel Age Hotel in Los Angeles. This was not a meeting of minds, but a meeting of two introspective individuals who, despite their mutual lack of communication skills, got through to each other. As Depp writes: 'After sharing three or four pots of coffee, stumbling our way through each other's unfinished sentences but somehow still understanding each other, we ended the meeting with a hand shake and a "nice to meet you".'

It was Depp's first chance at a big movie role, something that would involve a lot of exposure and if it worked would bring him to a lot of people's notice. He'd been working on ways to approach the role based on the script and meeting Burton had given him a whole series of new ideas – but he still felt the part was beyond his reach. 'My chances were slim at best,' wrote Depp. 'Better known people than me were not only being considered for the role, but were battling, fighting, kicking, screaming, begging for it [including William Hurt, Tom Hanks and Robert Downey Jnr]. I waited for weeks, not hearing a thing in my favour. All the

In love on and off screen – Johnny Depp as Edward Scissorhands and Winona Ryder as Kim Boggs.

while, I was still researching the part. It was now not something I merely wanted to do, but something I had to do. Not for any ambitious, greedy, actory box-office draw reason, but because this story had now taken residence in the middle of my heart and refused to be evicted.'

One particular physical aspect of Depp reached through to Burton when casting *Edward Scissorhands*. 'I like people's eyes a lot and, especially with a character like this who doesn't really speak, eyes are very important'

Depp need not have worried. Finally the call came from Tim Burton who said only one thing to his young star: 'You are Edward Scissorhands.' Depp quickly realised the implications of his casting for his career: 'This role was freedom to create, experiment, learn and exorcise something in me. Rescued from the world of mass-product, bang 'em out TV-death by this odd, brilliant guy who had spent his youth drawing strange pictures.'

For Burton there really was no other choice. At the initial meeting with Depp he'd seen much personally and professionally in the actor which reflected the character and soul of *Edward Scissorhands*. 'Johnny is very much known as a teen idol and he's perceived as difficult and aloof. As a person he's a very funny, warm, great guy. He's a normal guy – at least my interpretation of normal – but he's perceived as dark and difficult and weird and is judged by his looks, but he's almost completely the opposite of this perception. So the themes of Edward, of image and perception, of somebody being perceived to be the opposite of what he is, was a theme he could relate to.'

Casting the other parts in *Edward Scissorhands* was somewhat easier. Burton settled on Winona Ryder – whom he'd worked with on *Beetlejuice* – for the part of

Edward offers his unique grooming services to Joyce
Monroe (Kathy Baker) and poodle.

Kim, the girl with whom Edward falls in love but cannot hold. It also helped that Depp and Ryder were all but engaged at the time, adding an extra resonance to the film. 'I like her very much,' said Burton of Ryder. 'She responds to this kind of dark material, and I thought the idea of her as the cheerleader, wearing a blonde wig, was very funny. I don't think their relationship affected the movie in a negative way. Perhaps it might have had it been a different kind of movie, something that was tapping more into some positive or negative side of their relationship, but this was such a fantasy. The fact that we were in Florida was helpful for the two of them to be together, because it was a pretty bizarre environment. They were very professional and didn't bring any weird stuff to the set.' Burton was aware of the dangers of his two stars having a personal relationship. 'I'm not a counsellor and had no intention of guessing how long their relationship might last, so I decided not to think about it. There was always a danger that they'd split up mid-shoot, but it never happened and their relationship helped the core romance more than it hindered it, in retrospect.'

Depp agreed with that assessment. 'The fact that we were together on the set of *Edward Scissorhands*, and in love, only fuelled what was going on between the character of Edward and Kim. The chemistry between us was even better for that.'

Dianne Wiest was cast as the Avon Lady Peg Boggs, who first brings Edward down from the castle to 'civilisation' and Alan Arkin played her husband, who seems totally unfazed by this new addition to the family unit. Anthony Michael Hall played the villain of the piece, the local teenage bully who sets about the corruption and destruction of Edward's character with glee. And, of course, there was Burton's idol Vincent Price, as the inventor who fails to finish his creation.

'It was a tough time for me,' said Depp of working on *Edward Scissorhands*. 'I was feeling really vulnerable – kind of insecure. Vincent Price was wonderful, he gave me great advice. And Alan Arkin and Dianne Wiest were real supportive too. They came to me when I was really doubting what I was doing, and how I was doing it. That I wasn't wrong.'

The first step in the production of *Edward Scissorhands* was to find a suitable location that would reflect the twisted fantasy of 1950s suburban California that Burton envisaged for the film. Burton and production designer Bo Welch settled on Florida, after scouting dozens of states for months at the beginning of 1990. A four-year-old housing settlement in Land O'Lakes, an area north of Tampa, was chosen, and the entire neighbourhood, consisting of 50 families, gave their consent for seven weeks of filming to take place in and around their houses. 44 out of 50 houses were given make-overs for the movie, including smaller windows and new details on the garage doors, as well as being repainted in a series of primary pastel colours, to fit in with Burton's fantasy twist on classic 1950s suburbia. It was also aimed at giving a sense of heightened reality, a sort of vision of this strange new world through the eyes of innocent Edward.

For the neighbourhood of Land O'Lakes, the arrival of Tim Burton, Johnny Depp and the movie making machine turned into something of a summer event in 1990. During the night scenes, families would surround the crew with lawnchairs and beer filled coolers to watch the proceedings. Some even went further, gaining parts in the movie as extras, including entire families, with kids and dogs in tow. Neighbours with cameras surrounded delivery men unloading the finished hedge

topiaries – in all manner of shapes and sizes, including a dinosaur, an elephant, a bear and a penguin, even Elvis – which Edward creates in the film.

For his part Depp had a difficult task ahead with *Edward Scissorhands*. The character he was to play had no grounding in reality. In the screenplay Edward was a totally fantastic creation, but one with clear emotional depths which the actor would have to communicate successfully to the audience if he were to make such a weird character work. To begin with Depp looked at the film as a *faux* fairytale, with Edward as an innocent, loose in a world he doesn't understand, but one in which he is keen to fit into, especially when he finds himself falling in love with Kim.

Burton noted, 'Johnny risked all by not making the character flamboyant or over the top. There he was on set covered from head to toe in leather, with few lines to speak. "Hmm, he's pretty restrained, blank almost," I said to myself, watching him perform. But when I saw the rushes, what he made come through, I just couldn't believe it. He'd glaze his eyes over and put across the subtle torment almost like a Walter Keane painting. The simple, internal style of acting he achieved was amazing.' Depp's first move was to throw out half the script and lose almost all of the dialogue Caroline Thompson had written for the character. 'Because Edward is not human, and not a robot, I didn't think that he would talk a lot,' said Depp. 'He would cut through everything, and have the most honest, pure answer with all the clarity in the world.'

'He plays it like a little boy,' commented Winona Ryder. 'You don't feel sorry for him, he just plays it with the honesty of someone who doesn't know how to put on a face. You know how little kids can blurt out the truth? That's what he does.' It is Depp's mesmerising performance that is the key to the success of *Edward Scissorhands* as both film and fairy tale. His touching and melancholy character revealed an actor who, although young, brought much that was serious to his work.

It was the first time that Depp turned to the work of the brilliant silent film

Show and Tell – Depp in his breakthrough performance as Edward Scissorhands.

comedian Charlie Chaplin as a research tool. Chaplin's shorts had set a standard for screen comedy which very few others were able to match, bringing pathos into his character as a core element. Depp developed Edward's walk, facial expressions and 'stranger in a strange land' approach to life from Chaplin's Little Tramp character. The decision to speak as little as possible is also drawn from Chaplin. For years, long into the sound period, Chaplin refused to have his Little Tramp character speak, and when he did it was in gibberish songs or nonsense dialogue. Depp's interest in silent comedians was also to fuel his character of Sam in *Benny & Joon*, where he drew on Buster Keaton as well as Chaplin.

Johnny Depp also had to come to terms with the costume and the physical limitations of the character he was playing. 'At first it was pretty strange working with no hands, but after a while it came to feel pretty natural. It was important to me that I found, as Edward does in the movie, not only the dangerous aspect of the hands, but also the stuff he could do on the positive side, such as the topiaries.'

When first approaching the physical practicalities of the hands, Tim Burton had toyed with having them operated entirely by puppeteers off-screen, but Depp's commitment to do as much of the role himself for real changed that. Stan Winston, an experienced movie creature creator, was brought on board by Burton to furnish Depp with a set of realistic, but non-lethal, razor fingers. 'The scissors had to be large,' said Burton, 'since I wanted Johnny to be beautiful and dangerous. We made him a pair and let him put them on and try to do something, and he learned better than just rehearsing what the feeling is like.'

The blades were made of durable plastic painted to gleam like chrome, with many back up sets prepared to cope with wear and tear and the odd expected accident or two as filming progressed. Each blade was attached to flexible urethane gloves, with each finger able to be moved independently, although Depp had to practise not to get the blades jammed in a tangle. Over time, the actor acquired the skill he needed to control his extended fingers, and the mechanical aided system was only used once in the finished film.

The wayward blades did sometimes prove difficult for Depp to control in reality. In one incident during a night shoot, when Anthony Michael Hall had to confront Depp as Edward, Depp accidentally punctured Hall's arm with his deadly fingers. Depp instantly apologised to the startled Hall, who saw his real blood dripping to the ground, mixed with the fake blood to be used for the scene. Hall's dazed response was 'It's cool, man.'

'I realised it was very important for Johnny to do it alone and really feel it,' said Tim Burton. 'He was in every shot and moving cables would have slowed everything down. Luckily, Johnny was sensitive to the problem and could artistically rationalise it, although it was hard for him to strike the poses and achieve an edgy mix of being beautiful and elegant one moment, and then by turn, dangerous and twisted looking.'

Edward Scissorhands was the first film to connect Depp overtly with oddball or freakish characters. 'The words "freak" and "freakish" have so many interpretations, and in a weird way he sort of relates to freaks, because he's treated as one,' said Burton of Depp. 'I think a lot of the character is him. He has this kind of naive quality which as you get older gets tested and has holes poked into it. I would imagine Johnny is somebody who would want to protect that to some degree.'

Depp was almost as enraptured by the presence of Vincent Price on the film as was Burton. 'One of the greatest things that Vincent Price, a very, very smart man, ever told me was "buy art,"' said Depp. 'That's a piece of advice I'll treasure forever. I haven't bought a home yet and I don't know if, when I do, it's going to be in the States. It may be in France somewhere. But I have bought a lot of paintings and drawings and some photographs. It's good to have things around that feed you.'

Like Burton, Depp was also in touch with Price up until the older actor's death in 1993. Depp came to regard Price as a father figure on the film. He was in awe of his achievements, for which he felt Price had never really received due recognition. His willingness to listen and heed Price's advice, to invest in art, to try at all costs to avoid typecasting – which had blighted Price's own career – was another aspect of Depp's continuing insecurity in his life. The fact that he spent his money – and he was now earning significant sums – on works of art rather than a permanent home reinforced Depp's rootless character. With money in the bank, he continued his habit of living in hotels and rented apartments which had developed during the shooting of *21 Jump Street* in Vancouver. Even his cars were rented, with Depp refusing to actually own one. 'We used to call him the homeless millionaire,' said John Waters. 'I'd say, "Where do you want me to send your mail? A Bench, Anywhere, USA?" Now he has an address, but I'm not sure he looks in the mailbox. I'm not sure he participates in the mail. He has a style that looks like he's not trying.'

Depp's *Edward Scissorhands* performance required a lot of effort, but he hoped that it came across as if he wasn't trying. Hailed by critics as a modern fairy tale with a cutting edge, *Edward Scissorhands* went on to gross over $54 million in America alone. The subject matter gave headline writers a field day, with the mostly positive reviews running under headings like 'a cut above'; 'a sharp act to follow'; 'blade runner'; 'cutting a dash' and even 'shear magic'.

'Looney Tunes gothic' was the tag that J. Hoberman attached to the film, writing in the *Village Voice* in December 1990, with *Edward Scissorhands* enjoying a Yuletide release. 'Depp's eloquently sad eyes seem a factor of his evident physical discomfort – hidden under a ton of make-up, hands encased inside an arsenal of implements out of a David Cronenberg film.'

Released the following summer in Britain, Burton's film had an equally welcome reception. Adam Mars-Jones, writing in *The Independent* noted astutely: 'Tim Burton has given Johnny Depp the best present a sultry, pouting teen idol ever had – an almost complete disguise.'

Depp briefly returned to his debut film with his brief cameo in *Freddy's Dead: The Final Nightmare* (1991). The film was to be the last in the Freddy Krueger cycle of horror flicks which had jump started Johnny Depp's career with the original film in 1984. In a favour to first-time director and *Cry Baby* producer Rachel Talalay, Depp appeared in a brief TV anti-drug promo, describing an egg frying in a pan as 'your brain on drugs'. He's credited on the film under the bizarre pseudonym of Oprah Noodlemantra. As well as providing a sense of closure – he was in the first, so it was fitting he was in what was supposed to be the last Freddy film – Depp's appearance was also in keeping with his work on public information films, and even the anti-drug stance of episodes of *21 Jump Street*. But you can't keep a good ghoul down, and Freddy was back from the dead in 1994, in *Wes Craven's New Nightmare*, a witty resurrection for the character ten years on by his original creator. Craven's new conceit was to have Freddy cross into the real world of Hollywood film-making to wreak havoc. Freddy was back from the dead yet again in the unnecessary *Freddy vs Jason* (2003). Johnny Depp didn't appear in either film – he had enough horrors of his own, dealing with the ending of his relationship with Winona Ryder.

Whatever both Depp and Ryder had felt about the attention paid to their relationship at the beginning, years of hounding by the press had taken their toll. It was hard enough to maintain a relationship when both their careers were developing so quickly and the couple spent so much time apart on different film locations. On top of that, both Depp and Ryder found themselves accused in gossip columns and film magazines of sleeping with their co-stars, of engaging in furious fights and of no longer being a couple at all. Ryder was clear on where she laid most of the blame for the eventual collapse of her romance with Johnny Depp. 'I remember us desperately hating being hounded. It was horrible and it definitely took its toll on our relationship. Every day we heard that we were either cheating on each other or we were broken up when we weren't. It was like this constant mosquito buzzing around us…Now, I feel like I have an identity, whereas before I was so used to people telling me who I was. I was Winona! I was precocious! I was adorable! I was sexy! These labels were being slapped on me, and I didn't have any life outside of it.'

The press romantically linked Ryder with her co-stars, including Gary Oldman on *Dracula* and Daniel Day Lewis on *The Age of Innocence*. After splitting with Depp, Ryder had thrown herself into movie work, completing *Bram Stoker's Dracula, The House of the Spirits* and *The Age of Innocence* in quick succession. 'I was desperately unhappy,' is how Ryder recalls the period. 'I couldn't sleep. There was so much drama in my life, I didn't have time for the little things that make life fun and make me happy. I had to get back to real life outside of my work. I know who I am now. I'm 23 and I want to act my age.'

In the spring of 1993, Ryder met Soul Asylum singer David Pirner at an MTV Unplugged gig. She and Pirner rapidly became an item, in a relationship that threatens to be as well documented by the press as her previous one with Depp. 'Our relationship is different from any I've ever had,' claimed Ryder. 'It's more casual, it's more of a friendship, really. What I'm basically saying is that it's not full of drama.' Ryder's later life would continue to be full of drama, especially the ignomy of facing a high-profile shoplifting charge in 2002.

Johnny Depp believes that his relationship with Winona Ryder slowly unravelled over time, the pressure of their film careers taking its toll. In June 1993, Depp said publicly: 'We split up a month ago. When you're with someone and you love them it's never easy to cut the string – to sever the connection. But, with us, it just came to seem the natural thing to do – a natural progression – just something that had to happen. I wouldn't say that our splitting was exactly a devastating experience for either of us, really. We're still friends. We still talk. And everything's fine: very amicable, very nice.'

Whatever he might have said in public, behind the scenes Depp was devastated by the ending of yet another of his relationships. 'It was a really lonely time for me,' he admitted. 'I poisoned myself constantly: drinking, didn't eat right, no sleep, lots of cigarettes. My feelings were close to the surface, so they were easy to manipulate. I did feel very lost at times, and very confused about everything.' A friend confided anonymously with *People* magazine: 'He was so desperately in love with Winona, that when they broke up, he wouldn't admit that it was over for the longest time.'

Although Ryder never expressed her views in public, it was widely believed that Depp's reluctance to commit to a longer term union in the form of marriage was the final nail in the coffin for an already rocky relationship. It wasn't the first time that one of Depp's romances had fallen apart because he refused to be tied down. He seemed to have a real difficulty in knowing his own mind or feelings. 'I've sort of always been in love and then, I've never been in love, really, when I look back on it,' he said, candidly. 'There were certain times in my life, when you get very close to someone because you're away from the unconditional love of your family, and you're sort of out there in the world alone and you need the love and attention and intimacy and a lot of stuff, and you confuse caring for someone – loving someone, even – with being in love. I've done that in the past…'

Whatever his own personal failings, Depp refused to accept them as the prime cause of the failure of his lengthy romance with Ryder. His own words suggested that he saw his relationships as replacements for his own shattered family, but would never admit that this may have caused their demise. For Depp, it was that old demon the press that had got to them. 'I've also learned that I'm never going to be able to have a normal relationship like most people get to have. There is always going to be someone chatting about us or reading about us in a supermarket somewhere…'

In a misguided move to deal with the voracious appetite of the celebrity gossips, Depp and Ryder had started out their life together being open with the press, in the hope that sated, it would slink away and finally leave the couple alone. It was never to be. 'It's very hard to have a personal life in Hollywood. In my relationship with Winona it was a mistake to be as open as we were. I thought it would destroy that curiosity monster. Instead it fed it. I had nothing but bad luck after talking about this stuff. It became such a public thing. Everyone felt like they were either a part of it, or owned a part of it, or that they'd somehow got the right to ask me about her. I hated it.'

However much Depp may have wanted to forget his time with Ryder, he couldn't escape the tattoo on his right arm: Winona Forever. 'Our break-up doesn't take away from the honesty of this,' said Depp of his troublesome tattoo. 'I meant it. If I were keeping a journal, I wouldn't go back and say "We broke up, so I'm erasing everything." The relationship was up and down.' In the years since breaking up with Winona Ryder, Depp had his Winona Forever tattoo removed, slowly but surely. At one stage it read Wino Forever, which gave the tabloids something amusing to write about. 'We were together for three years,' said Depp, 'and at the time, I really did think it would be forever.'

The biggest shock to Johnny Depp was being alone again after such a long relationship. 'Being lonely is scary. I've been lonely many times. Making one of my recent movies was four months of intermittent misery. It isn't that much fun.'

Johnny Depp with Winona Ryder – his highest-profile girlfriend before Kate Moss
– at the premiere of Edward Scissorhands.

CHAPTER THREE

King of Kook

HOLLYWOOD has been a magnet for expatriate European filmmakers since the early movie empires were built by East European Jews. This was especially true during the years of the Second World War, when many of Europe's finest actors, writers and directors fled the battlefields to practice their craft in safety. It was against this background that Serbian Emir Kusturica – once a controversial documentary maker for Sarajevo Television – set out to dissect the mythical American Dream, filtered through European eyes, in the wonderfully surreal *Arizona Dream* (1992). Kusturica won the Palme D'Or at the Cannes Film Festival twice, first in 1984 for his depiction of the national betrayals of Yugoslavia in the fifties seen through the eyes of a young boy in *When Father Was Away On Business*, and he won again in 1995 for his three hour epic *Underground*, which comments on the history of Yugoslavia from the Second World War through to the outbreak of the 1990s civil war. He also won the Cannes Best Director prize for his third film *The Time of the Gypsies* in 1989.

Kusturica found himself with an enviable reputation based on a slim body of work and was invited to teach a film course at Columbia University in New York. Fascinated by America and all that it offered, Kusturica eagerly accepted the post, with a view to devising a film all about America from an outsider's viewpoint. With $17 million of French money and two French producers, Claude Ossard and Yves Marmon, Kusturica developed a script first entitled *Arrowtooth Waltz,* later changed to *American Dream* and finally *Arizona Dream*. 'The American dream is the dream of everyone in Western civilisation,' said Kusturica, 'to have a car, a little money and a house. But when I was living in America for two years, I found that America itself was very different. People are unhappy and much poorer than I expected. There is a problem, then, because in destroying the illusion of the American dream you are destroying part of your youth, a childhood spent watching movies.'

The actual kernel of *Arizona Dream* came from a script idea of one of Kusturica's Columbia students. David Atkin's script contained 'a little piece about a young boy who didn't know what to do with his life. Somehow, I was interested in exploring the declining empire of the car industry in the States, because America is always the country of cars and movies. In this small piece I saw something similar to what I wanted to do.'

This basic scenario created another character ideal for Johnny Depp. He found himself unable to resist the offer to play Axel Blackmar, a twenty-year-old man orphaned when his parents die in a car crash. Blackmar has lost his way in life and holds down a job counting fish for the New York Department of Fish and Game. His low-level contentment is interrupted by the arrival of his Uncle Leo (played by veteran US comic Jerry Lewis), an Arizona Cadillac dealer who wants to off load his failing car sales business onto his self-absorbed nephew.

'I was thrilled to work with Kusturica because I saw *Time of the Gypsies* and it was one of the greatest things I've ever seen,' said Depp, happy to work with another director then little-known in America, who was willing to explore and experiment with his material. The role saw Depp playing another offbeat oddball who has taken a unique path in life. 'There's a part of me that always wanted to change,' said Depp. 'For example, ever since I was a kid, I was fascinated by the idea of time travel, of being someone else in another time. I think that's probably a normal thing – let's hope it is. What interests me is that so-called "normal" society considers them outcasts or on the fringe, or oddballs. With any part you play, there is a certain amount of yourself in it. There has to be, otherwise, it's just not acting. It's lying. That's not to say that I feel different than others. Maybe they have a more difficult time saying "I don't feel accepted" or "I feel insecure." These characters are passive: I see them as receivers. I've identified with them since I was very young.'

The production of *Arizona Dream* was a mammoth undertaking, with shooting in Alaska, Arizona and New York, a temperamental cast and an even more temperamental director. Cast alongside Depp and Jerry Lewis were Faye Dunaway and Lili Taylor as Elaine and Grace Stalker a mother and daughter with whom Alex Blackmar gets involved. Alex finds a new way to live out his dreams in their

Life as a used car salesman? Depp ponders his future
in Arizona Dream.

company – after all, one wants to fly and the other wishes she were a turtle. Also featured is actor Vincent Gallo, once a 1970s underground New York musician and an accomplished painter.

Kusturica suffered what he later called a nervous breakdown during the shooting of *Arizona Dream*. After weeks of exhausting night shoots, with an escalating budget, an increasingly erratic cast and looming money-men, Kusturica upped sticks and returned to New York, refusing to shoot any more of the uncompleted film until the financiers gave him more time, space and money to realise his vision. Such antics are generally described as the amorphous 'creative differences' which scupper so many Hollywood projects. Most films would have seen the director replaced and the movie completed, but the producers discovered that Kusturica had the cast, including Depp, on his side. The entire cast of the film refused to consider continuing with anyone other than Kusturica calling the shots.

'I'm a European director,' said Kusturica, 'not an American and I just wasn't ready for what they throw at you. They don't want imagination. They want a beginning, a middle and an end, with the end nice and convenient and happy.'

Kusturica was ready to acknowledge that his bizarre all-or-nothing way of working brought most of his problems upon himself. 'I don't know what's the matter with me. Perhaps I'm just crazy, but I have this vision and I just have to complete it, no matter what the cost. I'd hate to be my producer. With both *Arizona Dream* and *Underground* I thought I was going to die at least twice. It's too much of a strain.'

Vincent Gallo, a friend of Depp's since his *21 Jump Street* days, observed the behind the scenes mayhem on *Arizona Dream*. He'd also noted how much Depp had changed, had re-invented himself since being a rising TV star filming in Vancouver. 'He was dating Winona. They were wearing thrift shop clothes for the first time. He was tattooed and earringed and on a TV show. I just hated them,' commented the energetically wacky Gallo.

Their friendship suffered some strain during the making of *Arizona Dream*. According to Gallo, Depp found a soulmate in Emir Kusturica and began constantly to require his director's attention. 'And he was not completely nice to me to get it,' said Gallo, bitterly. 'Johnny has this need to be heavily involved with the director. It's almost like a love affair. Emir and Johnny carried around Dostoevsky and Kerouac books and wore black. They had never worn black in their lives. They kept everybody in the cast and crew awake all night, because they were blasting music and getting drunk.'

Kusturica had other problems with another member of his cast during the filming in Douglas, Arizona. Faye Dunaway was perhaps used to a different kind of treatment than that dished out to her by her European director, or perhaps she wasn't getting enough attention as Kusturica courted his young leading man. 'To understand Mrs Dunaway is actually not very easy,' admitted Kusturica. 'I didn't have clashes with her, but hers is a kind of method acting which is not co-acting. That's the problem with Hollywood.'

The strangely mixed cast that Depp found himself working with was an element of his director's take on the weirdness of America itself. Jerry Lewis had not worked in movies much in years, with the notable exception of his dramatic turn as the

kidnapped talk show host in Martin Scorsese's *The King of Comedy* opposite Robert DeNiro. 'I had heard a lot of bad things about Jerry,' said Kusturica. 'They must have been lies. For me, Jerry Lewis was crazy. He was extremely pleased because I was laughing at what he did, but at the same time I had to control him, because in this movie he is dying and has many very serious scenes. He is a very good actor.'

Kusturica and Depp ventured to the Cannes Film festival in France in 1992 to promote the unfinished *Arizona Dream*. It was a trip that Vincent Gallo believes was more to soothe Depp's ego than for the legitimate purpose of selling the film. 'Johnny had this need to go to Cannes and have everybody pay for him to get there, and to stay at the Hotel du Cap, and then refuse to do interviews, because he had read in an article that Brando refused to do interviews.'

All of Kusturica's four films had won awards – including *Do You Remember Dolly Bell?* which scooped the Golden Lion at Venice in 1981 – and *Arizona Dream* was no different when it was finally completed, winning the Special Jury Prize at the Berlin Film Festival in 1993. The commercial release of the film was sporadic, however, with America itself being denied a chance to see Kusturica's take on their land of dreams. The film enjoyed a successful and lengthy run in Paris, France, mainly because of the French infatuation with Jerry Lewis. *Arizona Dream* was finally released to art house cinemas in Britain in July 1995, only after Kusturica had taken the Palme D'Or at

Depp and co-star Faye Dunaway take a break during the filming of
Arizona Dream. Depp got on well with director Emir Kustirica, but
Dunaway didn't.

Cannes for *Underground.* It later enjoyed a strong afterlife on DVD.

Sight and Sound welcomed the belated release of the film: 'Johnny Depp is the visionary delinquent who refuses to accept the strictures of the adult world,' wrote Geoffrey MacNab. 'The film is by turns infuriating and inspiring: it has a random, haphazard quality utterly at odds with most American cinema. Like Depp and Dunaway who spend their time attempting to build primitive aeroplanes in the backyard, Kusturica feels free to experiment. It is as bizarre and original a film as any European has ever made about America.'

To Johnny Depp the leading role in the slight romantic comedy *Benny & Joon* (1994) seemed like ideal material for him. Like many of his previous films it gave him a chance to work yet again with a little known director. Depp's worries about his own performances – which had haunted him since *Platoon* – caused him to gravitate towards new, untried or maverick directors. He wanted the freedom to experiment that a young, inexperienced director brought him. He also wanted to escape the control that a well established director might try to impose on him. Depp didn't want an 'auteur' director cramping his patented quirky style. In fact, by this stage, many critics began to believe that perhaps Depp was in danger of painting himself into a corner with his choice of roles.

'Do I search out the weirdest thing I can find and then do it just because it is the weirdest thing I can find? Well, the answer is no. I just do the things that I like. However, I have to admit that what I like does tend to be left-field,' said Depp, whenever the topic was raised. 'I feel somehow much more comfortable playing it. I relate more easily than I do when I run across straight roles. I hate the obvious stuff, I just don't respond to it.'

Benny & Joon had gone through a variety of possible cast line-ups as it was anticipated in movie circles to be a well-received screwball comedy. The plot revolved around a charming, if offbeat, character falling in love with the leading man's emotionally disturbed sister. The first team in the roles of the offbeat charmer and the quirky sister were Tom Hanks and Julia Roberts. Both were hot properties, even though at that time Tom Hanks hadn't yet started his Oscar-winning streak which soon followed. That idea fell through and real-life Hollywood couple Tim Robbins and Susan Sarandon were approached to take on the roles. The pair had previously starred together in the baseball comedy *Bull Durham* (1988), with Kevin Costner. But that didn't work out either. Finally, the studio – MGM – settled on Depp, who'd been lobbying for the part, in the role of the unbalanced, but charming stranger, Laura Dern as the sister, and up-and-coming ex-*Cheers* star Woody Harrelson as the protective straight-laced brother.

Just when things seemed settled, the *Benny & Joon* curse struck once again, with two of the trio dropping out. Laura Dern had secured an Oscar nomination for her role in *Rambling Rose* (1991) and felt she could not put up with third billing after the two male leads, so she walked off the picture. Second to jump ship was Woody Harrelson. The *Cheers* star was desperate to establish his straight-man credentials in Hollywood and lose the *Cheers* comedy barman image. He'd entered negotiations with director Adrian Lyne to secure the hotly contested role of Demi Moore's cuckolded husband in the Robert Redford-starring thriller *Indecent*

Proposal (1993). With the role apparently in the bag, Harrelson left the *Benny &
Joon* team in the lurch, with the June shooting date looking rather precarious.

Depp was eventually joined by the much more dependable Aidan Quinn as
brother Benny, a down-to-earth garage mechanic and Mary Stuart Masterson as the
emotionally disturbed sister, Joon, who is under Benny's constant care. Quinn was
pleased to step into the breach, seeing the film as different from the usual run-of-the-
mill Hollywood production. 'It has a fable-like quality,' said Quinn. 'It's an unusual
story for a studio film. Benny's got the weight of the world on him. He's the mud of
reality, while the others are the sprites of magic. My character is very much a straight
man – I'd like to play fewer of them! A person gets typed as "Oh, he's a serious,
sensitive actor" and all that crap. But don't get me wrong – I love this movie.' At last,
after all the Hollywood bickering, shooting the picture could finally begin.

The initial concept for *Benny & Joon* originated with screenwriter Barry Berman.
Berman was a graduate of Ringling Brothers and Barnum & Bailey's highly
competitive Clown College in Venice, Florida. He'd earned his apprenticeship
touring the country in his big shoes and bright make-up, performing in the world
renowned circus. Between shows, he and his fellow clowns would screen hours of
classic comedy films, including many reels featuring Buster Keaton and Charlie
Chaplin. It was this experience that ultimately became the inspiration for Berman
to create the character of Sam, played by Depp.

It wasn't until five years after he left the big top and hung up his oversize shoes
and red nose that Berman actually got around to writing the screenplay, developing
the original story with Leslie McNeil, a collaborator from a previous project.
Together they worked on the script, developing details to fit into the story for a few
more years, until it came to the attention of first time movie producers Susan
Arnold and Donna Roth.

Susan Arnold herself felt an affinity with the character of Joon Pearl. The
producer had previously worked for several years with the Imagination Workshop,
a California-based arts program that worked with underprivileged and
disenfranchised people, as well as with psychiatric patients. 'My experience with
the workshop certainly peaked my desire to make a movie about someone who
had a little bit harder time in life than most of us,' admitted Arnold.

Barry Berman recalled that the character of Joon that so entranced the would-
be producers and finally got his film made did not emerge until several drafts into
the screenplay. 'Joon wasn't based on any person I knew,' admitted Berman, 'but
her existence created an element of independence between the characters that
enabled me to explore the general enmeshments that occur in just about all
relationships. Her emotional problems didn't limit my range for Joon's activities.
She could be totally lucid, just as easily as she could be slightly insane.'

After approving a final draft of the script, the next task for producers Arnold and
Roth was to find a director for the project. They knew they would need someone
who could capture on film the humour found within their sensitive and often funny
love story. It would be no easy task in blockbuster-dominated, career-driven
Hollywood. However, they did find their man in Canadian-born director Jeremiah
Chechik, whose career as an award-winning commercials director had won him the
opportunity to direct features, although his first shot was the lowest common

denominator (but box office hit) *National Lampoon's Christmas Vacation* (1989). 'Jeremiah passionately loved the script and, most importantly, the characters,' said Roth. 'Not only could he see the story's heart, but he understood its humorous side as well.'

Chechik was clear about what drew him to the *Benny & Joon* script. 'In the most simple way, it is a romance between two oddities who meet and fall in love. The story is universal because every human heart contains the potential for both pain and pleasure. The story has a fable quality to it, but it's also very believable.'

Chechik's first task was to sort out the cast for his film, with Johnny Depp the obvious choice for the role of oddball Sam. 'When I first met Johnny to discuss *Benny & Joon*, I began to understand how much he had brought to the role of *Edward Scissorhands*. He is so emotionally expressive, doing what seems to be so little. It was clear that he would bring a thoroughly original and exciting energy to the role of Sam.'

Producer Donna Roth concurred with Chechik's choice for the pivotal role. 'There is something magical about Johnny, there is no doubt about it. The first time we met him, it was like meeting a blind date at the front door and discovering, "My God, he is so wonderful." Johnny exceeded all of our wildest expectations.' In the film Sam is a big fan of Charlie Chaplin and Buster Keaton, dressing like Keaton and performing slapstick routines in the park to amuse Joon. For Depp, the role was too much to resist, especially as it gave him another chance to draw on the work of Keaton. He'd previously used silent comedy for his role as Edward Scissorhands, which Sam most closely resembled, while he'd flirted with the idea of playing Chaplin in Richard

Alone in the world – Depp often played characters like emotionally disturbed Sam in Benny & Joon.

Attenborough's bio-pic of the great comedian.

The opportunity to bring the work of Keaton to a whole new generation of moviegoers was a big attraction to Depp. 'I had such a great time rediscovering Keaton, Chaplin and Harold Lloyd. Comedy, especially when it is so physical, is extremely demanding. I developed an even greater respect for those guys as I began to try to do what they had accomplished in such a seemingly effortless way.'

Donna Roth felt that the actress playing Joon had to possess great skill to do justice to the part. 'One of the many things that shines through Joon is that she is really smart, and Mary Stuart Masterson is witty, intelligent and a wonderful actress who we knew could portray all sides of this unique character.'

Mary Stuart Masterson came from an acting family, headed by her father Peter Masterson, a director, and her actress mother Carlin Glynn. At the age of seven she'd made her film debut in *The Stepford Wives* (1975), opposite her father. She studied acting throughout her life, primarily in New York, although she did spend two summers at Robert Redford's Sundance Institute, working as an actress for hire for budding film-makers. She'd appeared in many films, but rarely in leading or starring roles, with her major appearance before *Benny & Joon* being in *Fried Green Tomatoes at the Whistle Stop Cafe* (1991). 'I wanted Joon to be someone the

Kooky kinship – Sam (Johnny Depp) and Joon (Mary Stuart Masterson).

audience could identify with and be moved by, without viewing her as a victim or a tragic character,' said director Chechik. He found all that in Mary Stuart Masterson. For her part, the actress was intrigued by the jigsaw-like nature of her role that involved piecing together a character from snatches of backstory. 'Joon is everything from a highly intelligent woman with a quick wit to a person with virtually no grasp on reality. It was really revealing to play a character whose confidence is shaken by the confusion she lives with everyday. My own insecurities came right to the surface as a result. But this story is basically about love. There are circumstances that are universal in this story, such as learning how much you can love someone and still allow them to be free.'

The final member of the *Benny & Joon* trio was Aidan Quinn. 'Aidan is a superb actor who is able to convey, in the most real and believable ways, the very delicate shades of this character's emotions,' said Chechik. Born into an Irish family, Quinn remained in the United States when his family returned from there to Ireland. Quinn started acting in the theatre in Chicago, before making his film debut in James Foley's *Reckless* (1984) opposite Darryl Hannah. He proved to be the ideal straightman for the quirky behaviour of the two other characters in *Benny & Joon*.

With the cast finally in place, research and training took over – especially for Depp and Masterson, who both had areas to study in order to ensure that their characters appeared authentic on the big screen. As well as watching many silent movies, Depp found himself in the hands of Dan Kamin, a mime, magician and silent film buff who served as his coach and choreographer in recreating the comedy of the screen legends who are part of Sam's life. Kamin had written the study *Charlie Chaplin's One Man Show* and also served as a consultant on Richard Attenborough's film life of Charlie Chaplin.

'Since Sam's brand of comedy is physical rather than verbal, in much the same way as his silent film heroes, we concentrated on a style of movement,' explained Kamin. 'We started with magic tricks, using sleight of hand and worked our way up to recreating Keaton's patented falls. The subtle movements are the hardest to capture, but Johnny did a marvellous job. He was really courageous and worked hard – even at the small things.' To recreate the style of the Keaton and Chaplin silent slapstick comedy, Dan Kamin helped Depp fine-tune his natural physical abilities. 'He gave me some pointers on movement,' said Depp. 'I enjoyed the slapstick parts of the movie, although I sustained some injuries.'

Many of the scenes of slapstick were new, inspired by something Keaton performed previously, but others were straight recreations of some great silent comedy movie moments. One such is the famous dancing rolls sequence, performed by Chaplin in his 1926 film *The Gold Rush*. The same sequence was recreated by Robert Downey Jnr in the role of Chaplin in the bio-pic for which Depp was once considered. For all his interest in Chaplin and other silent clowns, he would never play a straight recreation of their characters. Magpie-like Depp lifted bits of business or general approaches from Keaton and Chaplin to feed into characters he was creating from scratch.

Mary Stuart Masterson had in depth research to undertake in her attempt to make Joon's illness seem real. Her hours of preparation involved, among other things, reading a great deal of material about the mentally ill and meeting with members of the Imagination Workshop. The actress also extended her devotion to duty by taking up painting for the film – Joon's paintings often reflect her mental state – and several of the paintings seen in Joon's studio in the film were, in fact, Masterson's own works.

In the final two weeks of pre-production, Chechik called a summit meeting of his four principal actors – the three stars and Julianne Moore, cast as Benny's would-be love interest. 'It was important for me to create an atmosphere where the actors didn't feel at all inhibited about experimenting with ideas and contributing to the process,' explained Chechik. 'At the outset, I established very specific parameters for the story and its characters, but then, as rehearsals progressed, it became a mutual journey of discovery. I think the fact that we worked with a relatively small cast and crew who got along so well also helped to create a level of intimacy so important for this kind of story.'

The chosen location for *Benny & Joon* was Spokane, Washington. The city offered several backdrops for the film, from the lush Riverfront Park, where Sam stages some of his slapstick performances, to the airy suburbs and the grittier downtown sites. The interiors were shot on a soundstage converted from a recently abandoned warehouse. The major challenge for production designer Neil Spisak (who would later work on the *Spider-Man* movies) was in creating the visual look of *Benny & Joon*'s world, especially in the colourful playthings, antiques and trinkets found in Joon's art studio. The set was created twice, once on the makeshift soundstage and the second time as an addition to the real house used for *Benny & Joon*'s home, located along the Spokane River. Despite his music video background, reinforced by a similar background for cinematographer John Schwartzman, Jeremiah Chechik resisted swamping his fragile characters in flashy visuals. 'I wanted the visuals to advance the emotional life of the story, but I didn't want them to dominate. I wanted the camerawork to be beautiful, but naturalistic; to be poetic, but not to outshine the characters. Most importantly, I wanted the camera to give the actors a stage for their characters, not the reverse.'

Critical reception for *Benny & Joon* was overwhelmingly positive, though one or two reviewers noted that the almost magical realist nature of the script had been let down by Chechik's sometimes leaden direction. *Sight and Sound* had much to say about Depp's role: 'The idea that getting it together with Johnny Depp is an effective therapy for mental illness,' wrote Claire Monk, 'certainly holds more appeal than, say *Rain Man*. Depp's precision clowning makes for some moments of great visual comedy, as he punts across the kitchen using a mop and mimes his way into a job, his role looks increasingly like a consolation prize for not getting to play Chaplin.'

In *The Mail on Sunday*, Tom Hutchinson wrote: 'As the clowning minder to a mentally ill girl, Johnny Depp tenderly reinforces the role of eccentric outsider which has become his province. Delightfully played, it is a fable with a potential to touch the heart.'

Following *Benny & Joon,* Depp was beginning to worry that some of the parts he was being offered were being written especially for his kooky, offbeat cinematic persona. His public assessment was, however, upbeat – it had to be: 'Overall I don't think I'm limiting myself, because I'm doing things that are true to me. I see these

*The Keaton influence – Depp drew on the influence of silent era
comedian Buster Keaton for Sam in Benny & Joon.*

guys [his characters] as much more normal than what's considered normal. There seems to be this constant theme in the things that I do which deal with people who are considered "freaks" by so-called normal people. I guess I'm attracted to these off-beat roles because my life has been a bit abnormal. The only thing I have a problem with is being labelled.' The reason for this justification was Depp's next casting. He had been labelled as the ideal star to play the title character in the film *What's Eating Gilbert Grape?*, and despite any doubts he may have been harbouring about playing another lost, vulnerable, innocent soul, Depp signed up.

The film was based on the novel by Peter Hedges, who also wrote the screenplay. 'Gilbert Grape is stuck in Endora working in a grocery store and everybody's gnawing at him: his family, his friends, his lover,' says Hedges of the title character. 'Into the town rolls a girl who collides with everything that has been closed up inside him.'

The novel had only been published a few days, according to Hedges, when he began receiving phone calls from Swedish film director Lasse Hallström. Hallström had received an Oscar for Best Foreign Language Film *My Life as a Dog* (1985), as well as a Directors Guild of America Award. *My Life as a Dog* had also been awarded the Best Foreign Language Film Trophy by the New York Film Critics Circle. Hallström had made his American film debut in 1990 with *Once Around,* a little seen film which starred Richard Dreyfuss and Holly Hunter. To Hallström, Hedges' Gilbert Grape novel seemed like the perfect material to recapture the spirit of *My Life as a Dog* in an all-American setting. Like Emir Kusturica, he was another European exile intent on producing his vision of America.

'All of my movies have the ambition of being truthful,' said Hallström. 'If you want to imitate life, you have to blend drama and comedy since life is both dramatic and comedic.' The phone calls to Hedges were welcomed by the writer. 'This was great news for me, because *My Life as a Dog* is one of my favourite films. I realised that Lasse could bring great humanity to these characters where another director might make fun of them.'

Hedges was even more pleased when Hallström announced who he had in mind to play the title character. Having been impressed by Depp's oddball turns in *Edward Scissorhands* and, most recently, *Benny & Joon*, Hallström had found his Gilbert. 'Gilbert is very much an observer, a reactor in the movie,' said Hallström. 'Johnny Depp was the perfect actor. He has the sensitivity that Gilbert Grape needs.'

'He has an almost burning desire to make ugly choices,' said Hedges of Depp's film career. 'He comes with a physical beauty that's just astonishing, and at the same time he has no interest in being that. When I met him he had this really long hair. He showed up at the meeting, very quiet, really shy, and was teaching us magic tricks. I thought, I suppose he could be Gilbert…'

Depp himself was keen on the character, and almost instantly had a handle on the kind of laid back, naturalistic performance he wanted to give in the role. 'Gilbert Grape has had to leave his dreams behind because of circumstances,' explained Depp. 'He has a hostility that he can't express because of his duties and responsibilities to his family. To be able to deal with himself everyday, he's had to make himself sort of numb so that he's not affected too much by everything.'

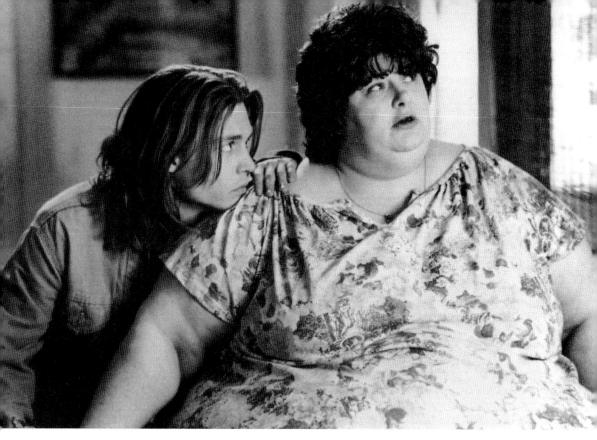

'There are things that have happened in my life that parallel things in Gilbert's life,' he admitted, referring specifically to his parents' divorce and the departure of his father, where the young Depp was the only one left to look after his heart-broken mother. Even at this stage in his career, Depp still found himself haunted by echoes from his childhood. In the story, Gilbert has been considered the man of the weird Grape household since his father committed suicide. He lives in a sprawling house with his mother (Darlene Cates), a 600 lb mountain of a woman whose huge proportions are playing havoc with the infrastructure of the house and who hasn't left the building for years. The other members of the Grape family are no help either to the struggling Gilbert. His brother Arnie (played by Oscar nominated actor Leonardo DiCaprio) is coming up to eighteen years old, but was never expected to have survived childhood and is severely mentally impaired. His older sister Amy (Laura Harrington) is a home-maker in the making who yearns for normal domesticity, while the youngest sister Ellen (Mary Kate Schellhardt) regards Gilbert as a surrogate father figure.

Gilbert's troubles extend beyond his family, to take in his friends, employers and customers in the tiny, middle-of-nowhere dead end town of Endora. He works as a clerk at the Lamson Grocery Store, which is battling against a big chain hypermarket on the outskirts of town; he's having an affair with Mrs Betty Carver (Mary Steenburgen); while his best friend Tucker (John C. Reilly) sees the opening of a franchise burger joint as the best job opportunity in Endora for many a year.

Crashing into his world comes Becky (Juliette Lewis), a caravanning tourist,

Depp with Darlene Cates, a non-actor who won Depp's admiration for her performance as Gilbert's mother in What's Eating Gilbert Grape?

temporarily stranded in Endora due to mechanical problems and forced to become part of the community for a short while. 'Gilbert is a guy who's walking around in his sleep through his life,' observed Juliette Lewis. 'He needs his eyes to be opened and there are a lot of people like that.' One of the biggest acting challenges in the film was not for Johnny Depp but his younger co-star Leonardo DiCaprio in the role of the mentally-handicapped Arnie Grape. 'I needed someone who wasn't good-looking,' said director Hallström, 'but of all the actors who auditioned for the role of Arnie, Leonardo was the most observant.'

DiCaprio, on the verge of teen idol pin up status when cast in the film, had been acting since the age of fourteen. He started in commercials and educational films, before moving onto episodic television. DiCaprio won great acclaim for his role as a young drug addict in 1995's *The Basketball Diaries*, as well as drawing many comparisons with River Phoenix.

DiCaprio followed in the footsteps of his acting idol Robert DeNiro, whom he'd featured opposite in *This Boy's Life* (1993), by delving into copious amounts of research for his character. He began by watching many mentally challenged young people on video, before meeting some in person. Hallström was instrumental in narrowing DiCaprio's focus to one particular autistic boy whom they had met during their research. 'I took a lot of his mannerisms and made them my own. I developed the character even more by adding the mannerisms of some of the other people I had met.'

The authenticity of DiCaprio's performance surprised and pleased the film-makers, according to the film's executive producer Alan C. Blomquist. 'Leonardo gives Arnie this child-like quality, playing him as very free and open and honest. He's a great

Brotherly Love – Gilbert (Depp) helps out brother Arnie (Leonardo DiCaprio) in What's Eating Gilbert Grape?

counterpart to Johnny's Gilbert, who is so solemn and serious about life.' Johnny Depp and Leonardo DiCaprio worked together easily on location in Austin, Texas, where Richard Linlaker had shot his Generation X underground hit movie *Slacker* (1991). 'We had a brotherly relationship on camera,' said DiCaprio of working with the older, wiser star name, who'd been through the teen idol acclaim that DiCaprio was just on the verge of experiencing. 'It was important to be just buddy-buddy with each other. Brothers don't necessarily have to say anything to each other – they can sit in a room and be together and just completely comfortable with each other.'

'He was extremely like Gilbert,' said DiCaprio of Johnny Depp. 'But it wasn't something Johnny was trying to do. It naturally came out of him. I never quite understood what he was going through, because it wasn't some big emotional drama that was happening on the set every day – but subtle things I'd see in him. There's an element of Johnny that is extremely nice and extremely cool, but at the same time he's hard to figure out. That makes him interesting.'

The most striking presence on the set of *What's Eating Gilbert Grape?* was that of 600lb Texas resident Darlene Cates. Cates was not a professional actress, but was spotted by Peter Hedges on a Sally Jesse Raphael chat show about obesity and the problems associated with it. Cates had more in common with her character as the matriarch of the Grape family – she really hadn't left her real house for a long time.

From chat show to movie star, Darlene Cates found herself having to act out her own nightmare for the sake of *What's Eating Gilbert Grape?* in a scene in which a crowd in the street stop to stare at her because she's such a spectacle. 'That scene was so real to me,' said Cates. 'I had to take time out afterwards because I burst into tears. But then so much of the film was real to me. An integral part of the story is letting people see how much bigotry and cruelty big people go through... I think she shares what many overweight people do – a feeling that we are unacceptable. I'm glad to say that I don't feel that way any more. I found out that I do have something to offer, just like everyone else.'

Juliette Lewis, the actress cast as Becky, later featured alongside DiCaprio in *The Basketball Diaries*. Born and raised in Southern California, Lewis is the daughter of actor Geoffrey Lewis and a graphic artist mother. She started acting at the age of twelve, in Showtime's mini-series *Homefires*, before guest-starring in a recurring role in the TV series *The Wonder Years*. Her film career has included Woody Allen's *Husbands and Wives* (1992), Peter Medak's gloriously funny black comedy thriller *Romeo Is Bleeding* (1994), *Kalifornia* (1994) opposite *The X-Files* star David Duchovny and then boyfriend Brad Pitt, and Oliver Stone's controversial *Natural Born Killers* (1994), opposite Woody Harrelson.

Juliette Lewis took her commitment to the role of Becky to the extreme of not really socialising with the other cast members in order to focus on her character. 'I just sat in my hotel room watching TV,' admitted Lewis. 'When I'm at work, I just sort of go. My purpose is to do the job as well as possible and not to go dancing or do all this other bullshit.' 'The job', as Lewis saw it on *Gilbert Grape,* was to make Becky 'real still. On this film I didn't want to fiddle so much and do a bunch of facial gestures. I didn't want to go crazy with her because she's the sane element in the movie. So I made a decision to be still and logical. My mind works like a computer. I can read scenes, and I'll know exactly how to behave – it just happens automatically.

I don't have to do a lot of outside stuff to figure it out.'

Johnny Depp saw much more to his role than Lewis saw in hers. 'Gilbert Grape would seem like a pretty normal kind of guy, but I was interested in what was going on underneath, in the hostility and the rage that he has and that he's only able to show a couple of times in the film. I understand the feeling of being stuck in a place, whether it is geographical or emotional. I can understand the rage of wanting to completely escape from it and from everybody and everything you know and start a new life.'

Depp invested his character with much more psychological material than might come across on screen, drawing from events in his own Florida adolescence, but it was information the actor needed to construct the character. 'For me, it's like Gilbert at some point or another allowed himself to die inside, slowly killing or martyring himself for his family, becoming a surrogate father – even to his mother. That kind of loyalty may start out as pure love, but it can work against you, with love and devotion turning into resentment and guilt and losing yourself, which is the worst thing anyone can do – because then you hate others because of what you have done to yourself.'

Depp did see an optimistic side to Gilbert's character arc, a slim glimmer of hope that meant that Gilbert didn't disappear entirely into a well of self-loathing and despair. 'It's optimistic, in that this girl comes into his life and gives Gilbert very simple, very direct information that begins to crack his shell – and he realises the mistake he's made. In life we tend to judge people harshly based on their appearance, whether they're overweight, handicapped, ugly or mentally-challenged. Sometimes these people are looked upon as freaks because they're different. What a lot of this film is saying is that they're human like everybody else. The first time I met Darlene [Cates] I looked beyond her size and I saw this sweet face and these soulful eyes, and I thought she was so beautiful. I found her to be very brave to unravel her emotional life in front of the whole world – and this from somebody who'd never acted before.'

Like Juliette Lewis, Johnny Depp found the location filming for *What's Eating Gilbert Grape?* to be less than ideal. Depp had gone straight from the recent break-up of his long term relationship with Winona Ryder into a series of films, including *Benny & Joon* and *Gilbert Grape*. The filming was his immediate way of escaping his troubles and dealing with being alone, but sometimes the cinematic therapy didn't work its magic. 'It was a hard time for me – I was having a weird time myself, practically, which kind of helped me creatively,' he said. 'We were shooting in Austin, Texas, which to me seems like what America must've been like in the fifties. But I was trying to escape from my own brain: I didn't know what was right and what was wrong; I didn't know who was who and who wasn't...it was all very confusing. I don't know if I subconsciously made myself miserable for a little bit because I knew that's what the character needed, or if it was just what I had to deal with at that particular time. I was drinking a lot – poisoning myself.'

Despite putting so much of himself into the film, the reviewers saw *What's Eating Gilbert Grape?* as one quirky role too far for Depp. Richard Corliss was kind in *Entertainment Weekly*. 'DiCaprio and Cates bring loopy authenticity to their roles, and Depp is, as always, a most effacing star. Here, as in *Edward Scissorhands* and *Benny & Joon*, he behaves wonderfully on screen.' For many, Depp was

repeating a well worn performance once too often. Here, as in *Benny & Joon*, was Depp doing *Edward Scissorhands* without the make-up. 'Gilbert is played by Johnny Depp, who might have been the next Tom Cruise except that his career choices are so wilfully non-commercial,' wrote Anne Bilson in *The Sunday Telegraph*. Quentin Curtis in *The Independent on Sunday* put his finger on the basis of Depp's latest performance: 'Johnny Depp plays the title role in *What's Eating Gilbert Grape?*, a rerun of his wistful romantic comedy *Benny & Joon*, down to the nowheresville setting and the loopy kid he looks after.'

Britain's *Sky Magazine*, however, pointed out in no uncertain terms the danger to Depp's acting career if he were to continue to plough this particular furrow. It was the proximity of both *Benny & Joon* and *What's Eating Gilbert Grape?* that put Depp's career under the spotlight. Dan Yakir wrote: 'Depp's avoided one kind of stereotyping, but he faces the opposite danger: will he still be playing kooks when he's 40? It's not something that seems to worry him overmuch – and after all maybe he's right not to worry. Would you, if the choice was between ending up like Christopher Walken or Don Johnson?'

'I've been real lucky,' was Depp's response. 'People have mentioned that I like doing offbeat roles, but I've been lucky in the sense that I haven't been typecast. It's important to keep changing. There's a lot of stuff that I just don't buy into, like being an actor who takes himself so seriously that he pretends to be this tortured artist…I think that everybody has pain and an actor doesn't necessarily have more of it than others…'

However, events were just about to bring Depp his fair share of personal pain.

Leonardo DiCaprio with Depp and Juliette Lewis in What's Eating Gilbert Grape?
DiCaprio was seen by many as Depp's heir apparent in the kooky misfit stakes.

CHAPTER FOUR

Love, Death,
& Demons

JOHNNY DEPP may have believed that actors have no more pain than other people, but late in 1993, Depp was to suffer more pain than most when one of Hollywood's rising young stars died of a drug overdose outside his club, The Viper Room.

At the age of 23 River Phoenix seemed the least likely Hollywood candidate to die of the 'live fast, die young' syndrome. Throughout his life, from his unusual South American childhood with his hippie parents through his ever increasing Hollywood stardom, River Phoenix had become an icon for a generation. This James Dean figure for the 1980s and 1990s preached an anti-drug, pro-animals, pro-life, vegetarian lifestyle. He was the politically correct movie star, a representative of Generation X who spoke out on the issues that concerned many of his fans. Yet, on October 31st 1993 he collapsed and died of a drug overdose on the pavement of The Viper Room on Sunset Strip in Los Angeles.

On the corner of Larrabee Street and Sunset Boulevard, The Viper Room was co-owned by Johnny Depp and rock star Chuck E. Weiss. Depp remodelled the interior of the small, dark and rather dingy club as a 1920s speakeasy, decorated in an art deco style. He even went so far as to hire cigarette girls to recreate an old Hollywood atmosphere. The prices, at $5 per drink, were certainly not of the old Hollywood variety. The Viper Room was so small that it only boasted five booths, one of which was permanently reserved for Depp's ICM agent Tracey Jacobs – clearly indicated by the gold plaque which reads: 'Don't Fuck With It.' The place was Depp's playground, with a corner stage where he and his musician friends could jam, enabling the actor to return to his musical roots and play at being a rock star instead – a dream he shared with River Phoenix.

With a capacity of just 200 people and a tiny dance floor, The Viper Room had no trouble becoming one of the 'in' spots on the Los Angeles night club circuit when it opened in August 1993. By October, the place had built up a regular clientele, featuring much of young Hollywood. 'My idea,' said Depp, 'was to play Louis Jordan and to segue to the Velvet Underground.'

Although not a close friend, Johnny Depp was a regular if casual acquaintance of River Phoenix. The pair had much in common: both had escaped the 'Brat Pack' actors' crowd of the 1980s, Depp by being slightly older, Phoenix by being younger.

They both chose an alternative path through Hollywood, away from the obvious mainstream.

Phoenix arrived at the club for a night of rest and relaxation on October 30th, with an entourage that included his latest girlfriend and *The Thing Called Love* co-star Samantha Mathis, his brother Leaf and sister Rain, and Flea (Michael Balzary), bass guitarist with The Red Hot Chili Peppers. Phoenix had been shooting what was to be his final, uncompleted film, George Sluzier's *Dark Blood*. His drug habit had become Hollywood's best kept secret, known to differing degrees by his intimates, but not yet tabloid fodder.

Although he was due to perform on stage that night, Phoenix didn't get the chance. Just after midnight, and obviously suffering, he was taken from the club to the sidewalk outside. His brother Leaf dialled 911 for the emergency services after the group had argued among themselves and with The Viper Room doorman over Phoenix's condition. By the time medics arrived, it was too late for Phoenix. He was declared dead due to a cocktail of drugs at 1.51am on Hallowe'en morning, October 31st 1993.

It was to be some time after the event before Johnny Depp could bring himself to speak openly in any depth about the incident. 'The thing is, he came with his guitar to the club. What a beautiful thing that he shows up with his girl on one arm and his guitar on the other. He came to play and he didn't think he was going to die – nobody thinks they're gonna die,' Depp recalled. 'He wanted to have a good time. It's dangerous. But that's the thing that breaks my heart – first that he died, but also that he showed up with his guitar. That's not an unhappy kid.'

Depp saw Phoenix's descent into drug abuse as nothing more than a dreadful mistake, one he himself could understand. 'He was a great actor and a great young man, a great human being. He had a great family, a very level view of life, and a promising view of the future. This is my quarrel with the press – they could have said, "Look, this was a normal guy, who had some things he was confused about, and he made a mistake. Anybody could make that same fatal mistake, and it could be any one of us. Watch yourself!" Nobody said that.'

Depp found himself on the receiving end of a rough ride from the media, who accused him of contributing to River Phoenix's death by running a club like The Viper Room in the first place and then by allowing back room drug abuse, which – the papers alleged – Depp knew all about. 'There was a lot of speculation going on,' said Depp. 'A lot of people were playing backyard detective and exploiting the situation to get ratings and to sell newspapers and magazines. The tabloids were complete fiction. It's really tragic and sad. How many times did we need to hear that 911 tape? How many times did they have to print that stuff? For how long does Leaf have to live with that rewinding in his head? We've become a society of ambulance chasers. Everybody focused on the bad, nobody's interested in the good…I've worked in this business for ten years, and to say I opened a night club to allow people to do drugs, even in the bathroom – do people think I'm insane? Do they think I'm going to throw everything away – even my own children's future, so people could get high in a nightclub? It's ridiculous.

'The press was trying to tarnish his memory in the minds of all those people who loved him,' said Depp of the reporting of Phoenix's death. 'What it all boils down to is a very sweet guy who made one big, fatal mistake. It's a mistake we're all capable of. What took place was so heavy that I didn't even retaliate on the accusations towards me. The fact is, I was there that night. The fact is, it was my club. I said, "I refuse to be a part of this morbid circus that you fucking ambulance chasers have going. Fuck off!"'

Johnny Depp's long-time friend Sal Jenko ran The Viper Room on a day-to-day basis. He and Depp had to deal with a second drug scandal when TV soap star and singer Jason Donovan also collapsed outside the club in a repeat of the River Phoenix incident. Donovan's drug problem was not fatal, but Depp found himself in the headlines again. The British Sunday tabloid, the *News of the World* ran with 'Depp's Den of Sex, Drugs and Death' as its headline on the Jason Donovan story.

'I run a place that is filled with drugs and people screwing on the tables,' said Depp of the caricature of his club in the tabloids. 'This is a night club – it's a decent place. The Mayor of West Hollywood is having her reception here, for Christ's sakes, why don't they write about that? Because it doesn't sell magazines – unless they get a photograph of the mayor with a syringe stuck in the back of her neck...'

The Viper Room's notoriety was not at all what Depp had in mind when he initially opened the place. 'It became a scene instantly when we opened it. I never had any idea that it was going to do that. I really thought it was gonna just be this cool little underground place. You can't even see the place. There's no sign on Sunset. It's just a black building and the only sign is on Larrabee, a tiny little sign, real subtle, and I figured it would be low key. What soured me was what happened after all that took place on Hallowe'en, the unfortunate passing of River. I closed it down for two weeks out of respect, so the kids could write their messages and leave flowers. I thought that was real sweet of them. I knew for the next month or so it was just gonna be a gawk fest, just filled with gawkers and tourists, Grave-line Tours, all that shit. I just didn't go around for a while. We've weeded out the gawkers – now it's back to being a good place.'

Publicly, Depp resented any suggestions that he felt a responsibility for the death of River Phoenix. Privately, his activities revealed otherwise: Depp did carry a burden from that October night. He has been said to wander up and down Sunset Strip outside the club at four or five in the morning, handing out 50 and 100 dollar bills to the groups of homeless people who huddle on the sidewalk. It seems to be Depp's way of clearing his troubled conscience.

It was in March 1994, a few months after River Phoenix's death, that the world discovered that actor Johnny Depp had a new woman in his life. She was the London-born supermodel Kate Moss. At the Los Angeles night spot Smash Box, Depp launched his eight-and-a-half minute surrealist film on the dangers of drug use at an 800 person *Vogue* benefit for the Drug Abuse Resistance Education programme. The film, entitled *Banter*, followed in the footsteps of the public information promo shorts he'd made during his *21 Jump Street* days. Now he could turn his personal experience into a film pleading with youngsters to stay clear of drugs.

Described by *Esquire* as 'a gruesome but provocative excursion into the world of hard drugs', *Banter* raised questions about Depp's own reported drug use, with the death of Phoenix fresh in the media mind. 'It's all in the past,' Depp claimed.

'I've been taunted by the press and put in a position of having to defend myself. I've done nothing wrong. I've even made an anti-drug movie. and I hope kids learn a lot from it, that drugs are no escape. There are other ways of escaping, like books, painting and writing.' It was at this event that Depp and Moss made their relationship public for the first time, although they'd been quietly dating for weeks. Within weeks the couple were seen publicly holidaying on St. Barts, followed by attendance at a Johnny Cash concert in Manhattan's Fez club. Depp was also more than happy to journey with Moss to Paris where she was due to appear on the catwalk at fashion shows. But he was still paranoid about the possibility of press intrusion ruining the relationship. After all, Moss was as much – or perhaps even more – in the public eye than Ryder. She wasn't an actress, but like many supermodels such as Claudia Schiffer, Linda Evangelista and Naomi Campbell, she was regarded as one of the new media stars, recapturing the glamour that many feel Hollywood had lost.

Kate Moss was born on January 16th 1974 in Addiscombe, Surrey. She grew up in Croydon, another London suburb, and was launched to international supermodel fame at the age of only fourteen in August 1988. Moss was 'discovered' at Kennedy Airport by Sarah Doukas of the UK's Storm Model Agency, who persuaded the waif-like girl to begin modelling during her school summer holidays. In 1989 Moss put in an appearance in the little seen British sexploitation film *The Inferno*.

It was 1990 before Moss took up modelling full time, with her first magazine cover – for *The Face* in 1990 – defining the waif look, soon hyped by the international media. By 1993 she had secured a $1 million contract with Calvin Klein. Her willingness to appear nude in their advertising campaign, as well as those for Yves Saint Laurent and Calvin Klein's Obsession fragrance, was a major factor in her rapid rise to world recognition.

Kate Moss found her sudden fame took its toll on her former relationship with photographer Mario Sorrenti. For the media, therefore, the Depp-Moss liaison was a match made in heaven, even better than the Depp-Ryder Hollywood relationship. It was the tabloid press that Depp feared most, but the fact that Moss was British gave the British tabloid press the excuse they needed to feature every move the couple made in great detail in their pages. 'At this point the press have said so many shitty things that I couldn't give a fuck anymore,' said Depp candidly. 'As long as they're not hurting my family or someone I love, they can say I have a fetish for midget amputees for all I care…'

Johnny Depp had learned from the way his relationship with Ryder had gone. Although he was willing to discuss his life with Kate Moss, it was a discussion that only went so far. 'I don't talk about it and she doesn't talk about it, 'cause it's nobody's business,' he stated firmly. 'This is a rumour-filled society, and if people want to sit around and talk about whom I've dated, then I'd say they have a lot of spare time and should consider other topics. Or masturbation.'

His first meeting with Moss in February 1994 was, he claimed, very ordinary. 'Sorry to disappoint you, but it wasn't all that romantic. I went in to have a cup of coffee at a restaurant in New York [the Manhattan bistro Cafe Tabac] and she was sitting at a table with some friends, and I knew one of them. I just said "Come over and have some coffee with me," and so that's how we met and we haven't been apart since. We're just having fun. A lot of fun. She's a real down-to-earth English

As Depp approached 30, he refused to conform to the thirty-something
image, retaining the trademark t-shirt and chains.

girl who gives me no chance to get big-headed about my life.'

The age-gap between Kate Moss and Johnny Depp was even greater than that between Depp and Winona Ryder, but Kate Moss was old for her years, made worldly-wise from a modelling career begun in her early teens. Her child-like qualities appealed to Depp's juvenile sense of fun. One of the things that the pair discovered was a mutual passion for funfair rides, a far cry from the Depp-Ryder fascination for Beat poetry and literature. 'We love going to Magic Mountain [a theme park outside Los Angeles] and doing all the fastest rides, but you have to go first thing in the morning, or you just end up spending all day signing autographs.'

Moss made a point of refusing to talk about her relationship with Depp, presumably upon his advice and a series of Ryder horror stories. But it didn't stop her from gushing about her new-found romance to the *Daily Mail*, in terms which must, for Depp, have had uncomfortable echoes. 'I can't believe it,' Moss had said 'It's like nothing that has ever happened to me before. I knew straight away, knew that it was different. I just never felt anything like this before. I knew, this was it.'

The whirlwind romance caught both stars and the media off-guard. Within months, Kate Moss was the latest in a long line of Johnny Depp 'fiancées', Mrs Depp-to-be. Depp refused to confirm that he and Moss were engaged: 'I don't know what that means. It's just something that gets reported.' Further reports that Depp had asked Moss to marry him during a holiday in the Caribbean in early 1995 were neither denied nor confirmed by either party. 'Kate as a wife?' reacted Depp, 'I would not be against that, but it's something that needs to be discussed in private.'

By 1995 Kate Moss's fame was superseding that of her actor boyfriend. With the publication of a book of over 100 photographs, imaginatively entitled *Kate,* Moss's superstardom was confirmed. On the celebrity interview circuit promoting the book, Moss sounded like she'd been taking lessons from Depp on hatred of the press. 'All those anorexic things really did bother me. I know I'm going to be called a waif forever. And I hate it.' She may have hated it, but at the age of only 21, Kate Moss was earning £2.2 million per year.

Depp's *Don Juan De Marco* and *Arizona Dream* co-star Faye Dunaway saw in the Depp-Moss relationship a reaffirmation of the actor's romantic nature which had taken a knock when he broke with Winona Ryder. 'He's incorruptible,' she said, 'he always believes in this pure way about love. He's got those kinds of values and it's instinctive with him. This isn't something he's worked out in his head. I love that he believes in love.'

'He's really wild,' admitted Moss on British TV about Depp, 'but wild in a nice way. I don't want to tame him. He's always surprising me. Johnny's a complete and utter romantic, and very original. He once said to me he had something down his bum but he didn't know what. So I put my hand down his trousers and pulled out a [£10,000 diamond] necklace.'

Despite his hook up with Kate Moss and his obviously happier state of mind, many still saw Johnny Depp on a similar self-destructive course as River Phoenix. Although no longer taking drugs on a regular basis, Depp had his own self-admitted demons and his own solutions. 'There have been times when I wasn't in a good place at all,' he said. 'I couldn't get a grip on what was going on around me – and I'd just get tanked. That's all right for a little while, but when it becomes a way of life, it's not good. It's really bad. And you spend all this time trying to recreate that first high you got – like when you're thirteen or fourteen and you get drunk or smoke a joint for the first time and it's the greatest – it never comes back. You're never going to get that feeling again.' Depp had taken a hard look at himself and saw something in his own make up of the psychologically addictive personality. Although he quit drinking when he met Moss, Depp had been fond of a bottle or two up to that point. 'I spent years getting loaded to escape. But I never escaped, not once. I've got my demons, you know, and alcohol or drugs – some drugs – can unleash those demons or open up the doors for those demons to fly around.'

Those who knew Depp and worried about him saw his wannabe rock'n'roll lifestyle as a dangerous contributor to his problems. Like River Phoenix, Depp hung out with the hard men of the grunge rock scene, playing in his own band called Pee, or sometimes just P. Shane MacGowan, formerly of The Pogues, Gibby Haynes of The Butthole Surfers, ex-Sex Pistols guitarist Steve Jones, Flea of The Red Hot Chili Peppers and Sal Jenko, Depp's lifelong friend, who performed as drummer in the band, were among those with whom Depp played music. Depp signed his band to EMI's Capitol Records in mid-1995 but nothing significant ever came of the deal. 'People tend to overlook that he was a struggling musician before *21 Jump Street*,' said collaborator and guitarist Bill Carter.

Depp had played with Michael Hutchence of INXS on stage at The Viper Room during Kate Moss's 21st birthday party. The party also featured a guest appearance – organised by Depp – by Gloria Gaynor singing her disco classic 'I Will Survive' especially for Moss. Depp was another successful young Hollywood star who really wanted to be a rock star. At least he'd tried to be a rock'n'roller before finding fame through acting. 'I think of it just as a goof, really, not as a second career – just to mess around with my friends. It's good to be involved in other areas. I wouldn't want to be just an actor for the rest of my life.'

Depp was a self-confessed amateur in the self-destruction stakes compared to some of those he used to hang out with. 'I don't know anyone else who would have survived the things that Shane and Gibby have been through apart from them. Those guys have gone into the ass of the devil and come out his mouth – and it's not an easy thing to do.' The deaths of Kurt Cobain, River Phoenix and Michael Hutchence were well reported instances that gave Depp pause for thought about his lifestyle. Those who knew and had worked with Depp didn't see a self-destructive streak in him – at least not one that he couldn't control. 'I'm not worried at all,' said director John Waters of Depp's riotous behaviour. 'Johnny is not killing himself. I think he is aware of that pitfall. He's certainly seen it.'

From the moment Johnny Depp checked into The Mark Hotel in New York City in September 1994, he had a bad feeling about the place. It wasn't that the $2200-a-night Presidential Suite wasn't up to scratch, but that the hotel was not one of his regular venues – his usual, The Carlyle, was full and beggars can't be choosers when looking for a last minute booking into the Presidential Suite.

Depp was in town to do a series of publicity appearances and interviews to promote *Ed Wood*. To make the film he'd passed up on the part of Lestat in the adaptation of Anne Rice's *Interview with the Vampire* (Tom Cruise donned the fangs) and the Keanu Reeves role in *Speed*. He was evangelical about the Tim Burton project, so was happy for once to do more than the usual amount of press. 'Let's just say, my stay wasn't particularly comfortable,' was how Depp would sum things up later. The problem was the night security guard, Jim Keegan.

Keegan was on duty in the hotel from midnight to 8.00 am each night, and between those hours he more or less ran the upmarket Mark Hotel. Keegan monitored Depp's comings and goings from the hotel at odd hours. Suffering from insomnia, as he often does, Depp had been out several nights during his stay in New York, his partying sessions overlapping with Keegan's on-duty hours. 'It seemed like the guy couldn't stand Johnny,' claimed Jonathan Shaw, tattoo artist and friend of Depp since the early 1980s. Shaw had been to visit Depp at the hotel on several occasions, and was aware of Keegan's observation. 'Johnny dressed in leather and jeans, not at all fancy like everybody else in the joint.'

'The guy was a little froggy,' Depp told *Esquire*'s David Blum. 'He decided he was going to "get in the famous guy's face". I don't really take too well to that.'

Staying in the hotel with Depp on the night of Monday September 12th through to the early morning of September 13th 1994 was Kate Moss. Depp claims not to have been drinking that night, nor to have been on drugs, nor to have been fighting with Moss – as reported in the newspapers.

It was about 5.00am when a commotion from Room 1410 summoned Jim Keegan from his post to investigate. The security guard later told police that he'd heard a series of crashing sounds from inside the suite and saw a broken picture frame in the hallway outside the room. Neither Keegan nor The Mark Hotel's general manager Raymond Bickson would discuss the incident with the press after the event. It had been revealed, however, that it was the occupant of the room next door who had complained of the disturbance from Depp's suite. That occupant, claimed the press, was none other than singer Roger Daltrey of The Who, much more famous than Depp for trashing hotel rooms in his time. 'The difference,' said Depp in response to this story, 'is that The Who would have done a better job and then been applauded for it. I was arrested and incarcerated. Age is a wonderful thing, isn't it? Keith Moon would have been very embarrassed for him…but he was probably used to being embarrassed for him…'

Depp claimed Keegan was keyed up from the start of their confrontation. 'The guy probably had one too many cups of coffee that night. He was particularly feisty. He decided to call the shots in a way that I didn't think was particularly necessary. If I walk into an antique shop and I bend down to look at something over here and I accidentally knock a pot off the rack, it's $3000, of course I'd pay for it. If I bust a piece of glass, I smash a mirror, or whatever, I'll pay for it. I can probably handle the bill. That's that.'

Depp's casual attitude probably helped wind Keegan up – to him, any amount of cash paid out afterwards would not make up for the disturbance caused to other guests. For whatever reason, Keegan took exception to the happenings in Room 1410 and told Depp he would have to leave The Mark there and then, or the police would be called. Depp offered to pay for any damage he'd caused, but didn't feel there was any requirement for him to check out. True to his threat, Keegan called the New York Police Department. Within 30 minutes, Depp was leaving the hotel after all, but in handcuffs and in the company of three officers from the Nineteenth Precinct.

Depp's stay in jail wasn't a long one, and he was released the next afternoon. During the night he spent time in three different cells at the Precinct house, at Central Booking and in the 'tombs' behind New York Central Police Headquarters. The scruffily dressed and unkempt actor was reportedly mobbed by women police officers at all three locations. He did have a confrontation with one member of New York's finest, Officer Eileen Perez. 'I don't think she likes me,' Depp was quoted in *People* magazine. 'But I bet if she saw me in a mall, she'd ask me for my autograph.'

In the official police report Keegan listed ten damaged items: two broken seventeenth century picture frames and prints, a china lamp stand, a Chinese pot, a shattered glass tabletop, broken coffee table legs, broken wooden shelves, a shattered vase, cigarette burns on the carpet and a split red desk chair. David Breitbart was the New York criminal lawyer who handled the case, a man who chose to play games with journalists on his client's behalf. 'Did Johnny do all of that? I don't know, and neither do they. That crazy damage figure they asked for was also for what he owed for the room two nights before, three nights after, something like that. This was a fucking shakedown. I wish I could have gone to court on this, because no-one saw him do a thing. They put together the list of damages while he was in custody. Anything could have happened in that hotel room.'

Depp didn't deny the incident, explaining it all away as a case of human frailty: 'It wasn't a great night for me. I'm not trying to excuse what I did or anything like that, because it's someone else's property and you gotta respect that. But you get into a head space, and you're human.' His arrest on two counts of criminal mischief resulted in $9767.12 in damages being passed on to Depp. The charges were dismissed by the judge, but he was ordered to pay the damages and stay out of trouble for six months.

Pictures of Depp's arrest shared the front pages of the New York newspapers and television reports with the American invasion of Haiti. 'I was just stressed out,' he said. 'I'm human and I get angry like everyone else. I get frustrated and I just lashed out. Big deal. We're talking about an actor who might have assaulted a piece of furniture. I found myself on the covers of all the newspapers, as if this incident was of more importance than the invasion of Haiti. Firstly, you should be allowed to be a human being. Secondly, you should be allowed to have emotion. Thirdly, you should be allowed to have a private life.'

Depp's mother was none too pleased with her son being locked up: 'She got over it,' he said. 'She didn't like seeing me in handcuffs on TV, but she knows I'm not a bad person.' More than the handcuffs, it appears that it was Johnny's clothes that caused most distress to Betty Sue Palmer (now married to her third husband, Robert Palmer) particularly his green knitted hat and sunglasses. 'She thought she'd taught me how to dress better than that,' he said ruefully. Other relatives were on Depp's mind too: 'I've got a teenage niece and nephew who have to go to high school and hear their friends say "Your Uncle Johnny is a fucking maniac." They gotta live with that stuff, too...'

Depp had kept in close touch with his mother, despite the difficulties of his teenage years. In fact, his movie stardom had allowed him to reconstruct part of his family around him. Depp eventually employed his sister Christi Dembrowski and

brother Dan (or DP) to handle his personal affairs. His loyalty to his family and those he has worked with, such as Buck Holland, his long-time driver and general factotum – was one of the traits that many people commented on when asked to describe Depp, but it was a loyalty borne out of the search for a secure family, for a father who would not leave.

With The Mark Hotel debacle, Depp had joined an ever growing list of celebrity hotel trashers – which probably began with composer Ludwig van Beethoven, who is thought to have thrown a chair through the window of a Vienna hotel room. 'Did Beethoven go to jail for it?' asked Depp. He had become convinced that the story was hyped up and pushed to the newspapers as part of some cynical ploy to promote The Mark Hotel. 'It's good for them,' he said. 'Now they can say they have this little bit of history, this ridiculous morsel of history. They can say "We had Johnny Depp arrested." Hotels are my home. I live in hotels more than I live in my house. If it had been you, nothing would have happened. They would have come to the room and said, "What's going on?" You would have said, "I'll pay for the damages, and I'm terribly sorry."'

Faye Dunaway agreed with Depp's view of the incident. 'Sometimes you feel like you've just got to kick over the traces, and The Mark took advantage of it. A publicity trip; it's outrageous. I would probably have smashed up the lobby after that. I think they should count themselves lucky that he didn't.'

'I thought it was funny,' Depp later commented. 'I had to go to jail for assaulting a picture frame and a lamp! The rags said "He was drunk and he was having a huge fight with his girlfriend." Complete bullshit. But, you know, let's say the guy over here in the bar, he's having a hard day, man, and eventually – one more stubbing of the toe – the guy's gotta hit something. So you punch a wall, or do this and that. Fuck it, I'm normal and I want to be normal. But somehow, I'm just not allowed to be. Why can't I be human? I have a lot of love inside me and a lot of anger inside as well. If I love somebody, then I'm gonna love 'em. If I'm angry and I've got to lash out or hit somebody, I'm going to do it and I don't care what the repercussions are.'

The Mark Hotel incident was not Depp's first brush with the law caused by his volatile temper. His past was littered with similar occurrences. He'd been variously reported to have been caught hanging from the five-storey Beverly Center parking garage in Los Angeles with Nicolas Cage; to have a propensity for blowing gasoline on to an open flame; he'd even been seen shouting at Kate Moss in the dining room of New York's Royalton Hotel, a journalists' hangout. During his *21 Jump Street* TV series days, Johnny had assaulted a security guard in Vancouver, Canada in 1989 but the charges were also dropped in that incident. In 1991 he was sued by a woman after he smashed a window of the Lone Star Roadhouse on New York's 52nd street, showering her with glass, following a drinking competition with the legendary punk rocker Iggy Pop. Depp was also charged in 1991 with jaywalking in Beverly Hills and got into a fight with the officer who told him to put out his cigarette. 'I've known some Nazi cops who've seen way too many episodes of *Starsky and Hutch*,' was his pithy comment on that confrontation.

In the months after his 'bad night' at the Mark, Depp displayed his mischievous sense of humour in interviews he gave to various magazines. Each time he told a

In the cold light of day – Johnny Depp with two of New York's finest, following his arrest for causing a disturbance at the Mark Hotel in September 1994.

different variation on his tale of what actually happened.

According to *The Sunday Times* Depp claimed 'I was sitting on the couch in my hotel room when a really big dachshund jumped out of the closet. I felt it was my duty to retrieve this animal, so I chased it for twenty minutes, but it wouldn't co-operate. Finally, it dived out the window…and there I was, stuck with all this evidence.' He told *Empire* magazine: 'I think it was an armadillo. It felt like it was an armadillo. It may have been an elephant.' He told *Sky* magazine: 'It had absolutely nothing to do with Kate. You want to hear the honest truth about what happened in that hotel? There was a cockroach in that room the size of a baseball, and I was chasing it around trying to swat it and kill it, and I missed.'

'There have been times that he has misbehaved,' confirms agent Tracey Jacobs of ICM, whose role in Depp's professional life has often involved functioning as a clean-up artist, smoothing the disasters left in the star's wake. It was to Jacobs that Depp made his one phone call from jail after being arrested. 'I'm very tough on him about that stuff,' she claimed. But Depp's continued brushes with the law seemed to imply that he regarded Jacobs' 'tough' attitude the way he did everyone else who tried to tell him how to run his life and behave – with a certain amount of disdain. It also didn't affect his popularity. One month later Depp was on the cover of *People* magazine, followed by cover stories in *Premiere* and gay magazine *The Advocate*. He was rated in a list of America's most desirable prom dates by *Your Prom* magazine and nominated for a Golden Globe for *Ed Wood* (which he lost to Hugh Grant for *Four Weddings and a Funeral*).

'The hotel thing hasn't hurt his career,' said John Waters, in *Esquire* magazine. 'He looked good under arrest. I loved the handcuffs – they always work. Criminal movie star is a really good look for Johnny. The success of hotel room trashing should be calculated by the amount of damage, divided by the amount of column inches.' Waters suggested yet another alternative reason for Depp's hotel antics – perhaps the room service was bad.

A few days following the incident at The Mark Hotel, Depp had recovered his belongings from the hotel and the police and relocated to another New York hotel. Unpacking in his new room, Depp discovered that the Marlon Brando autobiography he'd been reading had been defaced by someone at The Mark Hotel while he was in police custody. 'Fuck you, Johnny Depp' was the first, unwelcome comment the actor came across as he flicked through the 468 page book. There were others on many of the other pages. 'You're an asshole,' read one; 'I hate you,' ranted another. The comments continued throughout the book. Depp puts the blame on staff at The Mark Hotel. 'There are two kinds of fans,' he told *Esquire* – who reported in depth on the whole Mark Hotel incident. 'The kind who just want your autograph or to say something nice. But there are these guys who are too cool for autographs. People try to piss you off. They want your attention.'

The trouble on this trip to New York was not over yet for Depp. It seemed whenever he was involved in one widely reported incident, a whole stream of others attached themselves to him. Later that week Depp accompanied some friends to a downtown bar called Babyland. By the morning, Depp was the star of another headline in the *New York Post*: Depp Pals in East Village Brawl, bawled the newspaper. 'It didn't take long for Johnny Depp-lorable to show his wild side again following his hotel hijinks the other night,' ran the report on page six of the paper, alleging that Depp 'sparked a fight'. The paper quote a punter who claimed 'Depp slammed into me and said "Fuck you."'

As with all the incidents in which he featured, Depp's account is different to that which appeared in the pages of tabloids around the world. 'This guy walked past me in the bar,' said Depp, beginning another of his doubtful 'armadillo-daschund' tales. 'He pulled out what resembled a penis – but I've a sneaking suspicion it may have been a thimble, this goofy fucking guy – and said something like, "Suck my dick". I'd just gotten out of jail. They'd said, 'Stay out of trouble for six months'. My first instinct was to...we all have that animal instinct inside of us...your instinct is, go for the throat.' According to Depp, however, he resisted the instinct that he'd followed too often in the past. He didn't want to go back to jail for something like that.

Incidents like this followed Depp wherever he went. In The Globe, an underground club in London's Notting Hill, Depp got on the wrong side of a member of the British aristocracy. 27-year-old Jonathan Walpole, a direct descendant of Sir Robert Walpole and a photographer by trade – was in the club, when he mistakenly picked up a glass from the bar that turned out to be Johnny Depp's drink. 'He pulled both my ears,' wailed Walpole to London's *Evening Standard*. 'Very hard. I informed him that this was not the customary way of greeting people in England. Then some ape leapt on my back, put his arm around my neck and tried to force my head to the floor.'

Depp's wild man antics and hotel room trashing seemed to set off a wave of copy cat bad behaviour in other stars. Two months later another Hollywood bad boy, Mickey Rourke, whose career was on the slide, trashed a suite at the Plaza Hotel. In a *New York Post* report, Depp's friend Nicolas Cage, asked of Rourke, 'What's he trying to be? Johnny Depp?'

CHAPTER FIVE

Ed Wood

HAVING TURNED down leading roles in such blockbusters-to-be as *Speed* and *Interview with the Vampire*, as well as the lead role in Michael Mann's proposed biopic of James Dean, Johnny Depp perversely decided that his next film role should be as transvestite *Ed Wood*. 'Can your hearts stand the shocking true story of Edward D. Wood Jr?' opens Tim Burton's film biography, starring Depp as the ever optimistic Hollywood hack of the title, dubbed the World's Worst Film Director.

For Tim Burton the idea of doing a bio-pic of *Ed Wood* seemed like a natural move, and the notion that Depp would star as the director who never knew when to give up seemed equally natural. *Ed Wood* was the creative man behind such grade Z kitsch film 'classics' as *Plan Nine from Outer Space*, the cross-dressing melodrama *Glen or Glenda* (in which Wood starred as both Glen and Glenda) and *Bride of the Monster*.

Born in Poughkeepsie in 1924, Wood seemed to be convinced he was an artist of some kind and had a great contribution to make to the world of entertainment. He grew up watching B movie westerns and horror films in the 1930s and '40s. After Boy Scout meetings, Wood got out his home movie camera and was filming his own epics from the age of eleven. At the age of seventeen he enlisted in the Marines, six months after the bombing of Pearl Harbour. He became a Corporal and was a decorated war hero. His proudest achievement was parachuting onto a Japanese island wearing women's underwear under his Marine uniform! Leaving the service in 1946, Wood spent some time as the 'She-male' in a travelling carnival.

He drifted to Hollywood, where he wrote and directed a stage play about the war, entitled *The Casual Company*, which no-one went to see. Desperate to get into the movies, Wood managed to persuade a bottom-of-the-barrel drive-in movie producer to let him loose on a film about a sex-change operation. Wood managed to turn the film – *Glen or Glenda*, made in 1953 – into a personal, heartfelt examination of transvestism, a 'hobby' Wood indulged in.

Featured in *Glen or Glenda* was veteran horror star, Bela Lugosi. Wood met Lugosi in 1953 and immediately struck up a friendship with his childhood film idol. Since coming to fame as the title character in the 1931 Universal film of *Dracula*, Lugosi had almost disappeared into obscurity after twenty years of crummy horror flicks. Wood made use of Lugosi's tarnished star value in his own so-bad-they're-

almost-good productions.

Wood gathered around him a group of fringe Hollywood characters who appeared in his films, hoping one day to become stars. Among them were his girlfriend Dolores Fuller, TV horror show hostess Vampira (the stage name for Maila Nurmi), Swedish wrestler Tor Johnson and campy TV psychic Criswell. Although he died penniless and unknown in 1978, Wood's films were rediscovered at the dawn of the video age in the early 1980s. Celebrated in Michael and Harry Medved's book *The Golden Turkey Awards*, the films of Ed Wood became cult viewing, and he was awarded the dubious honour of being the World's Worst Film Director.

After working with Depp on *Edward Scissorhands*, Tim Burton had produced *The Nightmare Before Christmas*, a fabulous animated puppet feature film, the bizarre comedy-fantasy flop *Cabin Boy,* and an animated film version of Roald Dahl's book *James and the Giant Peach*. The connections between Burton and Wood were so strong that the director was immediately attracted to the idea of putting Wood's life story on film. Both directors managed to indulge their own madnesses on film: Wood was ridiculed for it, but refused to stop, while Burton was lauded, and likewise, refused to stop. Both directors had a connection with a fading horror film star, Wood employing drug addicted Bela Lugosi in his dying days, Burton providing a similar service for his idol Vincent Price.

The original idea for the film didn't come from Burton, however. Screenwriters Scott Alexander and Larry Karaszewski, whose previous claim to fame were the insufferable *Problem Child* films, had been discussing an Ed Wood project since the days when they were room-mates at the University of Southern California. 'We were both fascinated by his colourful character, his gumption and determination,' says Alexander. 'Even when we went out to write other projects after graduation, this one was always at the back of our minds.'

Johnny Depp as Ed Wood. The 1950s director's sets had been made out of scraps and plywood – but cost thousands of dollars to recreate in Tim Burton's biopic.

Tim Burton leapt at the material when it was brought to his attention by fellow film director Michael Lehman who had been at USC with Alexander and Karaszewski. 'I really felt close to him,' Burton said of Wood. 'There's something beautiful about somebody who does what they love to do, no matter how misguided, and remains optimistic and upbeat against the odds.'

The film covers the high points of Wood's lowly career, from the beginning of his friendship with the dying Bela Lugosi through to the premiere of what he thinks will be his greatest work, the risible *Plan Nine from Outer Space*. The film ends on this upbeat note, choosing not to follow Wood through his descent into alcoholism and pornography.

'I grew up watching Ed Wood movies on television,' recalls Burton. 'Like everyone else at first, I remember thinking "Wow, what is this?" But then I began to realise that even though they are bad, they're good. There's something poetic about them. Ed remained true to his work. He didn't let technicalities like visible wires and bad sets distract him from his storytelling. There's a twisted form of integrity to that.'

Although he'd originally agreed to produce *Ed Wood* with Lehman as director, Burton found himself drawn more and more to the story of the maverick, talentless director. His experiences in Hollywood had not been good since handing over the Batman mantle to Joel Schumacher for 1995's *Batman Forever*. Projects were falling through, he couldn't get the films he wanted made, and his recent efforts at producing had led to a series of unsuccessful films. Perhaps Burton was beginning to feel ever more sympathetic to the plight of Ed Wood.

Martin Landau won an Oscar for his portrayal of drug-addicted Bela Lugosi,
here taking direction from Depp as Ed Wood.

There was also the Vincent Price connection. 'There was an aspect of his relationship with Bela Lugosi that I liked,' said Burton. 'He befriended him at the end of his life, and without really knowing what that was like, I connected with it on the level that I did with Vincent Price, in terms of how I felt about him. Meeting Vincent had an incredible impact on me, the same impact Ed must have felt meeting and working with his idol,' said Burton. The key to the film for Burton was finding the right actor to portray the title character. He found himself turning to the actor who had previously played the title character in his most personal film to date: Johnny Depp, star of *Edward Scissorhands*. Burton's producing partner, Denise Di Novi, explained why they thought of casting Depp. 'Ed Wood was extremely handsome and loveable, as is Johnny. More importantly, Johnny is an actor who takes risks and gives unusual characters the special treatment and dignity they deserve.'

'Johnny liked the material, he responded to it,' said Burton. 'I feel close to Johnny because I think somewhere inside we respond to similar things. This was a chance after working on *Edward Scissorhands* to be more open. Edward was interior, this symbol come to life; Ed is more out-going. It was interesting to me, after working with Johnny before, to explore a more open kind of thing. He did a really great job, and he found a tone that I liked.'

Depp has clear memories of being approached by Burton to star in *Ed Wood*. 'I was at home when Tim called and asked to meet with me right away. He was real secretive: "How quickly can you get to the Formosa Cafe?" I go "twenty minutes." So I went there. He was sitting at the bar. We sat and had a beer. When he told me about the project, I thought it was an incredible idea. I immediately said "Yes, lets

Ed Wood (Johnny Depp) with Kathy O'Hara (Patricia Arquette) enjoys
a moment of glory at a film premiere – before the feature rolls!

do it." He'd called me at about 8pm, I was at the bar by 8.20. By 8.25, I was committed, completely committed. I was already familiar with Wood's films. I knew that nobody could tell his story better than Tim. Tim's passion became my passion. I've turned parts down and regretted them in the future, and I think I would have been as sick as a dog if I had walked away from this one.'

Approaching the title role of *Ed Wood* was difficult for Depp. There is very little visual material relating to Ed Wood, other than some black and white still pictures and, of course, Wood's own film appearance in *Glen or Glenda*. Depp was also able to consult some rare silent film footage of Wood in action behind the camera, directing his oddball cast. Depp had to rely on his own perception of what he thought Wood might have been like in real life, mixed with a little bit of Tim Burton. 'I read whatever I could get my hands on,' Depp explained. 'It was completely accepted that the details of Wood's life were a little muddled. Tim wanted to capture the spirit of the guy, and I had to exhibit that. I watched the films and then put different people together in my brain. I wanted to make him extremely optimistic, innocent and a brilliant showman all at the same time. He was a man who loved making films. It was his whole life, and he didn't allow anything to discourage him.'

Depp's performance as Ed Wood was easily the broadest and most theatrical he had so far given on film. With a constantly fixed grin on his face ('I couldn't shake that grin for months'), Wood bounds through one disastrous film after another, encouraging and cajoling his collaborators like some kind of demented 1950s game show host. 'Tim would say things like "Andy Hardy, Andy Hardy,"' said Depp. 'So I saw some Andy Hardy stuff. I had a couple of other things that spiced it up a bit. I came to him and I said: "Listen, Andy Hardy, but look: Ronald Reagan." And Tim went: "Wizard of Oz or Casey Kasem." We just boiled up this stew and shot it. We came up with a character that was the essence of what Wood was all about.'

Depp dismissed worries about the accuracy of his portrayal. It was the first time he'd played a part based on a real person, rather than a fictional character. 'I think it would be foolish for any film-makers to say they could hit the nail right on the head when trying to capture someone's life. Right from the word go, Tim and the writers wanted to make something that captured a real Hollywood icon. I think we did that. It isn't really about exploitation. This is a homage. A real weird homage, but nevertheless, a respectful one.' There were aspects of the role that would have proved troubling for most actors, particularly those dubbed with the Hollywood heartthrob tag. Dealing with Ed Wood's transvestism on film might cause some 'teen idols' to have second thoughts about taking the role, but not Depp who – in his usual style – embraced the challenge. 'I wasn't at all afraid of the idea of working in drag,' he said. 'I considered it an experiment to see what it would be like to wear lots of women's accoutrements. I have to say I have a much deeper respect for women, and for transvestites for that matter. I think Ed wore women's clothes because he really loved women and wanted to be that much closer to them.'

In fact, rumours circulated that Depp was taking his research a little bit too far, by wearing women's underwear in his everyday life just to get used to it. 'He was trying it out,' said screenwriter Scott Alexander. 'He said that when he was wearing his angora sweater he would grab the little hairs over his nipples and just try to twist them around, absent-mindedly, while he was pacing around.'

Dressing his leading man in drag worried director Tim Burton. 'I was concerned about the fact that Ed would have to be in drag through portions of the film. People in drag are real easy targets, but Johnny is so credible that he pulls it off without making it laughable. Besides, he really looks great in those clothes.'

Things were made easier for Depp in drag, by Robin Williams who had brought men in women's clothes back into the mainstream in *Mrs Doubtfire* (1994). Many years previously, Dustin Hoffman had taken the same route in *Tootsie* (1982). Both these actors, however, were middle-aged at the time, and had few worries about upsetting their teenage female fans by appearing to display a fondness for wearing their clothes. 'Before we started the film,' said Depp, 'I got a package from Miss Vera's Finishing School in New York City. They teach men to become transvestites, how to behave like women. It was a bunch of stuff, literature and photographs. The letter said "We heard you were doing this film. We could help you become a woman." I pondered the thought of going there to investigate what they were doing.'

For costume designer Colleen Atwood, transforming one of Hollywood's hottest young actors into an actress was something of a challenge, even if he could draw on hot dress tips from his girlfriend Kate Moss. 'When Ed is dressed as a man, he's a basic guy – with shirt, dark slacks, tie, vest. That way, when he's in drag, it's a very big shock, and the distinction is clear cut. When he's a woman, we pad out his hips and give him a bust and stuff. Actually, Johnny looks great as a woman. The first time we put him in angora we were saying "God, he looks beautiful."'

Depp was not convinced of his female good looks, however, banning a magazine from using a photo of him in drag as a cover shot. 'When I first looked in the mirror, I thought I was the ugliest woman I had ever seen. I mean, I looked huge in those clothes. Enormous!' However, comfort was an unexpected side effect for him. It led him to understand Wood better: 'It was spookily comfortable. The only time I felt weird was when I had to do a striptease. But I didn't have any fear about what the audience might think. It would have spoiled the effect if I had looked uneasy in any way. However, I am getting better at walking in high heels…'

Patricia Arquette, playing Wood's loyal wife Kathy, was equally bowled over by Depp in drag, as well as being pleased at the opportunity to work with the actor. 'He was amazing. He was a natural. I would give him tips on undressing, particularly with the bra strap. He was very strict who he undressed in front of. I think he energised everyone on set. He was as much a guiding force on the movie as Tim. We had these very intimate scenes together, and he would get right into the part and stay there for hours. I'm not that disciplined. I still have fits of laughter during a scene. But Johnny could do it straight.'

The rest of the casting for *Ed Wood* was completed fairly quickly, with Martin Landau cast as Bela Lugosi, a role which won Landau a Best Actor Oscar in 1995, as well as a Best Make-Up Oscar for the film's make-up team. The role was miles away from Landau's parts in the 1960s and 1970s TV series *Mission Impossible* and *Space 1999*. Landau had re-invented himself in the late 1980s as an accomplished character actor, winning excellent roles and critical acclaim for parts in films with Woody Allen (*Crimes and Misdemeanours*) and Francis Ford Coppola (*Tucker: The Man and His Dreams*).

'I tried to get under the skin of the man,' said Landau of his role as Lugosi. 'I

understand the ups and downs of the business; therefore, I have a compassion for some of the experiences he went through.' Burton was fascinated watching Landau turn himself into Lugosi on a daily basis. 'Martin has transformed into Bela Lugosi. When I watch him act, I see that Martin understands something about Lugosi on a very deep level.' Depp was equally happy to be working with Landau, and enjoyed the chance to explore the relationship between not only Wood and Lugosi, but also that of Burton and Price. 'With the kind of relationship Ed and Bela shared, I was afraid to force the chemistry. I found that working with Martin was so easy. Every scene we played together took on its own life and was more than just words on a page. Everything I felt for him was heartfelt and real,' said Depp.

Burton was initially set to make *Ed Wood* for Columbia Pictures, but his desire to make the film in black and white brought him into conflict with studio boss Mark Canton. The lack of total artistic control that he desired meant that the project was put into turnaround – which means it was available for any other studio to pick up once they'd paid Columbia's costs. There was a rush of interest in the film, which Burton, ironically, ended up making for Disney, the studio where he used to work as an animator. With a budget set at $18 million, *Ed Wood* was to be a low budget

Dolores (Sarah Jessica Parker, who would later become notorious for New York TV series Sex and the City) accepts Ed's transvestism in this recreated scene from Ed Wood's Glen or Glenda.

film by mainstream Hollywood standards, meaning that Disney could let Burton off the leash without taking too great a risk. After all, they had much to make up to the director after letting him go so early in his career.

The work of recreating 1950s Hollywood and scenes from three of Wood's cheesiest films – *Glen or Glenda*, *Bride of the Monster* and his magnum opus *Plan Nine from Outer Space* – started in earnest on August 5th 1993. One of the biggest challenges was building identical sets for those ultra low-budget films. Production designer Tom Duffield ended up spending far more money recreating Wood's wobbly sets than Wood spent on all his movies put together. A total of 68 locations in and around Los Angeles were visited by the cast and crew. Many of Wood's old stomping grounds were used for real, including Griffith Park, where Wood made *Bride of the Monster;* Musso & Franks Bar and Grill, where he hung out; and his last apartment in Hollywood. 'It was a very vibrant shoot,' recalled Depp. 'I mean, it was really tough. We were filming in some of the most claustrophobic, badly ventilated, most uncomfortable locations in Hollywood. My adrenaline was pumping all the way, but everyone from the ground up was giving the movie 200 per cent. I think it has to be the most ensemble picture I've ever made. I don't think I've worked on anything where everyone was so close knit.'

Woods' second wife Kathy visited the location filming unannounced. After watching some of the shooting, Kathy Wood was finally introduced to the man playing her late husband. 'It was a real eye-opener,' said Depp. 'She gave me Edward's wallet and his phone book. I was initially a little fazed by it, because I really didn't know how to take it. But it really took the sting out of meeting someone who really knew the person you are playing on film. The wallet and the phone book became real important to the way that I finally fleshed out the part.'

Depp had high hopes for the finished film, not something he was used to feeling during the shooting process: 'It's the first time that I'm actually looking forward to seeing something that I was in. I'm really excited as it was such a great experience. The whole time we were doing it, it felt like a really good departure from any of the other shit that I've done.' The production wrapped principal photography on November 17th 1993, but it didn't open in the United States till almost a year later, in October 1994. The reviews were overwhelmingly positive, but box office returns were rough. *Ed Wood* fared better in Europe, with a UK opening in May 1995, followed by a premiere screening at the Cannes Film Festival (alongside another Johnny Depp film *Don Juan DeMarco,* and Jim Jarmusch's *Dead Man*). J. Hoberman in the *Village Voice* commented: 'The film is nothing if not knowing. Depp plays Wood as a wide-eyed, wired enthusiast at once suave and disjointed, lips accentuated by a pencil line moustache, teeth bared in a ventriloquist dummy's idiot grin, illuminated by faith in his own dream. *Ed Wood* is flawlessly crafted – as fastidious as any previous Burton production.' Richard Corliss in *Entertainment Weekly* called Depp 'an exemplary actor who can't do much more than smile heroically in the face of every humiliation'. In its year end poll, *Ed Wood* came third in the movie category, after Oliver Stone's controversial *Natural Born Killers* at number two, and Quentin Tarantino's *Pulp Fiction* at number one. Britain's *Empire* magazine commented, 'Depp gives a truly mesmerising performance, both in and out of drag, notching up another distinctly oddball role that again reveals the measure of the young actor's talents. A sublime treat.'

Depp had a final word about Edward D. Wood Jr which seemed to be a plea for how future writers should look at the work of Depp himself. 'Ed was someone who was not afraid to take chances and did exactly what he wanted to do. He did the best he could do with what was available to him and he was able to put together images that were surreal, with moments of genius, I think. His movies were all his, and they were genuine. I hope Ed is remembered as an artist.'

The idea for the film *Don Juan DeMarco* sprang from the mind of novelist Jeremy Leven. Leven had previously adapted his own 1980 novel *Creator* for the screen. He claimed to have been writing in one form or another since the age of ten, leading to two published novels: *Creator* and the bizarrely titled *Satan: His Psychotherapy and Cure, By The Unfortunate Dr Kassler, JSPS*, and another produced screenplay, *Playing for Keeps*. In his time he had been a television director, schoolteacher, state hospital psychologist, a faculty member at Harvard University and a clinical psychologist. All of these diverse influences would feed into the writing and filming of *Don Juan DeMarco*. 'I always wanted to do a movie about women, love, romance and sex,' he explained, 'and I always wondered whether anyone had ever done a movie about Don Juan.'

The start of his research into the subject led Leven to a bookstore in his native Woodbridge, Connecticut. There he found a copy of Lord Byron's *Don Juan*, credited in the movie as the source material of the idea. The book inspired Leven to write another original screenplay. 'Byron's piece is a very long tome that has a tremendous amount of politics, but some absolutely wonderful scenes,' said Leven. 'I freely appropriated some of those scenes, and then worked them into a screenplay about another issue.'

Leven's background as a psychotherapist led him to blend his fascination with Don Juan with his own personal experience. For the script he created the character of psychiatrist Jack Mickler, who served as the catalyst for his exploration of the blurring of fantasy and reality. After 30 years of trying to solve other peoples problems, Mickler is burned out. Withdrawn, from both his colleagues and his long suffering wife Marilyn, Mickler is simply going through the motions, awaiting his imminent retirement. Things take a different tack, however, when Mickler takes on the most fascinating case of his career. The tales of Don Juan DeMarco are exactly what he needs to give a new boost to his professional life and his marriage.

Enter Johnny Depp as Don Juan DeMarco, a character as far removed from Hollywood loser Ed Wood as Depp could get. The film opens with a young man perched precariously on a narrow catwalk on top of a huge advertising billboard 40 feet above the street. His face hidden behind a mask, cloaked in a flowing cape and wielding a raised sabre, the figure claims to be Don Juan, the world's greatest lover. The seducer of over 1,500 women, this contemporary Don Juan is distraught. He's loved so many women, but the one woman he is actually in love with has rejected him. Convinced there is nothing left to live for, suicide seems an inviting option.

Enter Dr Mickler, writer-director Leven's alter-ego. Called in by the police, who believe they are dealing with a madman, Mickler succeeds in talking the cloaked figure down. On the verge of retirement, he nevertheless takes on this unusual case, intrigued by the young man he discovers behind the mask. Given ten days to evaluate his seemingly delusional patient, Mickler is supposed to offer a diagnosis and recommend a course of treatment. As the film unfolds, DeMarco tells Mickler a series of stories during his sessions with the psychiatrist. He outlines his life and adventures – outlandish tales which include a childhood in a small Mexican town, a journey to Arabia where he is secretly pressed into service in a harem and an eventual shipwreck, with Don Juan washed up on a desert island, only to encounter his one true love. The tragedy of his life is that, by being honest with her, DeMarco finds himself rejected because of his confession of inadvertent promiscuity.

Engaged and drawn in by the tales – related in the film as gorgeous, colourful flashback/fantasy sequences – Mickler finds himself being affected by his patient. As the therapy progresses, Mickler is convinced that only Don Juan himself could relate such glorious tales of love, passion and romance. Mickler finds himself examining the importance of love and passion in his own life, resulting in a rekindling of the long lost spark between him and his wife.

Don Juan DeMarco is a light, fantasy confection. Leven said, 'Don Juan, as Johnny Depp plays him, is someone who's just unmitigatedly in love with love, and whether or not he's the real thing is inconsequential. He causes a tremendous transformation in Mickler.' Leven had no thoughts for a potential cast when he finished the original screenplay. 'I was told Johnny wanted to do it,' Leven explained. This is not surprising; it was not difficult to see that Don Juan could be the ideal role for the heartthrob actor, with his dramatic, Latin good looks. Indeed, reviewing the film for *Empire*, Mark Salisbury commented, 'It's a role Depp was born to play, his beauteous looks and doe-eyes the perfect accompaniments to a lifetime of seduction and loving.'

Indeed, it seemed as if all the parts Depp had played previously had led him to this point. Although he'd rejected the 'teen idol' attention he'd initially received, Depp was acutely aware of his affect on women, both on the big screen and off. Here was the ideal opportunity to play the role the media had already created for him, yet he could have some fun with it. Depp was now also in a position to influence casting of the other roles. 'Depp said he'd only do the film if Brando played the psychiatrist,' said Leven. 'At that point I thought the project was dead in the water, only to receive a second shock, hearing that Marlon was also interested.'

Working with the legendary Marlon Brando had been a long term ambition of Johnny Depp's. Depp's name alone was enough to green light many low budget projects – but did he really have the clout to try and attract an actor of the stature of Brando to one of his almost trademark small-scale, quirky films?

As he entered his thirties, Depp found himself often compared with the young Brando as the 'greatest actor of his generation'. It was a comparison he must have relished, because he was a great admirer of the veteran actor, who had recently celebrated his 70th birthday. In a sometimes controversial career spanning over 40 years, Marlon Brando had made 35 films and could be said to have pioneered the now standard approach to American screen acting. Nominated seven times for Academy Awards as Best Actor, Brando had won twice, once for *On the Waterfront* (1954) and then for his part as Vito Corleone in *The Godfather* (1972). Brando had built up a body of work any actor would envy – especially someone as aware of his screen career

as Johnny Depp. Films as varied as *Viva Zapata!*, *Julius Caesar* and the controversial *Last Tango in Paris* sealed Brando's reputation. His $1 million fee for a fifteen minute cameo appearance in 1978's *Superman: The Movie* fitted his legendary status.

Brando worked with director Francis Ford Coppola on *The Godfather* movies and *Apocalypse Now*, Coppola's Vietnam-set version of Joseph Conrad's *Heart of Darkness*, starring Martin Sheen. The Coppola connection was important in convincing Brando to take on the part of the psychiatrist in *Don Juan DeMarco*. As one of the film's three producers, Coppola was in an ideal position to make Depp's dream of working with Brando come true.

Cast in the small but pivotal role of Mickler's wife, Marilyn, was Faye Dunaway. Dunaway had worked with Depp previously in *Arizona Dream*, so the two were far from strangers. She had not, however, shared the screen with Marlon Brando. Watching Brando and Depp at work during the shooting of *Don Juan DeMarco*, Dunaway sensed a kind of passing of the torch. 'Johnny's the heir apparent,' she claimed.

With over 30 films under her belt, *Don Juan DeMarco* was the icing on her career cake. The attraction of the role was the blooming romance between husband and wife. 'After just a couple of sessions Jack begins to change. He becomes attracted to Marilyn in a way that has been dormant for over twenty years, and at first she finds it rather alarming,' she said. Dunaway had firm views on her two male co-stars. 'Marlon's an idol, a dream,' she said. 'He's a myth to every working actor in the world. And Johnny's a close second.'

Developing a close relationship during the filming, Brando and Depp spent

Donning a mask for Don Juan DeMarco, Depp once again found an opportunity to disguise the good looks that constantly threaten to overshadow his acting ability.

much of their time together, both on and off the production. 'It was tremendously exciting working with Marlon and Faye,' said Depp. 'They are actors with incredible careers. I was privileged to work alongside them and learn.'

Depp quickly overcame any nervousness he may have experienced when confronted with the actuality of working with Brando. 'You just jump in,' he said. 'I was real nervous on my way over to his house. Then as soon as I saw him he just instantly, magically, put me at ease within seconds of saying "Hello." He became this great, wonderful guy I was working with. He was a big, big factor in me doing the film.' *Don Juan DeMarco* really had a dream cast – a point not lost on executive producer Patrick Palmer: 'Let's face it, we've got the most talented actor over the age of 60, the most talented actor under the age of 30 and one of the most acclaimed actresses in Hollywood.'

As with all the films he made, it was the script for *Don Juan DeMarco* that finally sealed the deal for Depp. 'Jeremy's script was brilliant,' he commented. 'It's incredible writing. My character's dialogue is so poetic and beautiful.' He continued: 'The challenge for me was creating a character who was slightly cocky and noble, but likeable. I needed to create someone who has a strong sense of himself, but is still lost.'

Jeremy Leven had his own hopes for the film. 'I wanted *Don Juan* to be about so many things – about what's important in life, and the connection between people. It's a story about life beginning again, and about humanity and the way we're all living. Most importantly, it's about staying alive in life.'

The reviews for *Don Juan DeMarco* were almost universally upbeat, with many enjoying seeing a screen legend like Brando returning to something resembling his previous form. This was all the more surprising, as earlier *Entertainment Weekly* had tagged the film as 'whimsical' and the 'big risk' of the year, dubbing the cast as 'the year's most unlikely romantic-comedy trio'. Most praise was reserved for the film's lead, Johnny Depp. 'Exactly the right mix of vulnerability and bravado,' said *People* magazine of Depp's performance. British reviewers were swept up in the whimsy of it all, too. Allan Hunter in *Scotland on Sunday* called Depp's performance 'utterly delightful. Depp seems permanently drawn to characters on the fringe of society and is perfectly cast as a man who takes boyish delight in the opportunities that life possesses.' In *The Guardian* critic Derek Malcom was pleased to see 'Johnny Depp stand up to Brando as the best young actor in Hollywood. The part seems to be made for him, and he plays it without narcissism or camp.'

Depp had completed another double whammy of successful movies, but it was becoming ever more doubtful that he would be able to plough the oddball furrow much longer. The pressure upon him to move towards the mainstream and star in a blockbuster action movie was becoming irresistible.

By the spring of 1995 Depp was riding high with two critically acclaimed movies, one of which was also a huge commercial success across the world. He ventured with Kate Moss to the south of France in May 1995 to attend the 48th annual Cannes Film Festival.

Sometimes known as Hollywood on the Riviera, Cannes had over the years attracted a large number of Hollywood stars, prepared to promote their upcoming films but happy to leave the winning of awards to the Europeans. This had changed

Critics agreed that the title role in Don Juan DeMarco was a part Johnny Depp, with his classic Latin looks, was born to play.

in the 1990s with American films like Quentin Tarantino's *Pulp Fiction* and the Coen Brother's *Barton Fink* taking the coveted top prize, the Palme D'Or. Depp had two movies screening at Cannes, Tim Burton's *Ed Wood* and his other black and white opus, Jim Jarmusch's mystical western *Dead Man*.

Former film student Jim Jarmusch first came to prominence with his quirky low budget black and white feature film *Stranger Than Paradise* (1984), starring John Lurie. His minimalist but hip style quickly brought the young director a growing cult following, who stuck with him through *Down By Law* (1986), which teamed Lurie up with Tom Waits and Italian comic Roberto Benigni as three on-the-run convicts; the colour multi-story film *Mystery Train* (1989), featuring a trio of foreigners staying in an American motel; and *Night on Earth* (1992) which starred Winona Ryder as a New York taxi driver.

Spending leisure time in France with Kate Moss, before doing his duty and attending Cannes screenings and press conferences, Depp was making the most of his trip to Europe. With both *Ed Wood* and *Don Juan deMarco* opening at cinemas across the continent in May, the timing was ideal. It became almost impossible to walk into a paper store or turn on the TV without seeing Depp's visage glaring off magazine covers, or being interviewed, wreathed in cigarette smoke. Although he claimed to hate the press for getting the facts about him wrong, or for appropriating a slice of him for their own ends, Depp was – like almost every other Hollywood star – happy to use the media when he had a new film to sell.

Ed Wood and *Don Juan deMarco* had been acclaimed, but *Dead Man* received a mixed reception at Cannes. During the film's screening towards the end of the Festival, one French viewer in the audience was moved to cry out his own, considered, critical opinion: 'Piece of sheet, Jeem!' Jim Jarmusch is one of those maverick independent film directors who ooze integrity – the ideal collaborator for Depp to seek out. *Dead Man* is a hypnotic, slow moving, sometimes astonishing Western, which shares more with films like Ingmar Bergman's *The Seventh Seal* than with any Hollywood gunfight film. Depp played a white faced, Keaton-inspired wandering accountant named William Blake who finds himself in the wild Western town of Machine. To Jim Jarmusch '*Dead Man* is the story of a young man's journey, both physical and spiritually, into very unfamiliar terrain. William Blake travels to the extreme frontiers of America sometime in the second half of the nineteenth century. Lost and badly wounded he encounters a very odd, outcast native American, named Nobody, who believes Blake is actually the dead English poet of the same name. The story, with Nobody's help, leads William Blake through situations that are in turn comical and violent. Contrary to his nature, circumstances transform Blake into a hunted outlaw, a killer and a man whose physical existence is slowly slipping away. Thrown into a world that is cruel and chaotic, his eyes are opened to the fragility that defines the realm of the living. It is as though he passes through the surface of a mirror, and emerges into a previously unknown world that exists on the other side.'

A kind hearted character, Depp's William Blake indulges in an act of gallantry, which results in him falling into the bed of a mysterious young woman. In turn he has an encounter with her fiancee – played by Gabriel Byrne.

Filming *Dead Man* in Nevada, Depp stayed at the Mackay Mansion, a three-

Depp's romance with Kate Moss was soon to collapse when she chose to put her career before his desire to have children.

storey Victoria house, reputed to be haunted by a little girl wearing a silk party dress with a blue sash. Depp had been interested in ghosts and 'visitations', and had regaled journalists several times with his experiences and fantasies. 'When I was a kid I used to have these dreams,' he said, 'but they weren't dreams. I was awake, but I couldn't move. I couldn't speak. And a face would come to me. Someone told me it was the spirit of someone who died that was very close and never got to say something that they wanted to say. And I believe it.' He even stayed in the room in Paris in which Oscar Wilde died. 'I didn't see Oscar. It was definitely the bed he died in – I'm not sure if it was the room, but there was all his furniture. I was a little paranoid that I might be buggered by his ghost at 4am.'

For *Dead Man*, Depp's agent Tracey Jacobs watched him go through the same process for Jim Jarmusch as he had for Tim Burton on *Ed Wood*. While waiting for the turnaround situation with Columbia on *Ed Wood* to be resolved, Depp was offered seven other films, but he turned them down to do Burton's film. Jacobs said, 'He had an allegiance to Tim and stuck with that process for almost six months. He did the exact same thing for *Dead Man*.' How much longer could Depp continue to be semi-bankable in Hollywood, yet refuse to play the blockbuster action movie game by their rules? Tracey Jacobs was asked if she was disappointed that he turned these projects down. 'No!' she replied emphatically. 'Do I want him to be in a movie that does $100 million? Of course – I'm not stupid! He wants to be in a commercial movie. It just has to be the right timing and the right one, that's all. Hopefully he'll be available when those come along again.'

Locations for *Dead Man* in Sedona, Arizona and Virginia City, Nevada taxed Depp's commitment to *Dead Man*. High winds and dry days made the weather a problem during shooting. 'Visibility was about like this,' admitted Depp, holding his hand in front of his face. 'You couldn't see the camera, couldn't see anybody. It was kind of nice, actually, I was standing in a fog somewhere.' There's nothing Depp likes better than to be cut off from his director – it allows him to go his own way, to indulge his own vision of the film and the character he's playing without interference. With an 'auteur' director like Jim Jarmusch – even if he was a friend – that distance was important to Depp. 'He really is one of the most precise and focused people I've ever worked with,' reported Jim Jarmusch. 'The whole crew is kind of amazed by that. It's a side of him that I'm not really familiar with, you know? I'm more familiar with seeing him fall asleep on the couch with the TV on all night. But it somehow fits, he's full of paradoxes.'

Jarmusch, who first met Depp five years previously, wrote the part of the leading character especially for him. 'What I love about him as an actor is his subtlety and very interesting physicality, which is under-played; he has amazing eyes, which he uses to great effect. I didn't appreciate his precision until I worked with him; he doesn't make false moves or overdo it.'

Making a Western was a great adventure for Depp, especially co-starring with one of America's most famous Western film actors, Robert Mitchum. Mitchum had made a minor comeback in Martin Scorsese's remake of the thriller *Cape Fear* in 1991, after starring in the 1962 original version of John D. MacDonald's novel *The Executioners*. Depp was almost overwhelmed by the ageing gunslinger: 'He's about seven foot tall and in great shape,' said Depp, who recalled Mitchum's 'Love'

*William Blake (Johnny Depp) is forced by circumstances to make the
transition from mild-mannered accountant to killer.*

and 'Hate' tattooed fingers from *Night of the Hunter*. 'It's still in his heart. Love and Hate. He's a tough guy.'

His role in *Dead Man* forced Johnny Depp to take stock of his career. Even with his string of recent successes, the actor was beginning to realise that he couldn't seek refuge in his oddball roles for much longer and the Hollywood machine would mean he'd have to start playing mainstream roles. But the prospect didn't worry him as much as it would have done when he was younger – his kooky image was beginning to get tiring. 'I hope this is the last of these innocents I play,' Depp said of *Dead Man*. 'It's a character that is, again, like a naive young guy who's trying to get his life together. He's trying really hard to make his life work and he ends up slowly dying. And he knows he's dying. It's a beautiful story, though.'

With glorious stunning black and white camera work from Robby Muller, who often worked with German director Wim Wenders, *Dead Man* is a beguiling and nicely paced would-be existentialist Western epic, with a dash of the classic *film noir DOA* (1950) thrown in for good measure. Critics at Cannes were not as harsh as the French viewer in the audience but clearly *Dead Man* was not a particularly easy film to watch. Derek Malcolm from *The Guardian* commented: 'What looks like an intriguing short story is stretched by Jarmusch into over two hours of slow burning and effortful watching, with its humour existing side by side with a kind of portentous visual philosophising.'

Depp left Cannes empty handed, with neither of his two in-competition films scooping an award. However, he was very pleased to learn that Emir Kusturica had been awarded the Palme D'Or for his three hour historical epic *Underground*, about the roots of the civil war in former Yugoslavia, his home country. The Cannes Film Festival visit and promotion of his current slate of movies was wrapped up shortly before Johnny Depp finally got some time to himself to celebrate his 32nd birthday on June 9th 1995. He'd taken time out from shooting on John Badham's *Nick of Time* to visit Cannes. *Nick of Time* was to be a rare concession to the Hollywood movie making machine, with Depp taking a fairly straight role, the nearest thing he'd ever come to playing an action hero in the Keanu Reeves or Bruce Willis mould. It was something he'd been avoiding all his professional life, but could resist no longer.

Nick of Time was a big budget remake of *The Man Who Knew Too Much*, co-scripted by Ebbe Roe Smith and Patrick Duncan. Alfred Hitchcock made the original not once, but twice, first in 1934 with Leslie Banks and Peter Lorre, followed by his own colour updating in 1956, with James Stewart and Doris Day. The original tale had a young girl kidnapped to prevent her parents from revealing their knowledge of a political assassination plot. In *Nick of Time* the story is skewed slightly, turning Depp into a young professional forced to carry out the political assassination to save the life of his small daughter. It was the only Depp movie likely to follow John Badham's others (like *Saturday Night Fever* and *Blue Thunder*) across the $100 million gross earnings barrier, turning the quirky, maverick, thoughtful actor into a bona fide A-list big grossing action hero.

Depp stars as Gene Watson, an unassuming accountant, approached at Union Station in Los Angeles by the official looking Mr Smith (Christopher Walken). Before he knows what's happened, he's under instruction to kill someone he doesn't know within the next 80 minutes or his daughter will die. As Depp's character takes up the challenge, this unusual film unfolds in real time as the audience watches. This clever conceit promised the film big audiences upon its November 1995 American release.

The attraction of the part to Depp was clear. Gene Watson wasn't one of his usual oddball kooky characters, but the plight of the mild mannered accountant would give any actor plenty of dramatic meat to chew on. It also emphasised Depp's ever increasing commitment to the idea of a family, which was bringing tensions to his relationship with career-orientated Kate Moss, just as it had with Winona Ryder.

'Gene goes from one extreme to another – from one emotion to the next – in the fraction of a second,' said Depp. 'To play the role I drew on what was accessible, and family is very important to me. I have nieces and nephews that I absolutely worship. If anything happened to them, I would go crazy and do anything to save them.'

Teaming Depp with character actor extraordinaire Christopher Walken was a key move by John Badham, since working with Walken was one more reason for Depp to succumb to the action hero mode of contemporary Hollywood. The ironic nature of *Nick of Time* was also enough to convince Depp to commit.

Shooting the film almost like a documentary was necessary for Badham to capture the realness of the situation and it gave Depp as an actor some new challenges. 'We did a lot of scenes that involved two or three cameras, which reduced the number of takes and kept freshness and spontaneity to the acting,' said Depp. 'You're not bound within frame lines and feel like you can go anywhere and do anything.' Shooting from April 2nd through to June 19th 1995, Depp spent much of his time in the Westin Bonaventure Hotel in the heart of downtown Los Angeles, the main location for filming, close to Union Station, where the film opens.

Some days when he turned up for shooting, however, Depp was not at his best, according to director Badham. 'Johnny would come in at seven in the morning and we would start to stage a scene, and I would think he was only propped up by a stage brace,' Badham told *Premiere* about his $4.5 million star. 'He would stand there looking a little shaken, but totally focused.' Badham didn't enquire what Depp had been doing the night before in his adopted home town of LA. 'Why ask the obvious? What I learned right away was, it didn't matter if he never went to bed, he was right on top of it.' Depp's *Nick of Time* co-star Gloria Reuben (from the TV series *ER*) didn't care if her leading man was a tearaway. 'He's a Gemini – very sensitive, a little shy and very funny. If he wanted to trash a hotel room with me in it, that would be just fine…'

Despite the real-time gimmick and Depp in action man mode, *Nick of Time* did not meet the expectations of the studio and was greeted with mixed reviews by the critics. *Entertainment Weekly* dubbed the film Depp's 'bid for mainstream action stardom'. Roger Ebert, writing in the *Chicago Sun-Times* didn't see *Nick of Time* as Depp's action movie at all: 'There is no danger Depp will turn into a surprise action hero; they cast Depp not Stallone for a reason. He tries to use his brain to figure out a way to save his daughter, without killing the governor. And his efforts are ingenious.' While deciding the film was overall 'too contrived', Ebert thought the real-time gimmick 'effective…It's a curious sensation, being able to look at the clocks on the screen to tell how much longer the movie has to run.'

Edward Guthmann in the *San Fransisco Chronicle* also called the storytelling technique 'effective…reminiscent of the paranoid nightmares that Hitchcock fancied – particularly *North by Northwest.*' Despite that, *Nick of Time* flopped in the United States and seemed destined to be released straight to home video in other territories.

Unexpectedly, Depp was then given the chance to rejoin Marlon Brando on a film; he was delighted to be reunited with his acting hero so soon after *Don Juan DeMarco*. For *Divine Rapture*, Depp was cast in the role of a journalist investigating religious miracles in Ireland, alongside Debra Winger and his *Dead Man* co-star John Hurt. In July 1995 he went to Ireland for location filming alongside 71-year old Brando, cast as a priest.

Divine Rapture was intended to be a black comedy about miracles, but instead it became a Hollywood joke. Debra Winger was cast as a fisherman's wife who dies and is brought back to life, while Brando was to play a local priest involved in assorted miracles, like fish raining from the sky. In an ironic touch, considering his attitude to the press, Johnny Depp was to play an investigative reporter sent to cover the alleged miracles, while British character actor John Hurt was cast as a local doctor. Shooting began in mid-July for what promised to be a tense and pressured eight week shoot. 'I've been over here for eight weeks already,' said director Thom Eberhardt, who'd supervised the pre-production process. 'Most of the time the weather was glorious. Then as soon as we got underway the rain rolled in.'

The first sign that *Divine Rapture* was in trouble came from God – via the Irish

On the set of Nick of Time with director John Badham.

Catholic Church. Two churches in County Cork had been selected as filming sites, but cold water was quickly poured on the plan by the local clergy who bluntly stated: 'Churches are not film sets.' The Bishop of Cloyne then forbade the use of Ballycotton's two churches, the Star of the Sea and the Immaculate Conception, on the grounds that Brando's priest character made Catholicism seem ridiculous.

It should have been taken as a warning by all those involved in the making of *Divine Rapture*, for much worse was to come. No-one could tell, though, from the enthusiastic welcome laid out for the film-makers by the 450 inhabitants of Ballycotton, County Cork. To them, the arrival of Hollywood filmmakers meant dollars in their pockets. It was to be hoped that some of Marlon Brando's $4 million fee would find its way into the local economy.

Indeed, local street sign-painter Brendan Ahern, who could double for Brando from behind and at a distance, was signed up by the production. He resigned just as quickly after one day when he discovered his Hollywood big bucks amounted to just £35. 'I can't afford the film business any longer,' he is reported to have said, before returning to his £45 per day sign painting business. All he got for his trouble was a chance to shake the real Brando's hand. Once again no-one saw the omens. No one realised that *Divine Rapture* was a doomed film. Marlon Brando moved into a mansion in nearby Shanagarry at a reported cost to the production of over £4,000 per week, and to the disappointment of the locals he didn't come out much, despite his new found enthusiasm for all things Irish. 'I have never been so happy in my life,' he'd declared upon his arrival at the airport. 'When I got off the plane I had this rush of emotion. I have never felt at home in a place as I do here. I am seriously contemplating Irish citizenship.'

The shooting schedule continued to be delayed, but eventually Depp managed a couple of days work, taking a few photographs and climbing over fences. Mobbed by fans, he signed a few autographs after filming and was then spirited away in a limousine to the exclusive Ballymaloe House where he was staying. Although he was expected to be joined by Kate Moss within days, Depp's publicist said the actor was feeling homesick and missing his newly acquired pet pit bull terrier named Moo, a gift from Kate. Depp did have one friend in town to help drown his doggie separation sorrows – new *Batman* star Val Kilmer, whose tempestuous marriage to British actress Joanne Whalley appeared to be on the rocks again after the birth of their first child.

After a few days' shooting, *Divine Rapture* was shut down due to 'financial difficulties' on July 17th. The $16 million budget – low by Hollywood standards – was not all in place and doubts were being raised about whether the backers, French company Cinefin, would be able to pull the cash together. Brando had been paid $1 million up front, but the rest of the cast and crew, including Depp, were not so lucky. 'Basically, what you have,' said director Thom Eberhardt, ' is a roomful of question marks and upstairs another roomful of producers, where the problem now lies.'

The film was in limbo for a week, until July 24th when production was officially cancelled. Pay cheques made out on the previous Friday for the cast and crew to cover – in some cases – several weeks work, were deemed to be worthless. Eberhardt saw his seven years of planning the film collapse over one weekend. The producers issued a statement, condemning the financial backers. 'With deep regret,' ran the statement, 'we have had to cease production of *Divine Rapture*. In spite of continuing assurance of financial backing from our backer, the funds have not been forthcoming.'

'Along with the cast and crew, we are shocked at the situation and deeply saddened by our inability to continue with this wonderful project. We wish to thank the people of Ballycotton who showed us so much support. We will be doing everything we can to compensate them for their time and effort.'

The cast and crew were not the only ones out of pocket. Fishermen, hoteliers and food suppliers were all owed money by the film company when the production collapsed. The Bay View Hotel, where many of the cast and crew stayed, was due payment for up to 20 rooms. The hopes of local hoteliers for fame and fortune had been dashed by the failure of the film. 'We hoped it would keep the hotels and guest houses full for years when the fame of the area spread throughout the world because of the film,' admitted star-struck hotelier John O'Brien. Even the English owner of the Shanagarry mansion where Brando was staying was out of pocket. Adrian Knowles stated: 'I did receive a cheque on Saturday morning that I understand will not be honoured, but I too have been assured that I will be paid.' Brando promised that he would meet the costs of his gardener, cook and two housekeepers personally until he left, which he did rather quickly a few days later on Tuesday July 25th.

Johnny Depp had already given up on the production when filming was first suspended on July 17th. A weekend trip to France with Kate Moss turned into a permanent departure from *Divine Rapture*. Depp did not return to the location and had not been paid for any of his work in the twenty minutes of completed film.

One of the producers, Barry Navidi, foretold of years of legal action between the producers and financiers over the collapse of the movie. Although Navidi personally lost around £1 million in the project, he was more saddened at its curtailment: 'The tragedy is that we have quite amazing rushes of the movie, with incredible performances from the stars,' he said.

With the collapse of *Divine Rapture*, Depp had a summer break before he was due back in Britain in September 1995 to play a part in *The Cull*, a film written by *Performance* co-director Donald Cammell. *The Cull* was about a Gulf war veteran whose life is threatened by government assassins because he plans to reveal details of chemical warfare. It was also to be produced by Cinefin, but the company was financially crippled when *Divine Rapture* collapsed. The final fate of the movie was sealed by the gun-shot suicide of writer-director Cammell in 1996.

Other projects which came Depp's way at the time were a role in Francis Ford Coppola's proposed film version of Jack Kerouac's *On The Road*. So keen was Depp on the part that he bought an old raincoat once worn by Kerouac at auction for $9,000, more than the cost of the damage he'd caused at The Mark Hotel. Depp was also being pursued to take on the role of the comic book super hero Speed Racer.

For a long time, Johnny Depp had harboured thoughts of leaving the US and relocating to France, only returning to Hollywood or London for film roles. Paris was one of Depp's favourite cities, one he often visited. He was still without a permanent home. His rented house in Laurel Canyon had been damaged in the 1994 LA earthquake while he was in London. It took seven months to repair, forcing him to live in a hotel. Depp claimed that at one time or another he'd lived in every hotel in LA. His flight from America to a possible European home was only the latest in a long line of manifestations of this initial trauma. 'It's a different thing in Paris,' explained Depp of the attractions of life in France. 'It's more about the work than anything called celebrity.' Little could he have known that these vague musings about relocating to France would eventually lead him to a whole new life and a dramatic change in career direction before he turned 40.

Even as he talked of moving to Paris, Depp invested in property in Los Angeles. He'd been talking of buying a Hollywood property for some time, but he had special requirements. Just any Hollywood house wouldn't do. 'I would love to buy Bela Lugosi's old house,' he said, shortly after visiting the ruins of Harry Houdini's home. 'Or Errol Flynn's. Or Charlie Chaplin's. I want some old, depressing history to call my own. Plus, I love the idea of a view.'

Depp finally made up his mind in October 1995 with his $2.3 million purchase of Bela Lugosi's old Los Angeles mansion called 'The Castle.' Home to Lugosi in the 1930s at the height of his success, it's a walled and gated 9,000-square foot estate on a 2.5 acre plot near Hollywood's Sunset Strip. 'They shot part of *The Wizard Of Oz* there, and those things are very interesting little tidbits, nice to know,' said Depp of his new investment. 'I just loved the house; it's such a strange design, very unusual architecture. It is like a weird little castle in the middle of Hollywood, but I'm hardly ever there.' Depp finally had his 'depressing history' to call his own, one he knew well from co-starring with Martin Landau in *Ed Wood*.

With his property investment and talk of having a family, Depp finally appeared to be on the verge of settling down. However his equally career-minded partner Kate Moss had no intention of giving up her globe-trotting lifestyle. By the end of 1995, their relationship was over. In a repeat of the split from Winona Ryder, the pressures

In October 1995 Johnny Depp finally bought Bela Lugosi's old Los Angeles mansion on Sunset Boulevard at a cost of $2.3 million.

of being part of a world-famous couple took their toll. While Moss took to the catwalks of New York, Depp retired to Viper Room seclusion, attempting to drown his romantic sorrows by surrounding himself with 'bimbos', according to tabloid reports.

'It's my own fault Kate left me,' Depp finally admitted. 'I can be a real pain in the butt and act really irritating. Especially when I'm working on a movie and it isn't going the way it is supposed to be. I shouldn't have taken my worries home with me. Or at least, I shouldn't have kept going on about them. It was enough for Kate.'

Depp's growing desire for a family of his own was to prove the final straw. 'I wanted to become a father. The time was obviously right for me. I started to talk about it with Kate. I thought she would react really enthusiastic, but she didn't. Kate immediately said that children weren't an option at the moment. That came as a shock to me. I never considered the fact that she might not be ready for it. Will I ever find someone I like as much as Kate and who wants to give me a child? There was nothing else to do than finish it.'

Getting over the break-up, Depp threw himself back into work delivering one of his best film performances and realising a long-held dream to direct a movie. His desire for a family would not go away, though. It just took a back seat for a while…

Mob thriller *Donnie Brasco*, based on Joe Pistone's 1989 memoirs of his days as an undercover FBI agent infiltrating the Bonnano mafia family in New York, saw Depp take on another real life character. The film gave Depp the chance to play an adult character in a gritty real-life situation. The actor was attracted initially to the role by the dense, over-long screenplay by Paul Attanasio. Despite the echoes of his fame-winning part as an undercover teen cop on *21 Jump Street*, Depp was captivated by *Donnie Brasco*. Attanasio was more interested in the effect the deep undercover work had on the detective himself and his family. The role-playing involved could go on for years, as Pistone took time and care to establish himself as a 'made man', an accepted member of the organised crime families. For Depp, the parallels between Pistone's undercover work and acting were obvious. However, as Depp pointed out, if he screws up he can retake a scene. Pistone had to be line perfect and have his character spot-on every single day: one slip-up could have ended his life…

Depp's first task was to get to know the real Pistone. Unlike when he'd played Ed Wood, here was an opportunity to meet the guy he'd be playing onscreen. 'He's got an interesting rhythm to his speech,' said Depp. 'I did my best to get that. I put great pressure on myself to make it right. I was just pretending, but he'd lived it.'

Several screenplay drafts later, *Donnie Brasco* had a director in British film-maker Mike Newell (hot off the unexpected success of *Four Weddings and a Funeral*), a $40 million budget from Columbia Pictures and a shooting schedule to run between February and April 1996. As filming approached, Depp felt great pressure to be true to the realities of the life of an undercover New York cop and the members of the criminal gangs that were infiltrated. 'These are real people in real situations,' noted Depp after spending time on the fringes of the New York mob scene researching the role. 'They're very strong family guys with a tremendous sense of pride and strength – it's just that they're on the opposite side of the law.'

Depp poses as a small-time jewel hustler who slowly wins the confidence of Lefty Ruggiero (Al Pacino), a low-ranking mafia insider. Admitted to Ruggiero's

inner circle through his willingness to go one step further than most, Depp's character finds his loyalties increasingly divided between his mentor, government employers and his own family who remain blissfully unaware of his activities.

For Newell, who came to the project after Depp, the star was the only choice for the role, despite his previous soft-hearted, quirky characters. 'We were concerned when we looked at his work,' admitted Newell, 'but Johnny is one of those actors who performs like a long distance runner. In any film, you stay with him throughout in anticipation of the finale. Here he plays a young man who pretends to be someone he isn't. His underlying character is initially very cold, but the prolonged exposure to Lefty ultimately makes him human, a transformation takes place.'

'He's a very polite, very gentle person in all sorts of ways,' said Newell of Depp. 'But I also think he has a devil in him. Underneath this wistfulness, you feel violence. There's terrific mental energy going into keeping these two mutually antagonistic things in balance.' It was perhaps this inner 'devil' that Newell identifies that allowed Depp to give the fine performance he does in *Donnie Brasco*. It is a very different film compared to the kind of projects he'd tackled up to that point, 'When I did *Donnie Brasco*, people within the industry said, "He finally played a man." And I didn't particularly get it. It's like, why was I a man? Because I punched a couple of guys? Because I kissed a girl, had sex? I guess that's it. I was fascinated by that.'

Rolling Stone's Peter Travers noted: 'Pacino and Depp are a match made in

Playing Donnie Brasco, Depp was able to actually meet the man he was based on, Joe Pistone. His research resulted in one of his most mature and realistic performances...

acting heaven, riffing off each other with astonishing subtlety and wit. Depp, an actor of admirable restraint brings out the artful slyness in Pacino. The delicate balance of Depp's performance ranks him with the acting elite.' The film was a critical success but really only a modest hit in box office terms, going on to accumulate almost $42 million in the US following its February 28th 1997 release.

The ambition to direct a film had been growing in Depp for some time, but he had previously had neither the time nor the inclination to pursue it. He'd previously helmed a few pop videos for friends, such as Red Hot Chili Pepper's John Frusciante. Depp had also directed an eleven-and-a-half-minute film in 1993 called *Stuff*, one long tracking shot through a house full of junk with a rock'n'roll soundtrack. He followed that with an eight-and-a-half-minute anti-drug short entitled *Banter*.

This all proved to be useful preparation for directing his first full-length film *The Brave*. With his brother Dan – or DP as he preferred to be billed – Depp adapted a previously written screenplay of Gregory McDonald's (*Fletch, Fletch Lives*) novel *Raphael: Final Days*. 'Since I've stolen as much as I can from the film-makers I've been fortunate to work with – Tim Burton, John Waters, Emir Kusturica, Lasse Hallström, Jim Jarmusch – I thought I'd try directing once,' said Depp.

Depp's choice of *The Brave* was, indeed, a brave one. The story was not exactly blockbuster material. 'It's about a young Native American guy who lives in the desert in Arizona in this weird little makeshift village with his wife and kids,' Depp

'These are real people in real situations,' noted Depp of his realistic approach to Donnie Brasco.

explained. 'He's a two-time loser; one more strike and he's in jail for life. And he can't really face his family, because he's so ashamed that he can't rescue them from poverty. He gets an opportunity to make a lot of money. He gets involved with these people who make snuff films.'

Depp decided that as well as directing, he'd play the part of Raphael, the victim in the snuff film within the film. 'I'm the one who is supposed to get killed. But in a way there's a hopefulness to it. My character makes this deal, but the money gives him a certain freedom. He spends some beautiful time with his children, and the movie is about the last few weeks of his life.'

The script for *The Brave* had been around for a while and had an unfortunate history already attached to it before Depp and his brother got their hands on it. Wannabe film-maker and troubled man Aziz Ghazal had developed the project before killing his wife and himself at the end of 1993. About a year later, the script was in development again and found its way into the hands of Johnny Depp. 'I read it and I hated it!' claimed Depp of his first encounter with *The Brave*. 'It was full of clichés, a kind of Christ allegory with not even a drop of humour. The hero, Raphael, was kind of dumb. Despite all these mistakes, I found the idea rather interesting. I met the producers. We talked a lot, until I said: "If you want me to star in it, I want to direct it as well."'

Depp and his brother Dan rewrote the screenplay from page one, producing a much darker take on the initial idea. Not only was Depp committing to direct – a large enough undertaking on it's own – but he was going to write and star, too. 'Something in the story touched me deeply,' said Depp. ' The idea of sacrifice – how far will you go for those you love, for your family? It's a theme I'm fascinated by. If I only directed the movie, the budget would be $1 million. If I also played Raphael, the budget would be $5 million.'

Knowing he faced an uphill struggle, Depp surrounded himself with people he felt comfortable with, relying on professionals from his previous movies to fill key roles. The director of photography was Vilko Filac, from *Arizona Dream*, while his script supervisor came from *Dead Man*. He managed to rope *Don Juan DeMarco*'s Marlon Brando in to cameo as McCarthy, the man who commissions the snuff movie. The film also features Frederic Forrest, who appeared in the first seven episodes of *21 Jump Street*. Depp's friend, musician Iggy Pop contributed the soundtrack and popped up in a blink-and-you'll-miss-him cameo.

The movie started shooting in the autumn of 1996, with seven weeks in Ridgecrest in the Mojave desert as the shanty town constructed around a dump site. This was followed with ten days of studio work back in Los Angeles. Depp's low-rent production base was the seedy Hollywood Suites Motel, located at the western end of Hollywood Boulevard. Depp found the first day of shooting particularly difficult: he was not used to being the go-to-guy on a film set. The number of questions he was being asked was overwhelming, as was the task of acting at the same time as staying highly focused on the wider issues of making the film. 'The first day of shooting, I was feeling overwhelmed. I had a lot of trouble explaining clearly what I wanted. I never imagined how difficult it would be to act and direct at the same time,' admitted Depp. 'It requires two opposite attitudes: when you direct, you have to be able to control everything down to the last detail. When you act, on the other hand, you have to forget everything, even lose control of yourself. It's hard to go from one to the other.'

Another unanticipated problem for Depp was having to watch himself in the daily footage, known as rushes. 'You know what really messed me up was seeing me on the screen for the rushes for the first fifteen days. That was really painful. I hate seeing me on the screen. I never go to the rushes as an actor. For *The Brave*, I had to face myself almost every night! For two weeks it totally blocked me and I wasn't able to judge anything.'

Floyd 'Red Crow' Westerman played Depp's father in the film. 'At first I thought Johnny was taking on more than he could handle. I've only seen one other guy who directed and acted in the same film: Kevin Costner in *Dances With Wolves*. I'd seen Kevin crack a couple of times and get mad. I haven't seen that in Johnny. He goes beyond getting angry. He likes off-centre, artsy roles as an actor, and he's that way in his personality too.'

Carrying the overall responsibility for everything on *The Brave* was wearing for Depp, but also a first-class filmmaking education. 'I thought I was going to die, every day,' he told *Esquire*. 'I would shoot all day and act as well, then go home; do rewrites; do my homework as an actor; do my homework as a director. Go to sleep and even then I'd dream about the film. It was a nightmare.'

Things changed quite substantially between the script and the material shot. Depp viewed his screenplay as little more than a blueprint for the movie, one he was happy to deviate from as ideas came to him during shooting. 'I would say that 70 per cent of what we shot wasn't originally in the script,' said Depp. 'It was in it, but not developed. It really came up on the set.'

Similarly, working with Brando meant the character of McCarthy changed substantially from the version in the screenplay, as did the climax of the movie. Brando, although appearing without a fee as a favour to Depp, was only available for two days, so his material had to be tailored to the actor's notorious moods. 'I think it's impossible to direct him,' Depp said of Brando, the day before shooting the star's scenes. 'He's ready when he arrives. I'm thrilled with the idea of working with him again. I feel like a student, fascinated, facing a great teacher.' Brando adds some mystique to the film as McCarthy, but he delivers another of those rambling, bizarre performances that have come to define the actor's later career.

There was other, more personal, fall-out from Depp's overwhelming commitment to getting his first film as director made. '*The Brave* needed me to be there all the time and that can get a little sticky for your private life,' said Depp of the all-consuming shoot, a self-imposed exile which he admits contributed to the end of his relationship with Kate Moss. 'Not just with my girl, but my family as well. You're working seventeen, eighteen hours a day. My mom is in Kentucky and my girl [Moss] would be in London or somewhere and they don't know what you're going through. They don't understand until at a certain point you say, "Look, here's the deal – this is what's happening to me and you've got to help me. You've got to be there." I know I've been going nuts, just trying to finish my movie. It was a crazy thing to do – that's not to say I regret it because I don't. But I would say it's not the most rational decision I've made in my life. I'm proud of it, but it was much more work than I anticipated.'

The Brave was badly received during it's screening at the 1997 Cannes Film

Festival, which means it might be a while before Depp directs again, but he does consider the film to be one of his most personal. 'I totally invested me in this movie, so I had to put much more about myself in it than in any other. There is a very dark side in the movie. It's such a weird subject. I'm fascinated by the way a person is going to act knowing he's living his last week of his life. I directed this movie honestly, without embellishment. Sure there'll be people who won't like it or who won't understand the humour I've put into it, but at least it will be a film that's like me.'

The harsh critical reception afforded the film at Cannes really stung Depp. '*The Brave* was an amazing experience for me because it was a great insight into how things really work,' he told *Dreamwatch* magazine. 'Unfortunately, I was preparing the film with the pressure that I had to get it ready for the Cannes Film Festival. That kind of thing I would never do again. If I'd had more time to edit the movie, it would have been a different film. So I made a huge mistake there. I went to Cannes, having worked really hard on the thing. I was very passionate about the film. It was screened for the public at the premiere and got a ten-minute standing ovation. I received compliments from people I admire, like directors Emir Kusturica and Bernardo Bertolucci.'

'The next day the reviews came back,' continued Depp. 'A couple of people started to trash the film and others followed suit. That made sense to me because there are more lemmings in the world than not. I did a little research, because I didn't understand how 2,500 people at the premiere could enjoy the film and then fifteen critics go for my throat because I had the audacity to think that I might have a brain. I found out the film was screened at 8:30am. That seems a little bizarre to me, because people in Cannes are out till 5:30am. They ate me alive. It was vicious. I was totally, totally shocked.' The finished film was never released in the US but a recut edition eventually appeared on DVD across Europe in 2003 which Depp had edited to his satisfaction. 'There are actors who did great work for me and I had to cut them out because they don't add up to what the film needs to say. When I was editing the film before, I knew that certain scenes didn't need to be in the movie, but I couldn't bring myself to cut them out because I didn't want to hurt the actors' feelings.'

Even in this revised form, *The Brave* is an uneven film, but one that shows a lot of influence from Emir Kustirica in the depiction of the shanty town community. Raphael's windfall is used to build a children's playground which becomes a facility for all. He throws parties and treats his wife and kids. Never far away, though, is Larry, the film's enigmatic death figure, prepared to use any method to ensure Raphael upholds his end of the Faustian pact. By the end of the film, he's prepared to fulfil his bargain. In a clever move, Depp is oblique about exactly what Rapahel has committed to for much of the film and the audience never see the actual process that Rapahel faces...

With no cinema release in the US, *The Brave* never had a chance to engage major critics who, away from the hothouse of Cannes or the need to trash the well-intentioned efforts of a neophyte director, may have been kinder to the film.

'He put an awful lot of his own money into this movie,' said *21 Jump Street*'s Patrick Hasburgh. 'That's a pretty honourable thing. I don't have that kind of courage.'

'The film hurt a lot to make' admitted Depp of *The Brave*. 'Will I direct again? Yes, definitely. I don't think that I would direct again and be in it, or be the lead role in it. But I will definitely do it again.'

CHAPTER SIX

Exorcising Demons

The final years of the twentieth century would see Johnny Depp working as hard as ever, but would bring major changes in his life, changes that would see his film career moving in a new and most unexpected direction. Appointments in Las Vegas, Paris, outer space and the spooky town of Sleepy Hollow awaited but it would be that trip to Paris that would have the most profound effect on Johnny Depp's life and career.

Hunter S. Thompson is just the kind of character who would pique Johnny Depp's interest. Founder of so-called 'gonzo' journalism – a freewheeling drug-induced style of writing – Thompson was a writer for *Rolling Stone* in the early 1970s, whose articles chronicling his trip (in more ways than one) to Las Vegas to cover a motorcycle race were collected in the cult classic *Fear and Loathing in Las Vegas*. Thompson's *roman-a-clef* was a fictionalised account of his experiences with a dash of drug-fuelled fantasy thrown in. Thompson disguised himself as Raoul Duke who, with his unscrupulous lawyer Oscar Acosta in tow, embarks on an epic substance-driven odyssey through Vegas and back to Beverly Hills. The book served as an epitaph for 1960s hedonism.

There had long been interest in turning Thompson's adventures into a movie. Jack Nicholson, a contemporary of Thompson's, was one of the first in Hollywood to seriously try, and there was interest from novelist Larry McMurtry. The failure of 1980's *Where the Buffalo Roam,* which starred Bill Murray as Duke and Peter Boyle as Acosta, put a stop to any further attempts to do a 'straight' adaptation of *Fear and Loathing* for a further decade. Renegade director Alex Cox (*Repo Man, Sid & Nancy, Walker*) was the first to be engaged on the 1990's version of *Fear and Loathing*. Although he had managed to attract both Johnny Depp and Benico Del Toro to the film, the director dropped out of the movie citing a personality clash with Thompson. He was also against the involvement of Universal, a major studio which he felt would turn his intended low-budget independent film into a big-budget extravaganza not in sympathy with the book.

Johnny Depp was keen on making sure the film happened purely for personal reasons. *Fear and Loathing* was 'one of my favourite books since I was a kid,' said

Depp. 'I remember reading it at seventeen and cackling like a banshee. I loved it! I went on to read the majority of Hunter's writing. When the idea came to do it as a film, I jumped at the chance.'

Depp had already struck up a friendship with Thompson, who like Marlon Brando was one of the actor's heroes. He'd spent time with Thompson at his isolated Woody Creek compound and invited him in turn to perform at the Viper Room, an event which took place in September 1996, just when Depp was about to embark on *The Brave*. Thompson then invited Depp to a party to celebrate the 25th anniversary of *Fear and Loathing*, and promptly announced the actor as his favourite for Raoul Duke, ahead of hotly tipped Keanu Reeves and John Cusack.

The departure of Cox saw the film's would-be star directly involved in the search for a sympathetic replacement. 'Tracey Jacobs [Depps' agent] and I sat talking about possible guys [to direct] and we thought "Let's try Gilliam!" But it was such a long shot...' Gilliam was regarded by Hollywood as a maverick director whose films – like *Brazil*, *The Adventures of Baron Munchausen* and *The Fisher King* – often went over budget and out-of-control. However, a better meeting of subject matter and director would be hard to find.

'I met Hunter in the Chateau Marmont at about one in the morning,' Gilliam told *Rolling Stone*. 'He said, "You've got to remember: We were serious people. I was a serious journalist, he was a serious lawyer. And this book was only one weekend."' That 'one weekend' was about to become a movie, but first Johnny Depp had to become Hunter S. Thompson... or was he Raoul Duke? 'Raoul Duke is 97 per cent Hunter. I said [to Thompson] "I need to spend time with you, and when you get sick of me being there, just tell me and I'll leave,"' Depp recalled. 'I told him that I'd probably become a pain, because I'd be asking him a lot of questions and taping the conversations and writing things down. He never kicked me out, which was good.'

'Johnny was amazing,' noted Terry Gilliam. 'He was like some kind of vampire. Each time he'd come back [from seeing Thompson] with more of Hunter's clothes and things. He was stealing Hunter's soul, really, secretly.'

The research paid off, but there was still a physical transformation Depp had to make before he could step in front of Gilliam's cameras. That involved shaving his head to better match Thompson's look. 'The first thing I felt was the wind on the top of my head,' remembered Depp. 'It was very strange. Even though my baldness was only temporary, while we were shooting *Fear and Loathing,* it felt real weird. When Hunter first saw it, he said they hadn't gone far enough and wanted to fix it. So I let him shave my head. I trusted him. I really did.' With Thompson's help, Depp captured the Raoul Duke of the book on the screen.

Depp's make-over wasn't the only one required for the film. 'They're two romantics,' said Benicio Del Toro of the central characters, 'with no melody left to dance to. So they're quite afraid, lonely and full of anger.' Described in the book as being impressively overweight, the svelte Del Toro had to gain 35 to 40 pounds to inhabit Acosta's physical reality. He also grew his hair long and spent some time cultivating an impressive moustache. 'Benicio's physical transformation was incredible,' said Depp, approvingly. 'He really committed himself and focused and got in there and did it. He was very proud of his belly, like a Puerto Rican Buddha.'

With a script which Gilliam claimed he co-wrote with Tony Grisoni in just eight days (although the writer's guild credited the screenplay to previous adapters Alex Cox and his co-writer Tod Davies), the relatively low-budgeted $18.5 million production embarked on a 50-day shooting schedule which took in Los Angeles, Las Vegas and the Nevada desert.

Like the two stars, Las Vegas had to be significantly altered for the movie. The gambling capital of the world had changed dramatically since 1971, when the book was written and the film was to be set. The production also travelled out into the Nevada desert to recreate the Mint 400 off-track race, as well as extensive sequences of Duke and Acosta's anarchic journey through the wastes of California and Nevada. Heat stroke was a constant problem faced by the actors, reminding Depp of his struggles shooting *The Brave*. Following the completion of location work, the exhausted *Fear and Loathing* company returned to Los Angeles for several weeks of filming in and around the city, as well as elaborate interiors constructed at Warner Hollywood Studios.

By the wrap party, everyone involved in making the film felt they'd been involved in something special. 'No-one has enough money to pay for the experience I've had on this movie,' Johnny Depp admitted. 'Going into the project, I knew that this would be our one time – and one time only – to make it happen right. I think the whole crew felt that, so every day was an odd celebration. It was a whole lot of fun, and a whole lot of misery. We got it all – the fear and the loathing.'

Director Terry Gilliam came away from the project with a new admiration for his leading man: 'As far as I'm concerned, Johnny Depp is the best actor of his

Director Terry Gilliam saw Depp as 'some kind of vampire' who had captured the essential essence of Hunter S. Thompson in Fear and Loathing in Las Vegas.

123

generation. I think he's capable of anything – there's no limit to his abilities. What amazes me is that the critics are always surprised by Johnny. It's like they don't really watch what's there. They don't understand how good an actor he is. He doesn't cheat by giving you all those cheap emotions. He won't make you comfortable – for him that would be a foot in the grave.'

Terry Gilliam's movie of *Fear and Loathing in Las Vegas* is not to all tastes. It's not quite a full-on Gilliam movie, but neither is it really the book brought to the screen. The reviews were largely negative. Roger Ebert of *The Chicago Sun-Times* was scathing: 'a horrible mess of a movie, without shape, trajectory or purpose,' he wrote. 'Johnny Depp has been a gifted and inventive actor. Here he's given a character with no nuances, a man whose only variable is the current degree he's out of it. He plays Duke in disguise, behind strange hats, big shades and the ever-present cigarette holder. Depp doesn't look unlike the young Thompson, but can't communicate the genius beneath the madness.' Audiences agreed with the disdain critics showed Gilliam's movie and stayed away. The film totaled just over $10.5 million at the US box office, a very poor return on its investment.

Made during the time he was working on *Fear and Loathing in Las Vegas, LA Without A Map* is an odd little film in Johnny Depp's diverse filmography. His appearances as himself in this tale of trial and tribulation in Hollywood seems to have come about through a chance meeting with director Mika Kaurismaki at the Cannes Film Festival. Depp was a great admirer of the films of Mika and Aki Kaurismaki, Finnish directors of off-beat and often bleakly humorous movies. Kaurismaki, then preparing to shoot *LA Without A Map*, offered Depp a cameo in the movie, which also featured his *Arizona Dream* co-star Vincent Gallo. Depp leapt at the opportunity, and in lieu of a contract apparently ate a paper napkin to seal the deal!

The British-French-Finnish-German romantic comedy was adapted from Richard Rayner's autobiographical novel about a series of Hollywood misadventures. Vacationing in the North of England, aspiring Los Angeles actress Barbara (Vinessa Shaw) stops briefly in a village where she meets town undertaker Richard (David Tennant) – who is soon besotted with her. Flying to California, Richard arrives at the Japanese restaurant where Barbara is a waitress and begins a relationship. At the same time, Richard learns about Hollywood at the hands of various hustlers and agents.

It's here that Depp appears, both as a fantasy version of himself and as the real life flesh-and-blood version. One of Richard's sources of inspiration in Hollywood is his treasured *Dead Man* poster, featuring a shot of Depp. At various points throughout the film, Depp's image comes silently to life, as does his image on a giant advertising billboard. Later, he appears sitting on a bench in a graveyard in a sailor suit and talks with Richard. Finally, Depp appears at a film screening as himself. When thanked for his inspiration by Richard, the real Depp gives him the brush off having never – in reality – met him before.

In the original novel, from which Rayner wrote his own script, the Hollywood character offering Richard career inspiration is Jack Nicholson, but Kaurismaki wanted to bring the story up to date. 'For me Johnny Depp represents Hollywood at its best,' said the director explaining what Depp brought to his movie. 'He is very

The book was regarded as unfilmable, but Depp plunged whole-heartedly into Fear and Loathing in Las Vegas as he did with all his projects…

down to Earth and makes his own decisions, but he is still a big star. He doesn't give his life over to any agents.'

LA *Without A Map* was the first time the Finnish director had worked in the US, even though he didn't have American funding. 'It was shot in LA mostly, but it wasn't an American movie,' said Kaurismaki. 'It was an European co-production, low-budget. I didn't exactly enjoy working in LA. It's the capital of cinema, but it's the most complicated place to shoot... It's crazy.' Little wonder Kaurismaki and Depp were simpatico...

LA Without A Map is a slight comedy which was screened at several film festivals, including the 1998 Toronto Film Festival and was released in September 1999 in Canada and the UK, as well as Kaurismaki's native Finland. Like Depp's *The Brave*, it has never had a US release, but was available on video in Germany. Reviews were few and far between, but the critics were not kind. Melanie McGrath, writing in *Sight and Sound,* concluded: 'References to directors Jim Jarmusch and Andrei Tarkovsky seem pretentious, cameos by Johnny Depp, Anouk Aimée and the Leningrad Cowboys equally so, only adding to the general air of desperation. *LA Without A Map* was destined to end up as little more than a curious footnote in Johnny Depp's ever growing and ever more diverse list of credits...

In the late 1990s, Depp managed to indulge some of his interests by contributing to a handful of documentaries. He appeared in *The Source* (released on video in 1999), a look at the beat writers that benefited from a wealth of interviews with major figures. Interspersed with clips of Allen Ginsberg, Jack Kerouac, Neal Cassady and William S. Burroughs are montages of clips that set the beats in the context of their times. Telling the story of how the beats rebelled against American conformity in the 1950s, this documentary managed to find fresh ways to relate their views on life and writing. It was livened up with segments in which Depp, John Turturro and Dennis Hopper respectively portray, in direct-to-camera monologues, Kerouac, Ginsberg and Burroughs. *The Source* devotes considerable attention to the influence of the beats, and interviews with such notables as Ken Kesey, Jerry Garcia and Philip Glass, performance clips of Bob Dylan, and news footage from the 1960s establish how the sensibility of the writers influenced society. Director Chuck Workman had previously chronicled the life of Andy Warhol in 1990's *Superstar*. Depp also found time to narrate three documentaries in the Discovery Channel's TV documentary series *Top Secret*, covering the US National Security Agency, Britain's Scotland Yard and Israel's Mossad. He'd go on in coming years to contribute to other documentaries, notably *Charlie: The Life and Art of Charles Chaplin*, *Breakfast With Hunter* and *In Bad Taste*.

Following the production of *The Brave*, Depp became convinced that he really needed to do a 'commercial' movie, both to boost his bank balance and restore his box office bankability. He committed to *The Astronaut's Wife* purely because he believed it would enjoy a degree of commercial success and so balance out his focus on his directorial debut.

At the centre of *The Astronaut's Wife* there was a solid idea which attracted Depp: the question of identity. How can we be sure that those we love are the same

people we fell in love with? How can we be sure of our own identity? Astronaut Spencer Armacost (Depp) loses consciousness on a shuttle mission for two minutes. Upon returning to Earth and his wife Jillian (Charlize Theron), it's clear that things are not quite right. Pregnant with twins and plagued by nightmares, Jillian begins to think that whatever returned from space, it was not her husband – at least, not as she knew him. Is she the centre of a conspiracy or in the grip of some kind of out-of-control paranoia?

'I wanted to write a story that would carry the audience along on an impending sense of doom,' said writer-director Rand Ravich (writer of 1995's *Candyman: Farewell to the Flesh*). 'The audience enters the terror of Jillian, who senses something unnatural is taking over her life and pregnancy – and the one person she loves is at the centre of it.' Casting the lead role was an easy step for Ravich. 'Johnny Depp is in my mind the best actor of his generation. I felt he would bring a necessary element to the role of Spencer: truth.' Executive producer Mark Johnson also knew what qualities their proposed leading man could bring to the role. 'Depp's classic, rugged American good looks combined with that sense of mystery going on behind his eyes works incredibly well for this character. He brings that quality of underlying danger to Spencer, the sense of unpredictability, the feeling of never really quite knowing who this man is and what his true intentions are.'

While looking for a more commercial project, the attractions of the role in *The Astronaut's Wife* were pretty basic for Johnny Depp, prime among them being the

'It was fun to play an all-American hero gone wrong,' said Depp of the poorly received supernatural thriller The Astronaut's Wife.

chance to play a villain. 'It was fun to play a redneck, an all-American hero gone wrong,' said Depp. 'What interested me was not the idea of some kind of "being" possibly inhabiting his body. Whatever happened in space just allowed him to reveal who he really is. He's got this image of being an all-American guy, with bleached white teeth and sun-kissed hair, but he's an awful person. You want to like him, but slowly and surely, as he reveals himself, you get to a point where that's not possible. I definitely didn't like him, for sure.'

Charlize Theron was happy to be working with Depp and playing opposite his deeper take on a rather superficial character: 'Spencer Armacost is a man who gets to live out his dreams as an astronaut, which fascinates people because astronauts get to experience the unknown. But then he becomes a nightmare, which seems to go against everything you believe about him. Johnny is so talented he captures all of that. He's just beautiful to watch at work.'

While the performances in *The Astronaut's Wife* may be perfunctory – Theron carries the film, while Depp sleepwalks through it in a way that may be appropriate to his possessed character – it's in its look that the movie triumphs. Shot by cinematographer Allen Daviau (*E.T: The Extra Terrestrial*, *Empire of the Sun*, *Bugsy*, *The Color Purple*) and designed by Jan Roelfs (*Orlando*, *Gattaca*), the film's look does much to emphasise its strangeness. Shot on location in New York City and Los Angeles, the production utilised numerous well-known sites including Staten Island, Washington Square Park, Wall Street and City Hall on the East Coast and the Greystone Mansion, Santa Monica Civic Center and downtown Los Angeles' Unocal building on the West Coast. Production covered the four month period of January to April 1998.

Critic Roger Ebert was just as hard on Depp in *The Astronaut's Wife*, released in the US on August 27th 1999, as he had previously been on *Fear and Loathing*. Writing in *The Chicago Sun-Times* he pointed out: 'Johnny Depp has a thankless role, as a man who must spend most of the movie withholding information and projecting ominous mystery. The set-up is tantalising, the pay-off is a disappointment.' *Sight and Sound* critic Ken Hollings pointed out similarities in Charlize Theron's cropped blonde look and that of Mia Farrow in Polanski's satanic chiller *Rosemary's Baby*, concluding: 'Depp offers an acidic, unsettling study of "the Right Stuff" going horribly wrong. His sexual playfulness becomes brutally urgent; his bravado in the face of danger; a dead-eyed indifference to the sufferings of others. The biggest irony of his performance is that Armacost retains his masculinity long after losing all trace of humanity. Polanski would undoubtedly approve.'

Again, following *Fear and Loathing*'s failure, the US box office total on *The Astronaut's Wife* was a disappointment, hitting just over $10.5 million. If Depp had hoped for a commercial hit from this movie, his hopes were dashed by the film's final performance. Somehow, though, it's more likely he didn't really care…

Depp's long-held desire of re-location to Pairs was met in 1998. 'I came over here to make a movie, met a girl, got a place, had a baby,' said Johnny Depp of the unexpected events which followed work on Roman Polanski's *The Ninth Gate*. It was the beginning of a whole new chapter in his life.

'It's classic Polanski,' Depp said of the film that brought him to Paris, adapted

'He convinced me that age didn't matter that much,' said Director Roman Polanski of Depp who took the role of Dean Corso in The Ninth Gate, a character who is much older in the book.

from the novel *The Dumas Club* by Arturo Perez-Reverte. 'If you took *Rosemary's Baby* and *Chinatown* and mixed them together, it would be this movie. It's a thriller, it's supernatural and it's another character who's not a particularly nice guy. He's a greed machine.'

Depp plays Dean Corso, a cynical rare books dealer hired by Boris Balkan (Frank Langella), a scholar specialising in books on Satanism, to recover the only two remaining copies of *The Nine Gates Of The Kingdom Of Shadows*, a seventeenth-century text with cryptic illustrations supposedly contributed by Lucifer himself. Corso's investigation takes him to Europe, where he is pursued by a strange girl (Emmanuelle Seigner, Polanski's wife) who assumes the role of his guardian angel. Bizarre deaths, inspired by the book's morbid illustrations, befall all those who come into contact with the book – except for Corso…

Depp was first linked with the film as early as 1997, when he met Roman Polanski at the Cannes Film Festival, where the actor was in competition with *The Brave*. A fan of Polanski's acclaimed film work, Depp was intrigued by the script that the director said he was writing. He offered to send the script to Depp once it was complete.

Roman Polanski's life and career has encompassed horrors which are the source of other people's nightmares. Fleeing Nazi persecution in Poland, he ended up in the US pursuing a career as a film-maker. Critical and popular hits like *Rosemary's Baby* and *Chinatown* made his reputation. The death of his pregnant wife, Sharon Tate (who featured in his film *The Fearless Vampire Killers*), at the hands of the Manson gang brought Polanski an unwelcome notoriety which was compounded when he fled America back to Europe in the late 1970s after facing a charge of sex with an underage minor at the home of Jack Nicholson. In exile in France, Polanski returned to making movies. He still worked with top Hollywood talents (Harrison Ford in *Frantic*, Sigourney Weaver in *Death and the Maiden*) and even won an Oscar in 2003 for *The Pianist*, his follow-up to *The Ninth Gate*.

Originally, the character of Corso was supposed to be around 40 years old, so Polanski was reluctant to consider Depp for the role. Depp, then in his mid-thirties, was willing to fight for the part, using the strength of his own personality. 'He convinced me that age didn't matter that much,' Polanski recalled. 'I came to understand that people like Corso tend to mature very young. Their character and reputation are formed when they're in their thirties.'

The summer of 1998 saw Depp touring Europe making the film, shooting on location near Paris, France, at the Château de Ferrières; Sintra, Portugal; Toledo, Spain and at the Sudios Epinay in Paris. Depp and Polanksi formed a relaxed, mutually respectful working relationship. Polanski noted that Depp is 'very easy once he's on set, but it's a bit of a struggle to get him out of his trailer, where he's reading, talking on the telephone, drinking.'

Polanski felt his own experience on both sides of the camera helped him strike up a rapport with his leading man. 'There are no secrets. The fact that I've acted helps: I understand the problems. You can see the directors who started as actors often get good results with others. As a director, you try to get the maximum out of people, you try to inspire them. I think I manage to do that, so that people feel happy, that they're doing something interesting.'

That was the one criteria that Depp applied to all his work, the one thing he always sought out: 'something interesting.' He'd found that in *The Ninth Gate* and he was willing to go the extra mile to make the mid-range budget $30 million film work. 'Johnny has an extraordinary and spontaneous way of giving his own rhythm to a character,' the director said. 'It seems quite natural for him, and you never feel like he's making any effort. It's almost fascinating, because he comes on the set and does his thing almost casually, which doesn't prevent him from being very accurate. His work was brilliant, because the Corso you see on the screen is exactly the one I had in mind before hiring Johnny.'

One of the world's best cinematographers, Darius Khondji, most acclaimed for his work on *Se7en* and *The City of Lost Children*, brought his unique skills to bear on *The Ninth Gate* and had considerable influence on the film's look. Similarly, Oscar-winner Dean Tavoularis' clever production design brought life to settings such as Liana's (Lena Olin) library and Balkan's (Frank Langella) lair 'You can almost smell the books,' said Polanski. 'Most of the sets were made from scratch in the Epinay Studios, near Paris, but they look incredibly accurate.' Even the US street scenes and those featuring the skyline of New York were shot in Paris.

Polanski worked with four special effects teams to achieve the 200 effects-related shots in the movie. 'You won't be able to notice some of them,' said Polanski during post-production, 'as they're perfectly integrated in the film.'

Depp found other challenges: 'There was a close-up where I had to kiss Emmanuelle Seigner and Polanski [her husband] was standing behind the camera, at exactly ten centimetres' distance. I was looking at him and I was saying to myself "Is this thing gonna end up in a love triangle?" [laughs] I was about to kiss Emmanuelle and I thought this was gonna be a group kiss! And there's Polanski saying "Take it easy, Johnny, there's nothing wrong. You are actors, it doesn't matter."'

Depp found working generally with Polanski to be a struggle as the director insisted on guiding his performance as Corso in a much more focused way than most of Depp's previous directors. 'It was not an easy film to make,' Depp admitted. 'Roman is pretty set in his ways. There's not much opportunity for discussion or collaboration. He was definitely a bit too rigid for my liking.'

While generally liking the movie, and pointing out it's similarities in structure to the *film noir* thrillers of Humphrey Bogart, *The Chicago Sun-Times* critic Roger Ebert thought that *The Ninth Gate* featured 'Johnny Depp in a strong if ultimately unaimed performance,' while Bob Graham, writing in *The San Francisco Chronicle*, pointed out that 'Depp is the best reason to see Polanski's satanic thriller. He looks like a rogue scholar and behaves like a *film noir* detective as he discovers the volume may summon up the devil.' Graham goes on to claim: 'Surely no one underestimates Depp as an actor any longer? He generates heat that reflects off the actors he plays opposite. Depp makes Corso a roguish anti-hero, who smokes, drinks, cheats the gullible and plays around the edges of the legal.'

The Ninth Gate was a better performer for Depp at the US box office than his previous two films, reaching a cumulative take of just over $18.5 million. Not blockbuster territory, but the film did pick up something of a loyal following and fan base which allowed it to perform well on video and DVD release.

'Europe becomes him,' said Roman Polanski, the director who'd brought Johnny Depp to Paris. 'He doesn't look expatriated. He looks as though he really lives here. He's very much at ease.'

Depp had come to Europe to play what Polanski called 'the most mature role of his career,' little suspecting that he'd end up playing the same mature role in his private life. Leaving America and his failed relationship with Kate Moss behind him, Depp was expecting to enjoy a few months in and around Paris and then return to the US to continue pursuing his quirky Hollywood career. That all changed for the actor when, after a hard day's work with Polanski on *The Ninth Gate,* he met French singer Vanessa Paradis.

'I wanted to take the road with Roman [Polanski] because he made some perfect films,' said Depp, looking back on what had brought him to Paris in the summer of 1998, 'but also there was something pulling me here, and now I know it was in fact destiny. I was drawn here for some reason that was not apparent to me, and this city, and this girl who I met who's from this city, has delivered to me the only reason to take a breath, the only reason to live – my daughter, my baby.'

Known as the Lolita of French pop music, Vanessa Paradis was a star in France, virtually unknown in the US and singularly identified in the UK with her novelty pop hit 'Joe le taxi' from 1987. Her father, Andre, was an interior design consultant and her mother, Corrinne, a housewife. Paradis found new success in a 1991 Chanel perfume ad campaign in which she was the 'bird in a gilded cage'. She later dated rock star Lenny Kravitz, who produced one of her albums. Paradis went on to win awards, acting in a variety of French movies.

One evening in June 1998, Johnny Depp came across her with a group of friends at the bar of the Costes Hotel. Depp, Polanski and some of the crew from *The Ninth Gate* were having dinner. Depp was unaware that Paradis had auditioned for a role in the movie he was now making, but had failed to be selected. Apparently too shy to do the deed himself, Depp persuaded one of the his co-diners to invite Paradis over. 'She said she spotted him pretty soon after he noticed her,' recalled Paradis' biographer Alain Grasset. 'They were exchanging secret glances. When he invited her to his table, he made a place for her to sit down and she said she went straight for it.' Hours later, after the rest of the dinner party had departed, Depp and Paradis were still talking. Finally, as the night wore on Depp remembered he had an early morning call on the movie and the pair parted following a simple kiss on the cheek.

Paradis, however, claimed that the start of their relationship was a bit more complicated than that oft-repeated story. 'Johnny didn't make a pass at me in a hotel bar. We had known each other for a long time,' she said, hinting that Depp's relationship with Kate Moss wasn't quite over when they'd first met. 'We had seen each other often, but always in the company of others. I don't want our child to read the tabloids later and think she was a slip. She was not planned, meaning we didn't say: we are going to make a baby now. We agreed that we wanted children. To make a baby is more beautiful than making a CD or a movie.'

Depp wrote about their evolving relationship in the French magazine *Studio.* 'Around the time I was shooting *The Ninth Gate*, we saw each other every night and every day. We couldn't stay far away from each other for very long. You couldn't possibly tear us apart…' By the end of the month, Depp was renting an apartment in Monmartre to be close to Paradis.

Less than three months later, Paradis was pregnant and Johnny Depp was finally facing the reality of having his wish for a family come true. The pregnancy was unplanned, but Paradis and Depp decided that they had a future together. The pair moved to Paradis' parents house in Seine-et-Marne, outside Paris, for the duration of the pregnancy. To some journalists, though, their union didn't look as rock solid as the pair maintained. Depp was spotted in London in January 1999 having dinner with Kate Moss, during shooting of *Sleepy Hollow*. Moss had just left rehab the previous month, and so the British tabloid press naturally built up a Paradis-Depp-Moss love triangle. Additionally, Depp was also 'caught' clubbing in London with eighteen-year-old Christina Ricci, who'd appeared in *Fear and Loathing*, was co-starring with the actor in *Sleepy Hollow* and would again co-star with him in the Paris-set wartime drama *The Man Who Cried*. For her part Ricci was quite happy to be connected with Depp in the press: 'I really liked it. It was awesome – my first tabloid story. If you're going to have a tabloid story written about you, it might as well be with Johnny Depp.'

Again, this event was used to question Depp's commitment to Paradis and their unborn child. Questioned whether he felt blackmailed into staying with Paradis because of the pregnancy, Depp hit back at his critics. 'That couldn't be more untrue,' he said firmly. 'I was not put in a situation where I was obligated to do something. Obligation is no way to begin your role as a father. I would never do that to the girl that I'm involved with, to my kid. I wouldn't live that lie.'

Depp and Paradis, Depp and Paris: they seem to have been made for each other. Taking up residence in the city, the actor was far more relaxed than he'd ever been in Los Angeles or even London.

French privacy laws kept the press at bay, for a start. He also appreciated the culture of Paris, which prized the literary above the visual, the important above the facile. All were in keeping with Depp's own journey from TV pin-up to serious film artiste. 'You know, here in Paris people just don't care,' said Depp. 'Europeans appreciate art for the art. Movies here are about people. In America it's always about killers from Mars. Here no one is interested in me. It doesn't matter that my name is Johnny Depp and that I do something in the movie business.'

While he had embraced France, the French were happy to claim Depp as their own. In April 1999, having completed shooting on *Sleepy Hollow*, Depp returned to Paris to be awarded the annual Cesar Award (essentially the French Oscars) for his body of work and his contribution to cinema. Roman Polanski introduced Depp, while the award's recipient could only utter 'Wow, merci.'

'That was a weird little deal,' he said of the Cesar Award. 'I was really taken aback by that. It was the kind of thing you get just before you die, like a lifetime achievement award. I mean, I felt like maybe there's somebody somewhere who knows something that I don't, like they give me this award, and then tomorrow, wham, it's over. But I was really touched, because I'm not big on awards. I mean, I get the concept of awards, but the whole competitive nature of that kind of thing is too bizarre. And this felt like I was supposed to accept my award and then have a stroke and be gone.'

Sleepy Hollow, the update of Washington Irving's classic American spooky tale *The Legend of Sleepy Hollow* started with special effects wizard Kevin Yagher. Having worked on various movies over the years (including an abortive directing stint on a *Hellraiser* sequel), Yagher was looking to get a new version of *Sleepy Hollow* off the drawing board, done in the style of Britain's Hammer Horror movies of the 1950s and 1960s. *Se7en* screenwriter Andrew Kevin Walker had turned out a gruesome and violent screenplay which deviated quite wildly from the original tale. Tim Burton came to the project late, having directed *Mars Attacks!* after *Ed Wood* and spent years embroiled in the as-yet unproduced new *Superman* movie. When his version of *Superman Reborn* finally collapsed, Burton was on the look-out for a new project and came upon Walker's version of *Sleepy Hollow*. If ever there was a project tailor-made for Tim Burton, this was it.

'I liked the opposition between a character with no head and a character who lives entirely in his head,' said Burton. Although the director felt the screenplay still needed some work, revising it himself and having Tom Stoppard take a crack at a rewrite, Burton had no doubt about who he needed to play Ichabod Crane, recast as a New York State detective trying to introduce scientific forensic methods to crime detection in 1799. Step forward Johnny Depp. 'Playing Ichabod was a great challenge. This is a character we grew up knowing very well, and of course I incorporated all the stuff from the book. But Paramount wouldn't let me wear a long nose and big ears. Tim and I grew up with a very similar outlook, the same obsessions with things that seem perfectly normal but which, in fact, when you really look at them are perfectly absurd.'

Both Burton and Depp are men of few words who respond much more to visual stimulus than the verbal. They managed to communicate with each other through a form of short hand. 'It's nice with someone like Johnny,' notes Burton, 'who understand with only a few words – there's that connective tissue.'

From November 1998 through to April 1999, a couple of months after Vanessa Paradis fell pregnant to a few weeks before the birth of his daughter, Johnny Depp worked on *Sleepy Hollow* in London and the surrounding countryside. Burton and the film's crew built an entire eighteenth-century village about an hour's drive from London, their Sleepy Hollow. The site featured fully constructed houses, shops, an inn, a pub and a covered bridge with a rooster weather vane: all fake, but all suitably 'distressed'.

It's to this location that Depp's fastidious Ichabod Crane is sent to investigate a spate of decapitations. With a cast of much admired British character actors playing the town's elders – Christopher Lee, Michael Gambon, Ian McDairmid and token American Jeffrey Jones – Burton set about putting his own unique spin on an oft-told American folk tale. 'We really wanted to evoke the spirit of the old Hammer horror films, Vincent Price movies, Roger Corman's work,' Burton said. 'The heroes in those films are always kind of separate, ambiguous, absorbed in their work. They're there, but you don't know much about them. And Johnny is perfect for that; he radiates like a silent-movie actor. He hardly has to say anything. It's something you can't manufacture.'

Depp agreed with his director: 'In a way it's homage to all those Dracula and

Hammer House of Horror films of the 1960s, with a style of acting that's just on the verge of acceptable. Maybe it's a little over the top. It's hard to explain. I was trying to walk a tightrope. Tim is particularly amazing: he will give you suggestions and he'll plant certain seeds. Then you take that and you use that.'

Depp's reunion for a third film with Tim Burton was a great contrast to his work with Roman Polanski. 'Burton allows you complete freedom to create a character from the ground up,' he said. Depp spent some time watching the work of Peter Cushing and Christopher Lee in a variety of the Hammer Horror movies in preparation. Harking back to an older style of acting, whether it be silent movies for *Edward Scissorhands* and *Benny & Joon* or the Hammer approach for *Sleepy Hollow* seems to be a working method that appeals to the actor. 'Johnny knows as well as anyone could that things are not what they seem,' Burton said of his leading man's inscrutable performances. 'He makes you see the world from a different perspective. And even though this is the third film we've done together, we never fall into, "Let's go back to formula A or B." He'll always explore each thing on its own, and he does it so well.'

Rolling Stone thought that in *Sleepy Hollow*, Johnny Depp was 'at his heartfelt and hilarious best, revealing the frightened boy in the stern advocate of scientific reason.' *The San Francisco Chronicle*'s Mick LaSalle, however, went against the critical tide. In a ill-tempered slam of the movie, he wrote: 'Depp winces, blinks, sniffs, purses his lips and acts fussy. Sometimes an actor can either mock the proceedings or go down with the ship. Depp finds the comedy.'

The US box office take for *Sleepy Hollow* speaks for itself. After a series of

Sleepy Hollow was Johnny Depp's third film with director Tim Burton, following Edward Scissorhands and Ed Wood.

disappointments, Depp was pleased that Tim Burton's unconventional shocker took in excess of $101 million in the US upon it's release on November 19th 1999 and an additional $105 million overseas. This bonafide blockbuster went on to win a slew of awards, including an acting award for Depp – the Blockbuster Entertainment Award for Favourite Actor (Horror), and nominations for two others: the Golden Satellite Awards, Best Actor in a Comedy/Musical and the Academy of Science Fiction, Fantasy, and Horror Films Best Actor. *Sleepy Hollow* turned out to be Johnny Depp's first genuine blockbuster.

While working on *Sleepy Hollow*, Johnny Depp had a run-in with the press again which resulted in him spending time in a London police cell and providing the media with a handy bad boy follow-up story to the The Mark Hotel incident. Depp was dining out with Vanessa Paradis in London, when the actor realised that the restaurant was being besieged by paparazzi photographers. 'They wanted a photograph of me and my pregnant girlfriend,' recalled Depp of the incident. 'That angered me – that they would take something so sacred and try to turn it into a product.' Depp tried to tell the photographers that for this particular night, he wanted them to leave him and Paradis alone to enjoy their meal. 'And they said no – "We'll be here waiting for you,"' Depp told *Premiere*.

That was too much for Depp, who found a plank of wood nearby (he claimed it may have been a doorstop) and threatened the photographers with it after

Depp brought the fastidious Ichabod Crane of Sleepy Hollow to life just a few weeks before his life changed with the birth of his daughter, Lily-Rose Depp.

rapping one of their number over the knuckles. Then he dared them to snap away. He told *Premiere* that he'd said: '"Now take the picture. Because the first flash I see, the guy is gonna be the recipient of this." Six guys. Nobody took one picture. The beauty, the poetry of the fear in their eyes, in these filthy little maggots' faces, was so worth it.' One of the photographers had managed to call the police, who duly turned up and hauled Depp away in handcuffs, giving the waiting photographers exactly the kind of picture they knew they could sell to the tabloids. Depp, however, was unfazed: 'I didn't mind going to jail for, what, five, six hours? It was absolutely worth it.' He was held for a few hours and then released without charge.

While sympathising with his plight, Roman Polanski saw in Depp's behaviour a reaction mechanism he hoped the actor would one day out-grow. 'He reacts viscerally, and that's what they're waiting for. He falls into their trap. That's his teenager reaction. He should shake that off.'

Back in Paris in late spring 1999, Johnny Depp was faced with the prospect of growing up in a hurry with the birth of his daughter. He'd done his best to prepare for the moment, even buying a watch – something he was rarely to be seen with – in order to time Vanessa's contractions when the day came. However, 'When the contractions started coming, I was useless,' Depp admitted. 'I kept fumbling with these hideous little buttons [on the watch]. Giving birth's a powerful thing. If a man goes into that room and watches his girl do that, it does not get any heavier. Certainly I've never seen anything as strong as a woman during those moments.'

It was on the evening of May 27th 1999, at around 8.35pm that Johnny Depp's life changed with the arrival of Lily-Rose Melody Depp, his daughter with Vanessa Paradis. It was a moment which was to have a profound effect on the actor. 'I feel like there was a fog in front of my eyes for 36 years. The second she was born, that fog just lifted. Vanessa is the most beautiful woman in the world and my daughter is the most beautiful creature that ever existed. That ever drew a breath. I now care about what happens in 40 or 50 years. I don't think that I lived before. This baby has given me life.'

Where did Depp get the name for his daughter from? It turns out that Lily-Rose 'was the only name that we'd come up with for a girl,' said Depp on the *Charlie Rose* show. 'We both loved the name : "Lily", and I think Vanessa's mom suggested the "Rose" part. My mom's name is Betty-Sue and we wanted something that sounded kinda like "Betty-Sue", that sort of southern thing. So "Lily-Rose." And "Melody", which is her middle name, was after a Serge Gainsbourg song called 'Melody Nelson'.'

A confirmed smoker all his life, Paradis had managed to persuade Depp to at least severely reduce his 30-a-day habit, if not quite quit altogether. Other previous pursuits – drugs, drink, parties – were also to fall by the wayside, as he and Paradis settled down to something resembling domestic normality. Learning French was also high on his agenda. Paradis spoke perfect English, but Depp realised that his daughter would be bilingual and able to talk about her father right in front of him without him knowing. He was determined that would not happen!

The apartment in Monmartre went, to be replaced with a $1 million apartment in Paris and a $2 million property just 40 minutes from the Riviera's Saint Tropez in

Saint Aygulf. By this time too he acquired Man Ray, the restaurant off the Champs-Elysées that he co-owns with a few pals, including Sean Penn and Bono. However happy Depp was, the problems caused by the press were never far from his mind. 'I'm a father, I've got a girl, I got a family, and I want to be normal, that's all – and I don't want to be looked at like some kind of freak. If you want to turn me into some kind of freak or animal in the zoo, the anger starts to rise in me. I just don't like it.'

Director Terry Gilliam, still in touch with Depp after *Fear and Loathing* as he hoped to persuade the actor to take a role in his planned film of Don Quixote, had noticed a change in him. 'Oh, he's pathetic,' Gilliam said in jest. 'Totally doting, as if she's the only child ever born. "She's got a skin rash – Oh my God!" He loses all his wit and sharpness around her; she's reduced him to *blancmange*.'

With her father showing no desire to return to America in the near future, it looked certain that Lily-Rose would grow up in France. 'I used to think, maybe you could do it in the middle of the States,' said Depp of raising children, 'Colorado or somewhere. But no. Not when you've got cretins going into schools and shooting children. That country is out of control. I think it's imploding. I hate Los Angeles now. Los Angeles is a machine, and it can't inspire. That's what I love about Paris – everything is poetry.'

Being away from Los Angeles suggested that Depp was also removing himself from the film business. While he had no intention of giving up acting, he was certainly keen to be away from 'the business'. 'I'm happy to be removed. I'm happy that I made the decision to stop looking at magazines, that I don't see many movies, that I don't know who people are, in terms of the movie executives, or other actors and actresses.'

After wrapping *Sleepy Hollow*, Johnny Depp did find himself back in Hollywood to accept a most unexpected form of recognition: a star on the Hollywood Walk of Fame. 'I thought it was funny,' admitted Depp. 'There's something perverse that I like about it. Something absurd about it. I mean, a town that's never acknowledged my presence really… Hollywood being a place that I've been at constant battle with for the last fifteen, sixteen years, and suddenly they want to give me a star on Hollywood Boulevard! Well, a lot of people said to me, "Why would you take it," and my only answer was, why wouldn't you? It's like being invited to the White House. Even if you're drastically opposed to whomever was president, you'd go just to see what was going on there. Also, I have to admit that I was kind of honoured in the sense that it is one of the old Hollywood traditions, the star on the Walk of Fame, and it was touching, in a way. The strongest image that stuck in my head was the fact that my daughter, in 40 years or 60 years or 70 years, she can walk down that street and say, "Oh yeah, there's my Pop's star." There's something kind of nice about it as well. But, yeah, initially I was a little astounded by the offer.'

Despite being portrayed as the 'anti-Hollywood' star in so much press coverage, Depp was perversely very happy to fly into LA with Paradis in tow, meet up with his mother and step-father and do the Hollywood PR thing. Whether he'd been advised by his agent that it would be a good thing to do for his image or whether the arrival of his daughter and self-imposed exile in France had somewhat softened his attitude to the business of movies is hard to tell. Either way, Depp was there, smiling for the cameras…

Once an outsider, Depp was awarded the ultimate Hollywood accolade with his own star on the Walk of Fame, which he unveiled with Vanessa Paradis.

CHAPTER SEVEN

Art Attack

As a new century dawned, Johnny Depp at 36 was enjoying an unexpected new life in France. Living with Vanessa Paradis was turning out to be a kind of paradise for the sometimes troubled star. The relationship was not without its problems. There were arguments and separations: 'We've had arguments. My fault of course, but we make up. We have to, because I'm a father and she's a mother,' said Depp in the magazine *Avantgarde*.

Depp remained convinced that the birth of his daughter Lily-Rose had given him a new purpose in life: 'This baby has given me life. I see this amazing, beautiful, pure angel-thing wake up in the morning and smile, and nothing can touch that. She gives me the opportunity to experience something new every day. And to love, so deeply. She is the only reason to wake up in the morning, the only reason to take a breath.'

Despite his devotion to his daughter and her mother, Johnny Depp had other reasons to get up in the morning. He remained an actor much sought after since the blockbuster release of *Sleepy Hollow*. However, he had the tricky task of trying to maintain a career as a film actor from his Paris base. Depp was formulating a new approach to his career, one that would see him very rarely returning to Los Angeles. If he could make a movie around Paris or in London, then that film project would be much more attractive to him. He'd done some TV in Britain – guest appearances on comedy shows *The Fast Show* (in December 2000) and *The Vicar of Dibley*. This amused British audiences, confused by the fact that someone seen as a major Hollywood star should be 'slumming it' by appearing on low rent comedy shows, even if one of the appearances was for a well-supported charity event.

Depp's immediate answer to his dilemma was to take a series of cameo parts in low-budget or independent movies. If they were shot in the US, it meant him being away from home for a shorter period of time than if he was the lead and if they were shot in Europe, so much the better. Thus came about a trio of quirky Johnny Depp appearances in *Before Night Falls*, *The Man Who Cried* and *Chocolat*, all of them a long way away from Ichabod Crane in *Sleepy Hollow*.

New York artist-turned-filmmaker Julian Schnabel had burst onto the independent film scene in 1996 with his dramatised biography of artist Jean Michael Basquiat in

Basquiat. It was a film which Depp had loved and he'd sought out the director to tell him. Schnabel found his next movie in the troubled life of exiled Cuban writer Reinaldo Arenas. 'When he showed up [in my life], there was so much he had to say that touched me. I can't give you a logical answer why it was so important for me to tell this story…'

The resulting film, *Before Night Falls*, was based on the memoirs of the little-known Cuban writer. An acclaimed and award-winning author in his youth, Arenas was persecuted, imprisoned and finally exiled because of his sexuality and for publishing material outside Cuba without official permission. Suffering from AIDS, Arenas committed suicide in 1990 and his memoir, *Before Night Falls*, was published posthumously three years later. It's a captivating tale, clearly great subject matter for an important and moving film.

In casting Johnny Depp in the minor double cameo role as both outrageous transvestite Bon Bon and the repressive and repressed Lieutenant Victor, Schnabel was inspired by a recurring motif in Arenas' own work. 'In Reinaldo's writing, one character can be two, three different personages; somebody can be a man and a woman at the same time,' the filmmaker explained. 'I also like to think that Reinaldo would imagine that Lieutenant Victor and Bon Bon could be the same person – that Cuban State Security would go to such extravagant lengths to undermine the stability of the prisoners. The fact that Bon Bon/Lieutenant Victor could be Reinaldo's vision of beauty and his destruction is a constant in Reinaldo's work. Reinaldo's only real body is the body of his work – he turned everything into literature.'

Depp's take on Lieutenant Victor had more thought behind it than may come across in his brief scene. 'I wanted to try to express how a person changes when wearing a uniform,' said Depp. 'There are a lot of people who become a symbol of power. You can find such people among guards in hotels or department stores. Usually they are nice guys next door, but once they wear uniforms, they start abusing their power and bullying weak people. I wanted to play a scary person, someone who feels powerful wearing a uniform.' Equally, Depp's drag act was also a uniform which gave the character of Bon Bon her power. 'That's what acting is all about – getting under a character's skin,' he said. 'I had a blast – but the heels were hell.'

Depp supported Schnabel's endeavours and was happy to lend his star power to the film, as long as he was treated as just one actor among many. The real star was Spanish actor Javier Bardem as Arenas. Depp, alongside his Man Ray restaurant partner Sean Penn, would bring their names to the movie in minor character roles. Penn – in particular – is almost unrecognisable as Cuco Sanchez, a peculiar peasant who encounters the teen Arenas. Directors Hector Babenco (*Kiss of the Spider-Woman*) and Jerzy Skolimowski (*The Shout*, who'd also appeared in *LA Without A Map* with Depp) also turned in cameos.

For his part, Bardem was happy to have Depp's support. He didn't worry that such a big name might detract from his own efforts. 'Johnny did amazing work,' said Bardem, 'and he was very generous, very helpful. He really got into the mood of the character, Bon Bon, and that scene with him as Lieutenant Victor is something that will stay in my memory. I admire him a great deal.'

Bardem was equally taken by Depp in drag: 'When I first saw Bon Bon on the set, I didn't realise it was Johnny. I just looked at this girl with heavy make-up and

the big behind and thought, "Man, I could get into that." I still felt that way after I realised it was Johnny. He's such a beautiful guy – who wouldn't make love to him? I know a lot of girls who would kill to have Bon Bon's ass.'

Before Night Falls was shot in Mexico for 60 days in late 1999, primarily in Veracruz and Merida, though Depp was around for a fraction of that time and reportedly contributed his work without a fee. A lot of effort went into recreating a convincing facsimile of historical Cuba, with Schnabel drawing on the contributions of many Cuban exiles to ensure accuracy. Released in December 2000 to resoundingly positive reviews, Depp's performance was treated as part of the whole and not a grandstanding cameo. However, a lot of the reviews were accompanied with a photo of him in either of his dual roles. *Variety* noted Depp's unusual performances: 'In the film's most amusing sequence, Johnny Depp makes one of two brief but memorable appearances as Bon Bon, a gutter-glamorous transvestite with a talent for rectal smuggling, who shifts several chapters of Reinaldo's book out of the prison. *Before Night Falls* grossed just over $4 million at the US box office, a perfectly respectable sum for a low-budget independent feature of limited interest to the mass cinema-going audience, but of great interest to Johnny Depp fans.

The Man Who Cried was exactly the kind of film that Johnny Depp was looking for. It fitted in precisely with his new life in Paris. Sally Potter's wartime drama called for him to play the strong supporting role of gypsy horse-handler Cesar, alongside leading actress Christina Ricci. The film was to be shot in Paris in the fall of 1999. His new-

As Bon Bon in Before Night Falls, Depp caused heads to turn!

143

found lifestyle seemed to be working out. 'I've been away from the US for two years and spent about fifteen days in my house over there,' he commented. 'I was in Paris working on a Sally Potter film, and I had to fly to Mexico to play a part in a friend's film [*Before Night Falls*]. I had to make a stop in LA and flew with Harry Dean Stanton. We went to a restaurant, and within an hour, a guy showed me a script. And another one five minutes later. It's a madhouse. This obsession, it's not like in Paris. It's wonderful to live in a place where culture is allowed to exist, where people respect history and life. Art, architecture, everything.'

The Man Who Cried saw Depp reunited with Christina Ricci for a third time following *Fear and Loathing* and *Sleepy Hollow*. Ricci played the lead character, a Jewish exile raised in Britain who falls in love with gypsy Cesar just as the Nazis arrive in Paris. Forced to flee, she leaves her love behind to find her father in the most unlikely of places: Hollywood.

Ricci and Depp had first met on the set of *Mermaids* in which she co-starred with Winona Ryder, whom Depp was dating at the time. Ricci was only nine years old. 'I was totally charmed. He was so sweet and nice to me,' recalled Ricci. 'Working with him is wonderful, because he's one of the kindest people I've ever met, so passionate and sincere. He's such an amazing actor and really caring person. I was a bit awkward, though, because I knew him as a little girl and had admired him for so long. To be suddenly romantically linked to him on-screen was strange and uncomfortable.'

Depp was keen to work with Ricci again, having been pleased at her casting in *Sleepy Hollow*. 'I think Christina is one of the few actresses out there who is making brave choices – not just in the films she chooses, but in the work she's doing,' admitted Depp.

In both *Sleepy Hollow*, and even more so in *The Man Who Cried*, Depp and

For Depp, appearing in The Man Who Cried was a chance to make an art movie without having to carry the film as the lead.

Ricci were put together in romantic situations. 'Certainly one of the things that first popped into my head was "My God, I've known her since she was nine years old and we're going to be kissing and stuff!"' recalled Depp.

'In this movie, it's weird,' Ricci admitted in *Movieline* magazine. 'We're having sex in almost every scene we're in – and it's rough sex! The first time we tried to be serious about it, we both started laughing, saying "This is ridiculous!"' Somehow the pair managed to get through it, though the fact that they'd worked together again in sexually provocative roles did nothing to dampen unfounded newspaper speculation – not for the first time – that the pair had more than a professional relationship.

Depp saw *The Man Who Cried* as another significant art movie project he could take part in without having to carry the whole movie – and it was being shot in his adopted home town of Paris. 'Sally Potter, who did *Orlando*, directed and she is a really interesting, sharp, bright, deeply caring woman,' said Depp. 'The story is about what the Jews and the Gypsies had to go through during the occupation. Nobody ever talks about it, so I thought it was a great opportunity to get that information out there.'

The resulting movie is a thoroughly engaging piece of cinema that tells a simple story in a magical way. Depp doesn't have much in the way of dialogue, but he gets to smoulder on the back of a horse and to bed Ricci several times.

Released in the US on May 25th 2001 *The Man Who Cried* went head-to-head with all-out action movies like *Tomb Raider, The Mummy Returns* and *Rollerball*. The result was less than $1 million in takings at the box office…Similarly, the critical reaction to the film was somewhat mixed. 'This is an amazingly ambitious movie,' said Roger Ebert in *The Chicago Sun-Times*. In contrast, Mick LaSalle, writing in *The San Francisco Chronicle* put his finger on what he felt was the problem with the film: 'Ricci and Depp are boring. In scene after scene, it's just big eyes and the pretence of deep feeling under an impassive surface…'

For a while Johnny Depp had a lasting reminder of his time on *The Man Who Cried*. The two gold teeth he had put in for his part as gypsy Cesar remained in place for quite a while. 'I had them made by a guy who puts them directly on the tooth,' noted Depp of his bling-bling teeth, 'and it's a rather violent thing to get them removed again, so I think I'm going to keep them for a while longer. There just are some things I just want put off till later, and an appointment with the dentist is one of them.'

Later, still sporting the gold teeth, he once more cited fear of the dentist as his reason for keeping them, though it also seems likely that he'd become attached to having them. 'I'm deathly afraid of going to the dentist to get them removed because the process is more frightening – they have to grind them off. I'm not a big fan of the dentist!'

Following Christmas 1999 in the South of France with his family, Depp was straight back to work in February 2000 and back in the US with his family in tow. 'Having them around doesn't interfere with my job at all. The only way it interferes is when I'm physically on the set. That is the hardest, because I'm away from my loved ones. I've been trying for as long as possible to keep my distance from Hollywood, the competitive nature of the beast. All I want is for the opportunity to do my work as

best I can and hang around with my family, drink wine and smoke cigarettes. That's all it's about for me.'

However, Depp recognized an opportunity when he saw one. Offered the part of George Jung in *Blow* by director Ted Demme (nephew of *Silence of the Lambs* Oscar-winning director Jonathan Demme), Depp saw a chance to play a character who defined so much about the American dream and the impossibility of realising it. Based on a non-fiction account of the growth of cocaine use in the US over a 30-year period, especially the Colombian connection with Pablo Escobar, *Blow* had to be significantly simplified for the big screen. Covering 30 years of contemporary history was a hard enough task, Demme felt, without getting bogged down in other details. Much was changed for the movie, not the least of which was the role Hollywood had played in the process…

'We knew the key to the success of the role of George Jung would lie in the subtlety and intelligence an actor could bring to it. Somebody had to make him much more than a drug dealer – and that's exactly what Johnny did. He brings a cerebral quality to his roles that takes them in unexpected directions,' noted producer Joel Stillerman.

'The story of George Jung was, well, mind-blowing to me,' continued Ted Demme. 'It's the story of the American Dream gone terribly wrong, about a small-town boy who poured all his talent and dreams into trafficking cocaine. He was a guy who wanted to control his own destiny, to live by his own rules, like many Americans do, and he found a way to do it and get rich. A lot of people can relate to what George wanted, which was never to be told by anyone – not his parents or politicians or the law – what he could and couldn't do.'

For his part, Depp knew taking on the role of a living person was going to involve a great deal of research, just as he'd done with Hunter S. Thompson and Joe Pistone. Depp visited prison several times to meet with the real George Jung – serving time on drug charges until 2014 – to draw upon his insider knowledge about the unpredictable existence of a drug smuggler. Jung had never heard of Depp and had to ask around in the prison to see if this actor was up to the job. The next day, Jung called Demme to say, 'So, this Depp guy – the boys say he's OK.' Depp recalled: 'I was happy with that. It's nice to know I'm liked in prison!' In the process of talking with Jung, Depp became fascinated by his attitude, one that echoed Depp's own to a great extent. 'He really saw himself as a modern-day pirate. He didn't believe in the system or politics or rules or bosses. He just wanted to go out there and really live. He didn't want to end up in a cookie-cutter job like everybody else. He had a real vision of freedom. He just wanted to do it and go out there and live in a very intense way. But it swooped him up, and he lost everything, including the people he loved.'

Jung's experience reminded Depp of his own path to achieving what many would regard as the American dream: fame and fortune. 'It reminded me of when I started acting because I didn't want to be this at all when I first started out,' argued Depp. 'I started making money like I'd never seen before in my life. One thing led to another and suddenly I was on the rise and there was no stopping it. That's what happened to George. He was just following what looked – at first – like a promising future.'

In George Jung Depp had found another one of his patented 'innocent abroad'

Playing George Jung in Blow saw Depp inhabit the high life the drug smuggler was able to buy for himself, as well as the low life that eventually destroys him…

roles. Despite the fact that he'd be putting his own gloss on the character, he was also aware of playing a real person in a version of their real life. 'I feel a deep responsibility to George Jung because he's in a prison cell without the possibility of parole for a long time. I didn't get to spend that much time with him, but one day I just felt the character click into place. It's an exciting moment when you feel yourself thinking and moving and talking like another person.'

Executive Producer Georgia Kacandes noted: 'He really got Jung's body language, he even started to look like him in a weird way. There was a whole subtle shift in Johnny between the time George is in his prime to when he is actively deteriorating under the stress. His body just collapses into itself and it's amazing. He physicalises the role without make-up or wardrobe. It's all in his psyche.'

Co-starring with Depp was Penelope Cruz: 'She plays Mirtha as this beautiful wild horse who George wants to grab the reins of, even though he knows that he can't. I was deeply impressed by her as an actress,' noted Depp. For her part, Cruz was equally impressed by Depp. 'Johnny is one of the most special people I've ever met. He has that magic charisma and he doesn't have to force it. I don't know if someone's born with that quality or if you have to work at it, but it's very rare.'

As well as Cruz, Demme selected an international range of actors to fill out the main roles, including German actress Franke Potente, Spanish actor Jordi Molla and idiosyncratic American actor Paul Reubens. Cast as Depp's parents in the movie

'I feel a deep responsibility to George Jung,' said Depp of capturing another real-life person on film…

were Ray Liotta and Australian Rachel Griffiths, actors not that much removed from Depp's own age: Liotta is six years older, while Griffith is five years younger than Depp himself. Make-up and costume were used to give the impression of these characters growing and changing across the 30-year time period of the film.

Blow was shot on locations in both Southern California and Mexico between February and May 2000. Innovative production design by Michael Hanan allowed for the re-creation of dozens of locations in several different decades, including the states of Massachusetts, Florida, California, New York and Illinois as well as the countries of Mexico and Colombia.

Released on April 6th 2001, *Blow* was met with almost universally positive reviews. Joe Morgenstern in *The Wall Street Journal* suggested that Depp's performance was just too good: 'He's the source of the movie's power, but also the emblem of its fundamental problem,' he wrote. 'With George being played by an actor of such effortless charm, no slime ever seems to adhere to this man of little demonstrable insight or ability.' Critics were clearly divided over the character. On the one hand Lou Lumenick in *The New York Post* wrote: 'Rarely since the tale of the Corleone has a movie presented such a compelling, sympathetic portrait of a criminal lowlife.' On the other hand, Stephen Hunter in *The Washington Post* commented, 'You can't make an epic about a mouse.' Likewise Roger Ebert in *The Chicago Sun-Times* observed, 'Johnny Depp is a versatile and reliable actor who almost always chooses interesting projects. The failure is George Jung's. For all the glory of his success and the pathos of his failure, he never became a person interesting enough to make a movie about.'

The film accumulated almost $53 million at the US box office, a very good performance for a relatively low-budget movie which hinged almost entirely on Depp to bring in an audience.

There was a sad postscript to Depp's *Blow* adventure with the sudden and unexpected death of 38-year-old director Ted Demme on Sunday, January 13th 2002 of a heart attack. He died after playing in a celebrity basketball game in Los Angeles. An autopsy and toxicology tests proved inconclusive, resulting in a 'natural causes' verdict, though there was a suspicion that past drug use may have weakened Demme's heart. Depp attended the funeral in Los Angeles, calling Demme 'a fallen comrade' and said he was 'devastated' by his unexpected death, especially as they were about the same age.

At the start of the 21st century, Johnny Depp was rumoured to be up for a variety of roles, including the role of Robbie Burns in a biopic of the Scottish poet, called *Clarinda* after the estranged wife of a Glasgow lawyer who inspired the poet's 'Ae Fond Kiss'. The possibility of Depp playing the part caused a great deal of controversy. Many had assumed that *Star Wars* and *Trainspotting* star Ewan McGregor would secure the role, but producer James Cosmo offered the part to Depp believing his box office draw to be higher. However, the £28 million film remains unmade, scuppered by the revelation that convicted con-man Eric Rowan was involved in Alloway Productions, the production company behind the project.

Was it the fact that *Chocolat* was shooting in France and Depp had again been offered an extended cameo supporting role that made him sign up to the film? Was it the chance to work again with Lasse Hallström, the director of *What's Eating Gilbert Grape*? Or with Lena Olin, Hallström's wife and Depp's *The Ninth Gate* co-star? Or was it simply the opportunity to play the guitar on film, a first for the music-loving actor? 'It's the first time I really played. In *Cry Baby*, I only pretended to play the guitar. This time, I really played the guitar, which was shot on the spot. I checked some old blues records, and practiced them, which I enjoyed so much,' noted Depp. His role in *Chocolat*, as Irish-accented riverboat gypsy Roux, sees him appearing for less than twenty minutes of the movie's two hour running time, but having a huge impact on the story.

A fable based on the novel by Joanne Harris, *Chocolat* tells the tale of the mysterious Vianne (Juliette Binoche) who opens a chocolate shop during Lent in a religiously inclined, straight-laced community. Seen as a demonic outsider, Vianne's chocolates are soon having amazing effects on the local populace, causing them to become less repressed and rather freer than before…

Once again, the fall-out from Depp's political awakening on *The Brave* was clear in the choices he made in tackling the part of Roux in *Chocolat*: 'With the director I soon decided he should be a gypsy, a free spirit, who travelled all over the world with his guitar: gypsy culture fascinated me as I discovered it has many affinities with American Indians' history.' There were other echoes of Depp's pre-Paris life: 'Roux is a wanderer, who is moving from place to place. Roux doesn't have roots. He is a guy who isn't interested in staying in one place for a long time.'

This wandering gypsy role also appealed to Depp because of its echoes of his own childhood: 'I think that my professional choices have something to do with the way I grew up,' admitted Depp. 'When I was a child my family was constantly wandering from town to town and I can remember school was a torment. I've never felt accepted and that was hard for me to face.'

Depp had to admit that he'd never seen his previous collaboration with Hallström: 'I never saw *Gilbert Grape*. I was 30 when I made that film. And it was a hard year, although now I'm thinking that they're all hard in some way. It was a rough, rough period for me, personally and emotionally. And when Lasse came to me with the idea of doing *Chocolat*, I was very surprised. We had a good experience on *Gilbert Grape* but it was also difficult. I was surprised that he'd want to go through something with me again, thinking that I was some kind of moody, brooding, horrible guy… But I was so happy to work with him again, to redeem myself perhaps, because he's a very magical guy.'

Coming back to work again with Hallström was a big part of the attraction of *Chocolat* for Depp. 'Lasse is like some kind of magician,' Depp told *Dreamwatch* magazine. 'He has a quality about him as a human being that is so pure, so childlike sometimes. When he goes to the set everything he does as a film-maker, his signature, is all over it. When you're watching his films, you're watching a very big portion of the man.'

One problem he encountered during the making of the film was the need to be seen eating lots of chocolate. What some people might regard as a perk of the job, Depp quickly came to despise. 'I ate more chocolate than I wanted to,' he admitted. 'About three seconds more in the take and I probably would have been spewing.' Hallström added: 'Most of the chocolate was covered in dust, as we were shooting

there for weeks and weeks and we never really bothered to dust it off. We also had plastic chocolate; 50 per cent of it was plastic and people couldn't really tell. People kept eating it anyway and so there were big teeth marks in the plastic chocolate.'

Despite playing the romantic lead in the film, Depp felt that he wasn't the ideal actor for that part: 'There are a lot of people out there who are very good at the "boy meets girl, boy loses girl, boy finds girl again" stuff and good luck to them. *Chocolat* was fun, but I'm not sure I'm particularly good at it. I'd probably be bored to tears if I had to do that sort of stuff all the time. The appeal of a film like *From Hell* for me is that it is pretty dark and I've always been interested in human behaviour.'

For her part, *Chocolat* star Juliette Binoche saw through much of Depp's posturing and straight to the man inside, Depp's 'inner gypsy'. 'A gypsy needs his family and I think he found a family in the people he works with like Lasse [Hallström] and Tim Burton. I once asked him why he works so much, and he said, "I just have to keep my head busy."'

Chocolat was shot in rural France and at Shepperton Studios just outside London, wrapping in July 2000, around the same time as Depp was starting his work on *From Hell*. Roger Ebert of *The Chicago Sun-Times* wrote of *Chocolat*: 'Binoche reigns as a serene and wise goddess… [It's] the sort of movie you can enjoy as a superior fable, in which the values come from children's fairy tales but adult themes have been

Juliette Binoche was another actress attracted to working with Johnny Depp due to his track record: his good looks didn't do any harm, either…

introduced.' *Rolling Stone*'s Peter Travers was beguiled by *Chocolat*: 'A charming Johnny Depp drops in as Roux, an Irish gypsy who tempts Vianne. *Chocolat* may be slight, but don't discount Hallström's artful finesse. *Chocolat* is yummy.'

Released on December 15th 2000, *Chocolat* went on to clock up over $71.5 million at the US box office and thanks to skilfull handling by distributors Miramax, the film scored a total of five Oscar nominations including Best Film, and Best Actress and Best Supporting Actress for Juliette Binoche and Judi Dench.

While shooting on *Chocolat* and just before embarking on *From Hell*, the usual number of projects that failed to progress came Depp's way. Among them were plans to work with director Griffin Dunne on *Nailed Right In*, in which Depp would play a mobster (echoing *Donnie Brasco*). Depp was also connected with the role of game show host-turned-CIA operative Chuck Barris in *Confessions of a Dangerous Mind*, before the part was played by Sam Rockwell in the film directed by George Clooney. A potential role in *Ocean's Eleven* was also connected with Depp, probably that played by Brad Pitt. The actor also talked of reuniting again with Tim Burton for a fourth film, an adaptation of the cult novel *Geek Love*, a Warner Bros. property the two had discussed making years previously.

Based on the Alan Moore and Eddie Campbell graphic novel, *From Hell* was perceived by many as being *Sleepy Hollow 2*, but to Johnny Depp, it was much more than that. The graphic novel drew (literally) on almost every speculation surrounding the Jack the Ripper murders in 1880s Whitechapel to create a dense, literate meditation on murder and the modern age. The acclaim that greeted the original comic book publication meant that the movie rights to such a well-known subject would almost certainly be sold quickly. For years the film was stuck in Hollywood 'development hell', moving from Disney to New Line and finally to Fox. Jude Law turned down a reported $3 million to star and then Brad Pitt passed due to a scheduling conflict. Finally, *From Hell*'s directors Allen and Albert Hughes (*Menace II Society*) met with Johnny Depp, only to discover that Jack the Ripper was another of Depp's many obsessions.

'I was always attracted to things on the darker side, especially when I was young,' said Depp, confessing to a long-standing interest in the Ripper case. 'I must have some 25 books, maybe more, on the case. There are so many theories, any of them could be correct. It's impossible to know. I've always thought it would make a great movie if very carefully done.'

It didn't take much to convince Depp to sign up, but the attention to detail evident from the directing brothers was something the meticulous actor found to be reassuring. 'Allen and Albert have a great passion for the material and have done more research than almost any other director I've worked with,' he remarked. 'I'm very familiar with the story, I know the right questions to ask, and they know the answers.'

One of the first thing's Depp had to get to grips with was the English accent required. It's a process that had tripped up so many of his contemporaries, including Keanu Reeves and Brad Pitt. Depp employed an east london cockney accent for his character to 'magnify as much as possible Abberline's working class aspects. He was actually from Dorset, but it sounds too bizarre to use. It's a really weird accent, like a combination of Keith Richards, Pete Townshend and Bruce

Robinson [*Withnail & I*].' During a trip to London Depp followed the footsteps of the Ripper for two hours walking around the East End accompanied by ex-policeman and Ripper expert Donald Rumbelow. The pair rounded off the tour with a stop in the Ten Bells Pub, where one of the Ripper's victims used to enjoy a drink.

Depp was also fascinated by the conspiracy angle of the still-unsolved Ripper case. The *From Hell* graphic novel tracks the conspiracy right to the door of Buckingham Palace. 'Whether the British monarchy was literally involved in the Ripper murders doesn't diminish the power of the accusation levelled at the ruling class,' said co-screenwriter Yglesias. 'That the authorities refused to even consider the possibility the suspect might be wealthy speaks volumes about the Victorian era. Society's ills were viewed exclusively as the fault of the poor and the lower class.'

Depp located his character of Frederick Abberline in a particular psychological place, one that made his quest to prevent Mary Kelly (Heather Graham) from becoming the Ripper's next victim all the more meaningful. 'Abberline has been beaten up by life. He lost his wife and child, and relies on self-medication to get through the day. I liked Abberline because he is not a traditional policeman. He has to deal with the case and face his own demons, the drug addiction. He tries to escape from his own fears.'

From Hell was shot in Prague, between June and September 2000. The

As an aficionado of Ripper mythology, Depp leapt at the chance to star in the Hughes Brothers' take on the mystery, From Hell.

production team not only had to recreate a faultless Victorian London in Prague, but they also had to contend with extreme variations in temperature and some wild weather. From a high of 98 degrees, the hottest temperature recorded in Prague in 139 years to below 30 degrees Fahrenheit in mid-July, the weird weather was cause for comment. 'Everyone says this is unheard of here. If it had been this cold in London, Jack the Ripper would have stayed home,' complained executive producer Thomas M. Hammel.

Neither Prague nor London could provide a location which could double for 1880s Whitechapel, the original having changed beyond all recognition. Oscar-winning production designer Martin Childs built a replica of the whole area in the middle of a field just outside Prague, near the small village of Orech. 'The setting is extremely important in a film like this, very integral to the story,' said Childs. 170 carpenters worked for twelve weeks to construct the impressive set. The main structures of Whitechapel seen in the movie include the Ten Bells Saloon, Commercial Street and Christ Church, as well as specific sites where the Ripper's victims were found. These were made to appear just as they did in 1888. Depp was impressed: 'I was stupefied the first time I walked down these streets. It was

Depp found himself promoting From Hell in the wake of the 9/11 terrorist attacks on the US, an uncomfortable time to be travelling.

incredible. The Hughes brothers are sticklers for details, down to the position of the bodies, the cobblestones, the location of the broken windows. Martin [Childs] did an unbelievable job.'

Depp worked with five actresses playing the Ripper's victims: Heather Graham (Mary Kelly), Lesley Sharp (Kate Eddowes), Susan Lynch (Liz Stride), Katrin Cartlidge (Dark Annie Chapman) and Annabelle Apsion (Polly). Also in the cast were Robbie Coltrane as Sgt. Godley, who keeps an eye on Abberline's investigation, and Ian Holm as Royal Surgeon and Ripper suspect Sir William Gull, who replaced original choice Nigel Hawthorne after he fell ill. Body casts of the actresses and detailed special effects were used to create the bodies of the victims after the Ripper's attentions. So realistic were they, that some of the actresses refused to look at the mutilated versions of themselves.

The style and look of the film was very important to the Hughes Brothers, from the recreation of Whitechapel through the costumes to the impressive visual effects used to recreate the London skyline and to capture Abberline's visions and the Ripper's barely seen actions.

All the attention paid off, as the film was released to a welter of critical acclaim. Lou Lumenick in *The New York Post* called *From Hell*, 'an instant classic... a gripping and stylish thriller... the classiest and best-acted slasher movie of all time.' Chris Vognar, writing in *The Dallas Morning News* thought the film was neither one thing nor another: 'An occasionally awkward mix of art film and slasher flick, *From Hell* manages to make its luridness intelligent enough – and its intelligence lurid enough.' Less impressed, Steven Rea in *The Philadelphia Inquirer* wrote that the movie 'is about as convincing as a visit to a theme-park haunted house'.

From Hell debuted at number one on the box office top ten when released on October 19th 2001, taking $11 million. The film was released at a strange time, just a month after the terrorist attack on America on September 11th 2001. The performance of the film was particularly striking given the judgment by numerous critics and analysts that the country was in no mood for fictional violence after being a victim of the real-life variety.

Depp had expressed concern about flying after Bin Laden's attacks on the US, but made the fourteen-hour plane trip from Paris to America to promote the film. He commented: 'It's already difficult to have to sit around and talk about movies in the midst of what's happening. My immediate plans are to get back to my family to be with my girls, and then from there, I don't know. I can't say that I'm very comfortable putting my two-and-a-half-year-old daughter and my girl [Vanessa Paradis] on a plane.' Asked if audiences would enjoy *From Hell* despite the real-world situation, Depp responded: 'Movies are escapism, and if people want to go and get out of reality for a couple of hours, why not?' *From Hell* built to a US box office total of over $31 million and saw Depp nominated as Best Actor by the Academy of Science Fiction, Fantasy and Horror Films.

Things were looking good on the second day of shooting on Terry Gilliam's *The Man Who Killed Don Quixote* in September 2000. Pre-production had been underway since June and despite the usual problems with actor's contracts, working with horses, an uncomfortably low budget and little rehearsal time, things were shaping up nicely. After all, Gilliam had been attached to various versions of the project for over a decade. Now shooting was finally underway and the film's two stars, French actor Jean Rochefort and Johnny Depp were in front of the cameras in Las Bardenas, in the desert of northern Spain…

Then the rain came. 'It wasn't just rain,' remembered Johnny, 'it was enormous rocks of hail which hit me on the head and filled the pockets of my coat full of ice. I've been in torrential downpours before but this was insane – I've never seen anything like it. It was epic.'

As the cast and crew sat in their cars and vans watching sets, props and camera equipment floating away, some were relieved. The curse of Don Quixote had struck. If this was as bad as things got, then shooting the rest of the film would be easy. Unfortunately, the bad weather was only the first in a series of problems which would beset the production and lead to it being shut down less than two weeks into principal photography.

Depp was playing Toby Grosini, a modern-day advertising genius transported to the seventeenth century and caught up in the magical adventures of Don Quixote, essentially functioning as the Sancho Panza figure in the tale. 'I was just stupefied when I read it,' said Depp of the screenplay. 'It was like reading a really well written novel. I instantly just dove in. It's one of the most brilliant scripts I've ever read. Hysterically funny, deeply poetic, profound. A great, great story.'

Gilliam was obsessed with Don Quixote. He'd written a script which almost entered production in 1999 before collapsing when one of the financiers pulled out. Then came another version, this time with Gilliam's *Fear and Loathing* collaborator Tony Grisoni. Other directors had come unstuck trying to film stories based on Cervantes' tales of Don Quixote, the *faux* knight forever tilting at windmills with his aide Sancho Panza in tow – Orson Welles, the genius behind *Citizen Kane, The Magnificent Ambersons* and *Touch of Evil*, for one. Everyone working on Gilliam's movie was painfully aware both of the cursed history of Don Quixote movies and Gilliam's own difficulties on films like *The Adventures of Baron Munchausen* and *Brazil*. 'It was almost as if there was this strange dark cloud hanging over us,' remembered Depp.

Leading man Jean Rochefort, then 70 years old, fell ill. He flew to France after six days of filming for checks with his doctor and failed to return to the project. The weather and the F16 planes conducting practice bombing raids on the army test range location being used for the film were now the least of the crew's problems. Depp recalls that it was the departure of Rochefort that doomed the film to non-completion. With finances already a worry, an unresolved insurance claim in place for the equipment and time lost to the weather and a team of nervous investors and producers, Gilliam left the film and returned to London. 'I think I was one of the last to leave,' claimed a demoralised Depp.

The star was all the more upset because this film was to see him acting alongside Vanessa Paradis. 'It would have been the first film Vanessa and I had made together,' mused Depp. 'We were excited that we were all going to be together. We were also slightly freaked out about going to work together, having to "lie" to one another on camera. It was a bit strange, but I figured we'd get over that in the first couple of days.' As it turned out, Paradis didn't shoot any material, except for some make-up, hair and costume tests, before the film was abandoned.

There was a film that emerged from this debacle, but it wasn't *The Man Who Killed Don Quixote*. Gilliam had invited documentary filmmakers Keith Fulton and Louis Pepe (who'd made *The Hamster Factor* about the making of Gilliam's *Twelve Monkeys*) to capture the inside story of the production. Fulton and Pepe ended up with *Lost in La Mancha*, a 93 minute film documenting Gilliam's hellish experience trying to keep his Don Quixote movie in production.

'Terry was so excited, big and broad and just exploding with excitement and giggling constantly,' recalled Depp. 'He's an insanely passionate, curious and knowledgeable man. He was loving it, just loving it – then, day by day, you'd see him shrink. It was hard to see Terry like that; he looked beaten – and Terry's a hard guy to beat. It's really sad because it would have been like the "Best of Terry Gilliam". I felt really good about it. I felt I had come up with a really interesting, really fun character and Terry thought so, too.'

When *The Man Who Killed Don Quixote* was shut down, all the assets of the production – including the script – became the property of the insurance company. Gilliam was determined to buy back his script and eventually remount the film, and he still wanted Johnny Depp on board. 'It's hard to put your finger on why he's so extraordinary,' mused Gilliam of Depp, 'but technically, he's astonishing. He's absolutely brilliant, with the kind of technique you'd only get if you'd spent ten years at RADA [Royal Academy of Dramatic Arts] – and it's all self-taught. You don't want to work with anybody else once you've worked with somebody as good as that. For me, it was like working with [the *Monty*] *Python* [team] again – he's that fast and funny and inventive.'

The remount of the film may take so long that Depp ends up playing Don Quixote himself, but whenever it happens, he intends to be there. 'If Terry wants to pick this up and start again, then I'm ready,' said Depp with some enthusiasm. 'If he wants to make it happen, I want to be there. I think it's going to be a great film. I think we can do it, make a beautiful, very funny Terry Gilliam film. I would love to be involved on any level…'

CHAPTER EIGHT

Thrill Ride

After the collapse of *The Man Who Killed Don Quixote*, Johnny Depp retreated to be with his family. He'd been working almost non-stop since *Donnie Brasco* in 1995. Now he was happy to take some time off away from the cameras to be with his wife and daughter. As Vanessa Paradis explained, 'Having a child makes you a better person because you have to be less selfish. There's not so much time for you and there's so much time for her, which she deserves. As much as you want to teach your kids, they teach you so much about being real, being innocent, being happy.' According to Paradis, Depp had learned as much as she had about parenthood. 'Johnny is the best dad. He's as good a person as he is a father.'

Now was Depp's chance to be a full-time father. After a break at Christmas 2000, Depp and Paradis decided that 2001 would be a relatively quiet year for them. During 2000, Depp had been involved in Paradis' music, contributing songs and playing on her new album, as well as directing music videos for the songs 'Pourtant' and 'Que fait la vie?' Songs on the album, *Bliss* (which was released in Europe in October 2000) written by Paradis made reference to her life with Depp and her daughter Lily-Rose, whom attentive listeners may have heard featured on at least one track...

Even hiding away in France, with its strict privacy laws, Depp was still being plagued by the unwanted attentions of the press. 'The tabloids there are really nasty,' said Depp of the French press. 'They've got tougher rules in France, but they break them. I had an incident with a really dumb magazine called *Voici* where they printed a photograph of Lily-Rose, a long-lens shot from very far away, and I just went ballistic. You can sue them – I've sued a couple of times, Vanessa's sued and we win every time – but this time I was beyond suing.'

This time, Depp took the solution to his problem into his own hands, giving in again to what Polanski had called his 'teenage reaction': 'I just wanted to beat whoever was responsible into the Earth,' admitted Depp. 'I just wanted to rip him apart. I tracked him down and gave him a few suggestions about how to live life and stay healthy and he took my advice. Because that's just unacceptable. They can do anything they want to me – and most tabloids have – but not my kid, not my pure, innocent little baby. She didn't ask to be in this circus.'

The usual parade of possible parts came Depp's way in early 2001 and most of them fell by the wayside, either because Depp was not motivated to commit to them or the film's producers decided to take the project in a different direction. Among the roles which came Depp's way included a team-up with Jennifer Love Hewitt for a re-make of the 1940s comedy *It Started With Eve*. The $40 million movie was based around a son – Depp's role – who gets a girl to pose as his fiancee to please his dying father. His plans are turned upside down when his father makes an unexpected recovery. Albert Finney was being talked of to play Depp's screen dad. To date, the film has never progressed. Depp was also supposedly up for the part of *poseur* poet Lord Byron in a biopic after Jude Law passed on the role. Again, nothing has come of this project.

Variety reported that Depp was signed up to play poet and playwright Christopher Marlowe in a new £13 million British movie being made with German backing by Natural Nylon, the production company formed by Jude Law, his then off-screen wife Sadie Frost, Jonny Lee Miller and Sean Pertwee. The film was to be directed by John Maybury, who made *Love is the Devil*, and would focus on Marlowe's relationship with Shakespeare (to be played by Law). Since then Natural Nylon has been disbanded by the principals and Frost and Law have separated. Needless to say, there's still no sign of the film…

The only film Johnny Depp worked on during 2001 was another of his long line of cameo roles in a friend's project. Director Robert Rodriguez planned *Once Upon A Time in Mexico* as the third film in his *El Mariachi* series. Rodriguez had launched his film career with the ultra-low-budget action flick *El Mariachi* and its bigger, slicker sequel *Desperado*, starring Antonio Banderas and Salma Hayek. Having detoured into kid's movies with his *Spy Kids* series, Rodriguez decided to complete his trilogy, inspired by both the *Mad Max* films and the *Dollars* movies of Sergio Leone.

The film takes the same characters and actors from the previous movie and drops them into a new, more epic situation, and introduces a few new characters, one of whom was played by Depp. Haunted and scarred by tragedy, El Mariachi (Banderas) has retreated into a life of isolation. He is forced out of hiding when Sands (Depp), a corrupt CIA agent, recruits the reclusive hero to sabotage an assassination plot against the president of Mexico, which has been conceived by the evil cartel kingpin Barrillo (Willem Dafoe). But El Mariachi also has his own reasons for returning – revenge.

'The script is a combination of many different stories I heard from my uncle who was in the FBI,' claimed Rodriguez. 'Some are true, others have been twisted into fiction. It also contains flashback elements for the audience. It's almost as if it is part four of the story – only part three doesn't really exist. The flashbacks to the "phantom" movie contain scenes with Antonio and Salma's previously unseen adventures, which gives this movie a more epic feel.'

Depp found a great challenge in the role of the amoral CIA agent Sands. 'Here was a chance to play a guy who's a little against the grain of what you'd expect to see in a CIA agent. He wasn't someone who was clichéd or who I felt I had seen before. It was an interesting idea for Robert to create a man who's in the CIA, but stationed somewhere he doesn't want to be because no one likes him. Sands is a

man who has no regard for human life. I've never played someone like that before
– who's not a good guy in any way.'

Depp was one of the few stars Rodriguez knew of who would allow themselves
to take on the role of the corrupt, amoral Sands. 'Johnny's character is very edgy,
and you have to have an actor who's willing to embrace that, because so many
actors don't want to come in and be unlikeable,' noted Rodriguez, perhaps thinking
of Depp's roles in *Before Night Falls* and the uncompleted *The Man Who Killed
Don Quixote*. 'Johnny didn't seem to care about that as long as the character was
interesting. What's funny is that, no matter how vile we made him, Johnny still has
this incredibly likeable nature, so the character still ends up being sympathetic. I
don't think you can really hate a Johnny Depp character, no matter how rotten he
may be, and Sands is rotten to the core. Sands was my favourite part in the script,
and the first character I began developing for this movie. He's the character who
orchestrates the entire assassination plan and slowly watches it fall apart. Then
Johnny came in and took Sands to a whole other level.'

Depp clearly had a blast making it, despite being away from his family. Clearly
the time they'd spent together in the first half of the year prepared Depp for the
May to June shoot in the summer of 2001. 'It was great, man. Really great,' Depp
enthused. 'Rodriguez is really a good guy, a really fun guy. We shot it in high def,
which is like a digital miracle! It was incredible! You'd never hear "Cut!" you'd just
keep doing this scene until he said, "Do it again." You're basically working off a tape
that's 75 minutes long, so you can just go.' The director's technical innovations in
fast-paced digital film-making and post-production fascinated Depp and gave him
cause to believe that directors like Rodriguez would have bright futures in the
industry. 'Rodriguez is an amazing, interesting guy. He's going to be around for a
long time.'

Within Rodriguez's moral universe Depp also discovered wit and lyricism.
'Robert's action has a great deal of humour at the same time as it salutes the genre,
particularly the classic westerns of Sergio Leone,' said Depp. 'It's truly poetic and
beautiful that Sands becomes a blind gunfighter, someone with no eyes, who knows
he's going to die but still feels compelled to defend himself. Robert decided to put
Sands' fate in the hands of a young innocent boy, who turns out to be his only friend
and the only person Sands is concerned about saving.'

The friendship between Sands and the young boy also plays with the audience's
feelings about Sands, according to Rodriguez. 'Johnny took someone you should
despise and gave the audience a conflicting interest in him so that, by the end,
they're actually cheering for him. It was interesting to watch an unredeemable
character eventually become redeemable.' It seemed that particular character arc
was rapidly becoming a Johnny Depp speciality.

Shooting with digital high definition cameras meant that the making of *Once
Upon A Time in Mexico* was a fast-paced process, something that Depp certainly
appreciated. A seven week shooting schedule on such a major movie was almost
unheard of, and Rodriguez took on a lot of the roles behind-the-scenes himself,
including the director of photography, the production designer, the editor and the
music composer. The film was shot on location in Mexico, in the colonial town of
San Miguel De Allende. Depp had filmed in the country before, with Mexico

doubling for Cuba on *Before Night Falls*. Lots of stunt and action work was involved, though not much of it involved him. Gunfights seemed to be his forte. Make-up effects specialists Shannon Shea and Jake Garber were also asked to create a fake arm for Depp based solely on a tracing the actor had sent via fax from Paris. The whole fake third arm gag became a running joke through the movie and was possibly a reference to some Gene Wilder business in Mel Brooks' *Young Frankenstein*, just the kind of film that Depp would cite as inspiration for some of his acting choices.

When Depp arrived on location, he had certain ideas about his character. 'He said, "I imagine this guy wears these really cheesy tourist shirts,"' recalled director Rodriguez, who admitted he had no idea what he would be in for with Depp. Other ideas didn't take hold in quite the same way, such as his plan that his character would carry around a Judy Garland biography. 'I just figured that this guy might have a sideline obsession with Broadway,' mused Depp. He also wanted to be seen wearing an assortment of very obvious disguises; 'That's why I brought along all my wigs and fake moustaches,' claimed the actor. The fake moustache gimmick was trimmed from the final movie, but was included in the cut scenes on the DVD and featured in the 'making of' featurette.

Depp was able to contribute to the film in other ways. His *Chocolat* experience and his work on Vanessa Paradis' album had given the actor more confidence in his

Playing a corrupt CIA operative, Depp was surprised to see how much he featured in the finished version of Once Upon A Time in Mexico as he worked on the film for only nine days.

music again after years during which his band, P, had taken a back seat to his film work. According to Rodriguez, 'Johnny went out and wrote a whole piece for his character, which I use in the movie. I created new orchestral versions of it for whenever his character is on screen.'

When the film was completed and released some time later, Depp was surprised to discover how much he was actually in the movie. 'I thought it was like a cameo. You know – a bit, a small little in and out thing. Suddenly, it was my agent or my sister, someone saw the movie and said "Man, you're through the whole thing." I had no idea – especially after nine days of shooting.' Clearly, Robert Rodriguez had put those nine days of work by Depp to good use.

In fact, Depp had enjoyed the whole speedy process so much, he asked the director if there was more he could do. 'He'd never shot a full movie in eight or nine days and at the end of that he was like, "Is there anything else I can do, man?" He said, "Who's playing the priest?" and I said I hadn't cast it yet. He said, "How about I do a Marlon Brando voice and dress up as someone else? Can I do the priest before I leave?" So there's a confessional scene which wasn't supposed to feature Johnny Depp...'

Released on September 12th 2003, in the wake of *Pirates of the Caribbean*, *Once Upon A Time in Mexico* definitely benefited from the Jack Sparrow effect. His performance in *Pirates* had so endeared Depp to critics, that *Mexico* was given a stronger welcome than it may have otherwise had. However, there were some critics not too impressed with the latest entry in the *El Mariachi* series. 'The only thing missing is a coherent story – or even, for that matter, an interesting idea for one,' wrote A. O. Scott in *The New York Times*. Wesley Morris in *The Boston Globe* commented: 'The plot practically demands that you board a tour bus to navigate it.' But the actors received much praise, particularly Depp. Ann Hornaday in *The Washington Post* commented that Depp 'is quickly proving to be the most larcenous man in show business by stealing every movie he's in.' Similarly, Geoff Pevere in *The Toronto Star* concluded: 'For the second time this year, the actor transforms a moribund movie into a watchable one merely by being there.'

The film opened at the number one spot in the weekly top ten, taking around $24 million at the box office and bumping Depp's own *Pirates* down to number five with a weekly take of $4.6 million. That film though, was well on its way to crossing the $300 million mark, something *Mexico* would not achieve with a domestic box office take of just over $56 million and an additional $26.8 million from overseas. The film secured for Depp another award nomination for Best Supporting Actor in a Comedy or Musical from the Golden Satellite Awards.

Although based in France and taking time out from movies to be a family man, Johnny Depp still had time for his interests in Los Angeles, not least of which was the now-infamous Viper Club. Day-to-day management of the club had been handed over to Depp's childhood pal Sal Jenco, although the actor said he'd still personally take action if he ever saw anyone taking drugs there. Despite problems with the kind of people who frequented his venues, Depp was expanding his business interests. As well as the co-owned Man Ray restaurant in Paris, Depp decided to open a trendy bar in the heart of London. The Column was to be a

partnership with former British soccer ace Lee Chapman, later followed with plans for a London version of Man Ray.

Meanwhile, just as Depp didn't take to the idea of his daughter, Lily-Rose becoming an actress, neither was ex-model Vanessa Paradis keen to have her daughter follow her footsteps into showbusiness. However, Paradis recogised that there would be little she could do except love and advise her. 'You can't say "no" to a child. I mean, you can say, "Don't touch fire or you're going to burn yourself" – and that's what I do right now, because she wants to touch everything. But in the big decisions of your life, like "Don't fall in love with that person because he's bad for you," you can't say that. You can't forbid somebody; you can only be there to help them. So I'll be really scared for her, I'll be worried, but I'll be there for her if she wants me.'

Depp finally lost the part of comic book hero Ghost Rider, which he'd been connected to on-and-off for quite some time, to old pal Nicolas Cage. It gave Depp a chance to come clean with an admission. When Cage was being awarded the American Cinematheque Gala Tribute at a ceremony in Beverly Hills in October 2001, Depp sent a video tape greeting as he couldn't attend in person. The tape included a long overdue confession about the time they'd briefly co-habited when both were young struggling actors. Depp recalled one day when – hungry and completely broke – he'd rifled through Cage's drawers and found some Mexican money. Depp claimed he traded it in for American dollars and used it to buy some food. Having kept his guilty secret for years, Johnny asked for Cage's forgiveness. Cage's response to this revelation was not recorded.

The death of *Blow* director Ted Demme in early 2002 had struck Depp hard due to the similarity in their ages, but February 2002 saw some good news for the Depp family: they were to be joined by a new member. Rumours had been circulating for some time that Vanessa Paradis was pregnant once more. The giveaway came when Paradis pulled out of playing a prostitute in Anne Fontaine's film *Nathalie Ribout*, which was due to shoot that summer. Depp was similarly keeping his schedule clear in anticipation of the arrival of his second child due in the summer of 2002. 'I haven't any film projects until after this summer. I chose to relax and to take care of Vanessa and my daughter Lily-Rose.'

Paradis said of their growing family, 'Of course I want Lily-Rose to have lots of little sisters and brothers. Many.' She added, 'I have a life that I would have never dared dream of. I would have thought I was asking for far too much.'

It wasn't long from the belated public announcement of the pregnancy to the happy day itself. Johnny Depp and Vanessa Paradis celebrated the birth of Jack John Christopher Depp III on April 9th 2002 in a hospital at Neuilly, just outside Paris. Depp's son weighed 7.05 pounds. Joining the tattoo over his heart which reads 'Lily-Rose', Depp added a new one on his right forearm, simply stating 'Jack', just beneath a bird in flight.

Depp described a typical family-oriented day for him: 'It's amazing. I get up and make a bottle of milk up for my son and then breakfast for my girls. Then we wander out into the countryside – we live in the middle of nowhere. We might come back to the house and paint and play in the sand box or on the swings. And in the evening I drink wine, drink coffee and go to sleep. That's my day and I love

Depp managed to steal every scene in which he appeared in Robert Rodriquez' Once Upon A Time in Mexico.

it.' This new family life had given Depp a feeling of equilibrium his life had previously lacked. 'I feel better about everything,' he admitted. 'For many years I was confused about all sorts of things: life, growing up, not knowing what was right or wrong. Now I know because Vanessa and my children have taught me, that the only thing that matters in life is being a good parent. I can't say the darkness has completely gone. It's still there, but I've never been closer to the light then I am these days.'

Depp was prepared to be seriously involved as a father again, having made sure his work commitments remained clear for most of 2002. 'I've been on a break for a long time,' he said. 'I haven't worked since I shot *Once Upon A Time In Mexico* in June last year. And before that, it was the Don Quixote movie. Before that it was *From Hell*. So I've been unemployed for quite a while. It's nice.'

When it came time to think about returning to work, Johnny Depp was not short of offers and opportunities, despite his time away from the screen. He was in contention with Andy Garcia for the part of Simon Bolivar, the man who freed Venezuela and Ecuador from Spanish rule in the nineteenth century, in a biopic. Depp's *Once Upon A Time in Mexico* co-star Salma Hayek was lined up to play Bolivar's wife. The £30 million film of Bolivar's life had the working title *The Vision*. Producer Edgar Meinhardt-Iturbe had spent a decade trying to make a movie about Bolivar and favoured Depp for the part. A source on the movie told online news service Ananova: 'This could be one of the most important films to ever come out of South America, so there is much tension surrounding the production. The person who plays the role also has to be politically acceptable.'

Somewhat closer to Depp's own real-life experiences – and an opportunity for revenge on those who had plagued him over the years – was the part of showbusiness gossip writer A. J. Benza in a movie of his book, *Fame: Ain't it a Bitch*.

Then there was the possibility of returning to directing. Although he'd had a tough time on *The Brave*, Depp's natural inclination to want some degree of control over his projects (usually just expressed through his performance) led him to contemplate getting back behind the camera. One project in particular had piqued his interest. 'I'm preparing a movie whose title is *It Only Rains at Night*. There's a script by Neil Jimenez,' he admitted. This was a project he'd talked about in 1999 when promoting *Sleepy Hollow* and it was obviously still on his mind. In 1992, *Movieline* magazine had listed *It Only Rains at Night* in its Top Ten Unproduced Screenplays feature. Jimenez, who'd written the early Keanu Reeves movie *River's Edge* and wrote and co-directed *The Waterdance,* had crafted a screenplay which was 'an odd mix of Kafka, Jim Jarmusch and a funky, Max Fleischer version of *Who Framed Roger Rabbit*.' The story was about a lonely, bland bachelor who by day beheads society's 'enemies', and by night practices gourmet cooking while listening to old Jack Benny radio shows. He falls in love with the severed head (which can talk) of one of his victims. It's easy to see what might appeal to an actor who'd been directed by Tim Burton in three movies.

'It's one of those projects that development and middle-level [studio] executives just love, but that their bosses think is just too weird,' admitted producer Midge Sanford, who was known as an advocate of edgy material. 'It is weird, wonderful, and with Johnny starring and Neil directing, it will someday make a very special movie.' That day has yet to come…

Hopes that Depp and Paradis would co-star in a movie after their failed attempt with Terry Gilliam were dashed when it was made clear that, despite rumours, Depp would not appear in Paradis' next film, based on Serge Bramly's *Le Reseau Melchior*. Another possible project which was revived and then disappeared again was the Griffin Dunne-directed mob drama *Nailed Right In*. The film gained its financing and Depp was being courted once again to play the small but important role of a mobster who shows the ropes to a couple of wannabe 'wiseguys', much like Pacino did for Depp in *Donnie Brasco*. Depp was reportedly being offered $2 million for a couple of weeks work. As shooting had been due to begin in September 2001 in New York the project had stalled once more in the wake of the World Trade Center terrorist attacks.

Johnny Depp's acceptance of the lead role, as *Peter Pan* author J. M. Barrie, in *Finding Neverland* was the first sign of a new direction for his career, one that would lead him to his biggest film hit in *Pirates of the Caribbean*. With Lily-Rose now two years old, and his newborn son in mind, Depp decided he should make some movies his kids would be able to watch in years to come. In March 2002, just before the birth of Jack Depp, Depp Sr signed to make the Marc (*Monster's Ball*) Forster-directed movie. It was based on Allan Knee's play *The Man Who Was Peter Pan*, an imaginary series of conversations between Barrie and his four young friends, the Llewelyn Davies brothers, who inspired him to write *Peter Pan*. By the time Depp had arrived in London in June 2002 for shooting, he'd also signed up to tackle *Pirates of the Caribbean*. His new family-friendly movie strategy was firmly in place.

Finding Neverland director Marc Forster was looking for 'something magical' to follow *Monster's Ball*, when Academy Award-nominated producer Richard Gladstein brought him David Magee's screenplay. Forster was drawn to the story, which re-imagined the circumstances and the emotions behind the evolution and creation of *Peter Pan*, an archetypal fantasy tale still widely read today.

Inspired by Barrie's real-life friendship with the Llewelyn Davies family, *Finding Neverland* explored the same themes that made Barrie's original play so influential: the power of imagination, the allure of nostalgia for childhood innocence, and the need to believe in something beyond the mundanity of everyday life.

'I saw the film as a story about the power of a man's creativity to take people to another world, and about the deep human need for illusions, dreams and beliefs that inspire us even in the face of tragedy,' explained Forster. 'For me, it is about the transformative power of imagination – being able to transform yourself into something greater than you are, even if nobody believes in you.'

Magee's screenplay was adapted from Allan Knee's stage play, but, according to the screenwriter, it was 'not a factual retelling of what happened to James Barrie when he wrote *Peter Pan*. I wanted to tell a story about what it means to grow up and become responsible for those around you. I hope people see the film as a respectful tribute to Barrie's creative genius and come away with a feeling that as human beings, we can grow up without losing all aspects of childhood innocence and wonder.'

For Magee, the story he was writing became more personally relevant as the process went on. 'My first child was about to be born when I started working on this material, and my father was coming to the end of his life after a long battle with cancer, so I was really thinking intensely about what it means to grow up and to become aware that time really is chasing after all of us,' he elaborated. 'For me, this story is about a man who is starting to face these issues in his own life.'

These themes also resonated with family man Johnny Depp. For Marc Forster, there was never any other choice for the role of J. M. Barrie, despite the fact that *Peter Pan*'s author was Scottish. 'Johnny is perfect to represent a man who never wants to grow up because you can see that he has this very accessible child inside him from the choices of movie roles he makes. He brought something very special to the role, underplaying it in a way that really pays homage to the man we both believe Barrie wanted to be.'

For Depp, *Finding Neverland* was the latest in a series of unconventional choices, yet it would also be a film his kids could relate to. 'The film never seems to go quite where you expect it go,' he said of the unconventional, seemingly chaste romance Barrie enjoys with Sylvia du Maurier, mother of the Llewelyn Davies boys, as played by Kate Winslet (*Titanic*, *Eternal Sunshine of the Spotless Mind*). 'It never turns into a sentimental love story of two people destined to be together, or that sort of thing. Instead, it's a much more complicated and moving relationship between two people who need each other on a level that's really beyond explanation or words.'

Freddie Highmore played Peter, the principal child role in Finding Neverland,
he and Depp developed a deep relationship, both on and off screen.

Most of all, Depp was drawn to the role by the simple and enduring magic of *Peter Pan*. 'It's truly a work of genius,' he noted. 'It's a masterpiece of imagination, and the result of the most remarkable inspiration. It's one of those rare perfect things in the world that will always be with us and this was a wonderful opportunity to explore where such a powerful story might have come from.'

While location shooting took place in and around London during June and July 2002, eager crowds gathered to see Depp at work – particularly at Richmond-Upon-Thames, a suburb 30 minutes to the west of central London. A corner of Richmond Green was dressed as a period location for the film, complete with a couple of vintage cars. Shooting took place at the interior and exterior of Oak House and the Old Palace Terrace, with more substantial filming at the Richmond Theatre, doubling for the Duke of York theatre in London where *Peter Pan* premiered in 1904.

Filming at Hyde Park in central London also drew a large number of curious onlookers. Suitably for a family film, the shooting of *Finding Neverland* became a family event as Depp brought Vanessa, Lily-Rose and Jack along with him, while Kate Winslet had her two-year-old daughter Mia with her.

Winslet and Depp had met for the first time for dinner in London in June, to break the ice. 'In truth, they were in love and did have a form of a relationship together,' she remarked of her role as the young widow who grows close to Barrie. 'But the movie is very much about his relationship with her and, as a consequence, his relationship with her four sons. It's through the relationship he had with these boys and the times they shared together that he was able to conceive of the story of *Peter Pan*.'

'It's a brilliant piece of casting,' she praised Depp's seemingly unlikely role as Barrie, 'because you immediately pull out of the period world and put it in somewhere that is much more kind of edgy and interesting.'

Winslet had played Wendy in a theatre production of *Peter Pan* at the age of fifteen, so she was no stranger to the material that inspired *Finding Neverland*. She found further inspiration in her co-star. 'Johnny was so able to be a child on the set that it was sort of like working with five children for me! He made me and the boys constantly laugh with his cleverness which is exactly what we needed to create the spirit of the story.'

Winslet was also fascinated by her own character. 'Sylvia is such an interesting person, because she's a very modern mother in an era when the view of children was just starting to change. Most people still believed children should be "seen and not heard", and children were typically kept away from the adult life in the household. Sylvia does things differently, and she reflects a change in how children were raised. She's very involved in her children's upbringing and she encourages them to be free spirits. I love the fact that she's such a non-conformist.

'But Sylvia is also a recent widow,' Winslet continued, 'so there's a lot of buried grief and anger in her, and I think that's part of what makes Barrie so intriguing to her. He's this larger-than-life character who couldn't be more different from most of the men she meets in her social circle. She's really magnetically drawn to this man, not because he seduces her, but because he welcomes her into his incredible fantasy world. I do believe at the end of the day, this is a love story, but it's about the love between Barrie and a whole family.'

One worry for Depp was the gentle Scottish accent he'd have to adopt. Never willingly shying away from accents (Irish in *Chocolat*, middle-European in *The Man Who Cried*, Cuban in *Before Night Falls*, cockney in *From Hell*), he struggled to master it himself until, two weeks before principal photography, he called in a voice coach. 'It's the hardest one I've ever had to do,' he told *The Observer* during production, 'but I'm getting there.' Producer Richard Gladstein felt that Depp's adopted accent helped him get to the heart of the role. 'Johnny brings out a natural sense of mystery in his portrayal of Barrie, sparking the audience's curiosity about what's happening in Barrie's mind,' he said.

Also in the cast of *Neverland* were Dustin Hoffman (who'd played Captain Hook in Steven Spielberg's Peter Pan movie, *Hook*, in 1991) as theatrical producer Charles Frohman and Julie Christie as Emma du Maurier, the mother of Kate Winslet's character. Radha Mitchell (*Pitch Black*, *High Art*) played the role of Mary Ansell, Barrie's wife in an unhappy marriage.

Hoffman was drawn to the film by the dual attraction of Forster and Depp. 'I saw *Monster's Ball* and have wanted to work with Marc Forster ever since,' he claimed. 'I also knew that James Barrie was going to be played by Johnny Depp and I think he's one of our greatest young actors. He has a quality that I highly admire – he tries everything in his power not to be a star. He takes chances on the roles he chooses and eludes being a pin-up, despite being so handsome.'

Pivotal to the success of the film was the casting of the four boys who inspire Barrie – particularly Peter Llewelyn Davies. From the beginning, it was clear to the filmmakers that the casting could make or break the film. After extensive auditions, they were able to narrow the search down to a few dozen exceptional young actors. Then, instead of holding individual readings, the filmmakers had groups of boys read together in search of that chemistry – a mix of rivalry and closeness – that occurs between real siblings. 'It was very important that the boys get on together just like a real family, since I wanted very natural performances from them,' recalled Forster. 'The boys we chose are all very special and gifted. Each one came to the set with a rare depth and sensitivity – as well as a sense of fun – which made telling this story so much easier.'

For Depp's part, he did his bit to bring out the mischief hiding just beneath the young actors' professional manners, relying on a favourite old practical joke to break the ice. 'You'd expect that these little boys would be climbing the walls on a movie set, but they had incredible concentration and focus. In fact, sometimes we had to loosen them up,' he claimed. 'For the dinner party scene, for example, Marc and I planned in advance that I could use my fart machine at certain moments. We hid the machine under the table and waited until the boys' close-ups and then I just started nailing them, and it worked like a charm!'

Freddie Highmore played Peter, the principal child role and the one with whom Depp had to develop a deeper relationship, both on and off screen. Despite his youth, Highmore had a tremendous grasp of his role. 'Peter is always thinking about his father and he doesn't think it's right that Barrie should come in and take over,' he noted of his character. 'But then Barrie shows him things he didn't know – like that he can write. Peter isn't really like "Peter Pan" because he's ready to grow up. Actually, I think Barrie's the child who never grew up because he was always taking

the boys off and playing pirates and cowboys and stuff. No matter what he says, Barrie is the real Peter.'

Filming on *Finding Neverland* wrapped at the end of August 2002, allowing Depp and his family to return to France once again. But he was happy to film in Britain. 'It's so good to be working in London again. Living in Paris, London is the nearest place I can work without that Hollywood crap. It's easy for my family to join me and I'm really excited about going up to Scotland for some filming. Maybe we'll stick around up there for a holiday, as Paris is empty in August.'

Scheduled for release several times by distributor Miramax, the film would finally see daylight in the UK on 31 October, 2004 – some two years after it was filmed – followed by a low-key 14 November, 2004 US release. Limited to just eight cinemas, the film initially grossed only $240,956, with distribution widening to 57 cinemas a few days later. It wasn't until the end of November that *Finding Neverland* opened wide in the US, hitting number eight in the box office charts with a take of $4.7 million. By April 2005, it had grossed in excess of $51.5 million in the US, with the UK contributing a further $3.3 million.

The historical liberties taken with the real-life story of J. M. Barrie would become an occasional critical stick with which the film (otherwise very well-received) was beaten. The movie's plot, wrote Manohla Dargis in *The New York Times*, 'hews closer to Disney than Barrie'. Jami Bernard, in *The New York Daily*

Playing opposite Depp in Finding Neverland, Kate Winslet claimed, 'Johnny was so able to be a child on the set that it was sort of like working with five children for me! He made me and the boys constantly laugh.'

171

News, added, 'The movie is so determined to wring laughter and tears – and it succeeds, there's no question – that it makes of Barrie's life a fiction on the order of flying children and pirates with hooks for hands.'

Philip Wuntch in *The Dallas Morning News* gave a warmer response: 'Despite opportunities to turn soft and clammy, the film is moving but not maudlin, whimsical but not cloying.' Most critics would regard Depp's central performance as Oscar-worthy. Michael Wilmington in *The Chicago Tribune* suggested there were few other actors who 'can play a child-man [like Barrie] without seeming effete or precious . . . The absolute ease and empathy with which he plays this part guide us smoothly into the tale's emotional thickets.' The ever-reliable Roger Ebert, in the *Chicago Sun-Times*, wrote that, for Depp, the movie 'is the latest in an extraordinary series of performances . . . It is commonplace for actors to play widely differing roles, but Depp never makes it feel like a reach; all of these notes seem well within his range.'

The film would be garlanded with award nominations, short-listed for seven Oscars: for Art Direction, Costume Design, Editing, Best Music, Best Writing, Best Picture, and Johnny Depp as Best Actor – his second Academy Award nomination. Despite strong lobbying by Miramax, the film ended up with just one Oscar, awarded to Jan A. P. Kaczmarek for Best Achievement in Music Written for Motion Pictures, Original Score. Depp was fated to leave the 2005 Oscar ceremony empty-handed, once more.

In 2002, Johnny Depp made a move that shocked many of his fans by taking the role of Captain Jack Sparrow in the blockbuster movie *Pirates of the Caribbean: Curse of the Black Pearl*. This role would bring him much acclaim and a whole new fan base, yet he took the role for only two reasons: Lily-Rose and Jack.

'My four-year-old Lily-Rose saw me in *Edward Scissorhands* and *Benny & Joon* and she saw the trailer for *Pirates*,' said Depp, 'which she loved. She made me rewind it over and over again, so she could see me dressed as a pirate [laughs]. It's funny but it's never really registered with her that mummy and daddy are actors. She knows that mummy is a singer and now she believes that I'm a pirate. She's absolutely convinced. I couldn't bring myself to tell her that I was only playing a character in a movie. It was obvious in her eyes that a pirate with golden teeth was so much more fascinating than a mere actor, and I didn't want to let her down.'

Depp's desire to star in a movie that his daughter could watch (and one for Jack when he's older) led him to the biggest hit of his career and accusations of having 'sold out' due to that success. 'Johnny told me that selling out was really quite pleasurable,' claimed Terry Gilliam, who still harboured hopes that the success of *Pirates of the Caribbean* would help him kick-start *Don Quixote* once more.

'Isn't it every boy's dream to be a pirate and get away with basically anything?' Depp asked rhetorically. 'Who wouldn't want to play a pirate? When I was first offered the role, I thought it was a joke. Why would Disney [the film was based on a famous Disney theme park ride] want to cast me? I was more shocked than anyone. But ironically while we were making it, it never felt like we were doing a blockbuster on a giant budget. In fact it wasn't until I saw the first trailer that I went, "Oh my God, what's that?" It would be nice to have a hugely successful

film… especially one that you did because you loved doing it. I don't get offered too many.'

The second big attraction was the quality of the script, the basic way that Depp judged most of his film projects. There was no point being a pirate just for the sake of it: Depp wanted to star in a quality pirate movie. The talent behind the camera – Jerry Bruckheimer producing and Gore Verbinski directing – was just as important, as were the writers. 'The mere mention of the names of Ted Elliot and Terry Rossio, who had written *Shrek*, which I had loved, gave me a good feeling right away. I also liked the idea of a pirate film – that's something that hasn't been visited for quite some time. On top of which they were taking that structure and stretching it out. All that was in the screenplay; so that's what did it for me. With Jerry's background and Gore's intense focus, I knew the film had strong shoulders to stand on. When I read Ted and Terry's screenplay, I was pleasantly surprised; they'd exceeded my expectations. They brought a great amount of humour to the story and created building blocks for the actors to elaborate on, to really stretch the character.'

Getting Depp on board in the first place was a huge gamble on behalf of Disney and producer Jerry Bruckheimer. After all, *Pirates of the Caribbean* was designed from the outset to be a blockbuster, and Johnny Depp had gone out of his way to ensure he never became 'blockbuster boy'.

'The way you get an audience to really embrace a movie is to cast against the grain,' said Bruckheimer, explaining his tactics. 'You find someone the audience

Alongside Orlando Bloom, Johnny Depp was to see his career and profile boosted to new commercial heights thanks to Pirates of the Caribbean.

would never expect to see in a Disney movie. I went after Johnny Depp. Johnny is an artist who's known to take on quirkier projects. He's a brilliant actor. He's not out to create a fan base for himself, or to simply select work based on salary; it's clear he needs to find a role that gives back to him artistically. I think he also wanted to do something specifically for his kids.'

It seems that Depp had to wait until he was verging on 40-years-old before he'd feel comfortable taking on such a high profile role. Despite wanting to do the movie for his kids, ironically Depp's character wasn't exactly the kind of guy he'd want his kids to emulate. 'Jack Sparrow is basically a con man – he's lazy,' said Verbinski. 'He's a great pirate, but he is not going to fight if he doesn't have to. He's always going to take a shortcut. I think the big thing for Sparrow is his myth. He's his own best agent – he markets himself very well.'

For Johnny, his character came together during the costume fittings, make-up and hair tests that traditionally take place a few weeks prior to filming. 'The first day I was in full make-up and wardrobe, seeing the guy for the first time, I was very pleased because I knew it was Captain Jack,' he remembered. 'Gore came in, looked and said, "Yeah, that's it." He got it immediately; he knew where I was going with the character. He supported it, he understood it and he got the humour. It was the beginning of a great relationship.'

On his own, Depp had his dentist cap four teeth: one in fourteen-karat gold, one in eighteen-karat gold, another in 22-karat gold, and the last in platinum. 'It's

Depp had tackled movie swordplay before while making Don Juan DeMarco, so the action in Pirates of the Caribbean came easy.

mathematics. He's a pirate. You expect it. I wanted more, but Jerry wasn't particularly enthused,' he admitted. As before, on *The Man Who Cried*, Depp would keep the gold teeth for a considerable time after the movie wrapped. Again, the rationale was his fear of dentists.

Depp's bizarre take on Jack Sparrow was to combine elements of Keith Richards with Warner Bros. cartoon character Pepe Le Pew and even Rastafarian culture. He also set out to walk with a rolling gait, even when on land. 'In preparing any role, I become the victim of my imagination,' he admitted. 'I invariably get a flood of messages. So early on I thought that maybe Captain Jack's brain has been affected by the intense heat of the Caribbean. So I spent a lot of time in my sauna. Living on a ship all the time, his sea legs would be uncomfortable on land – so that's why he sometimes seems on the verge of falling over. But then I thought to myself, the pirates of the eighteenth century… who would they be like in today's world? And it occurred to me… rock stars! Then I asked myself, "Who is the greatest rock and roll star?" and it's Keith Richards of the Stones. So I modelled my character on him and also on the cartoon character Pepe Le Pew, who was always someone able to run between the rain drops. Jack's got little trinkets hanging in his hair, so that was one of the inspirations. I like the idea that each one of these little pieces is a very vivid and extremely important memory for Jack.'

The thick mascara and camp approach may have worked on Verbinski and Bruckheimer, but it didn't go down well with everyone at Disney. 'There were a

'He was wicked,' said Keira Knightley of her more experienced co-star on
Pirates of the Caribbean.

couple of high-end Disney executives who were fine with what I was doing,' recalled Depp, 'but there were a couple who were very worried, like, "He's ruining the movie! Why is he acting like that? What's he doing with his hand? Is the character a complete homosexual?" There was a lot of that going on for a solid month and a half. I understand their worries, but I felt so in tune with this character and so confident that what I was doing was right that I had to say, "Look, I understand your fear. But you've hired me to do a job. You know what I've done before, so you know it's going to be something along these lines. So please trust me. If you can't trust me then you should probably replace me."'

Verbinski thinks Disney may have escaped lightly as some of Depp's earlier ideas were even more extreme. 'Early on, he said: "You know I was thinking that Jack had his nose cut off in a previous sword fight, so he has no nose. He's scared of sneezing because he has a fake nose and it will fall off..." and I was like: "I don't think we're going to sell that one."' The joke got switched to Mackenzie Crook's sidekick pirate character whose false eye keeps falling out and getting lost at inopportune moments.

Depp explained his unusual approach to Jack Sparrow: 'I'm all for playing a character straight if that's what the script calls for. You can't go out there and be totally irresponsible. There's a lot of money on the line, people's careers are riding on it, I understand that. But it's like, "This is my little circle here that I'm standing inside. You're welcome to come in. But if you start fucking with it, you gotta get out!"'

Depp not only managed to deliver a performance that would thrill his young family, but he got to be self-indulgent and mess with the heads of the executives at Disney. In the end the success of the film spoke for itself, but Depp knew the risk that was being taken in having him in the leading role. 'It was a different kind of role for me,' he said, while recognising what the film offered him. 'It was a great opportunity to invent this pirate from the ground up, to create a different kind of pirate than you have seen before.'

For his part, the producer who'd chosen Depp for the role seemed to know what he was getting himself into. 'Johnny's known for creating his own characters,' said Bruckheimer. 'He had a definite vision for Jack Sparrow which is completely unique. We just let him go and he came up with this off-centre, yet very shrewd pirate. He can't quite hold his balance, his speech is a bit slurred, so you assume he's either drunk, seasick or he's been on a ship too long. But it's all an act perpetrated for effect. And strange as it seems, it's also part of Captain Jack's charm.'

While making the movie, for the first time Depp found himself in the unusual role of elder statesman to his younger co-stars, who'd grown up watching the actor in his earlier days. Cast alongside Depp as his side-kicks were Keira Knightley and Orlando Bloom. 'I can't say enough good things about Johnny,' said Knightley, who played Elizabeth. 'It was a dream, it was a pleasure. I mean, he was wicked. Really cool.' *Lord of the Rings* star Bloom agreed: 'Johnny is a wonderful human being. I would go to him for advice on all sorts of things. I felt really privileged to work so closely with somebody who I've admired from afar throughout his career.'

Depp also got to work with Australian actor Geoffrey Rush as the ghostly

Captain Barbossa. Depp and Rush had only a handful of scenes with one another during the six-month shoot, but it was immediately clear from their interaction that there is a long history between Jack Sparrow and Barbossa – and a mutual admiration between the actors. 'Geoffrey's a very interesting actor, a renegade,' said Depp, who recognised a kindred spirit. 'I love his work. He never sticks his neck out in quite the same way. He likes to throw ideas out there and try new things, and so do I. This was just as important as any other truly serious film for Geoffrey; he didn't hold anything back. He's deeply committed, which is one of the reasons I was excited to work with him.'

For his part, Rush was somewhat taken aback by Depp's choices in the way he portrayed his role. 'Jack is probably the pirate that everyone wants to be; he is freewheeling, he is absolutely his own man, he's hilarious – he's like Johnny,' commented Rush. 'It was extraordinary to watch Johnny create this character. It was such a cool performance, very masterfully done. He is a brilliant actor.'

To maximise authenticity in the film, all of the actors playing pirates and some playing British naval officers spent weeks training with stunt co-ordinator George Marshall Ruge and his sword masters, Robert Anderson and Mark Ivie. Having starred in *Don Juan DeMarco* several years earlier, Depp had already received some training in the art of fencing. 'I remembered the fencing I'd done as a total body workout,' recalled Depp. 'It's a beautiful sport, very balletic and precise. On

Depp's bizarre take on Jack Sparrow was to combine elements of Keith Richards with Warner Bros. cartoon character Pepe Le Pew and even Rastafarian culture.

this film, the sword work, putting the "oomph" into the attack, was much more involved. It was a lot more work and more moves to learn. Some of the fights felt like they lasted ten minutes. It was all about the choreography in those scenes, the words came later.'

As well as the sword play, stunt work involving Depp also got very complicated. Stealing the British naval ship Interceptor became much more complex when Verbinski decided Jack Sparrow should be at the wheel, captaining the ship, while Will (Bloom) hoisted and trimmed the sails. Unfortunately, the actors had no clue how to do any of these things. Verbinski yelled across to the Lady Washington crew who were actually sailing the Interceptor to duck and hide so that only the two actors were visible on deck as the two ships passed one another. 'The cameras were rolling, next thing I know the captain disappears and it was just me by the ship's wheel, so I had to grab it,' remembered Depp. 'No-one told me I'd be steering the ship. It was trial by fire. On the second take, I thought we were going to hit the Dauntless barge, and then Gore says to me, "Johnny, come closer, bring the boat closer." I thought, "Oh man, I just steered a massive ship for the first time at what felt like breakneck speed! Come closer?" But we survived.'

There were other trials for the lead actor in the fast-paced production. 'Attempting to swim fully clothed in pirate gear with boots strapped to your legs was

'Johnny's known for creating his own characters,' said Pirates of the Caribbean producer Bruckheimer. 'He had a definite vision for Jack Sparrow which is completely unique.'

more difficult than I'd imagined,' pointed out Depp. 'The stunt work on this film was infinitely more intense than other stunts I've done, and I was dragged on the ground for blocks by a team of horses in *Sleepy Hollow*! Luckily I had a great stunt double in Tony Angelotti who took care of me and made me look good. I just stepped in and made faces. Like pirates, I don't work for the money or treasure, but for the adventure and pleasure.'

When shooting wrapped, Depp's weird pirate ride was not over, as he discovered when he arrived in Los Angeles for the premiere of the film. 'The premiere felt like being pushed into an alien space craft,' he said of the massive event run by Disney. 'I'd never seen anything like that in my life. I was very shocked regarding the film's box-office success, too. It's not something I'm used to and I was very touched that people liked it so much. I figure I might as well enjoy the ride while I'm on it.'

Pirates of the Caribbean: The Curse of the Black Pearl turned out to be Johnny Depp's biggest film yet. At the US box office the film took three times as much as *Sleepy Hollow*, previously his most commercially successful film. A US cumulative total of $305.5 million confirmed its status as a genuine blockbuster (right up there with Disney's *Finding Nemo*, also released to great business that same summer) and the overseas earning of another $349 million just served to confirm that Jack Sparrow was popular, no matter the language.

Released on July 9th 2003, critics were enchanted by Depp's performance in *Pirates of the Caribbean: The Curse of the Black Pearl*, giving it a generous overall endorsement. Roger Ebert in *The Chicago Sun-Times*, said, 'the movie made me grin, and savor the daffy plot, and enjoy the way Depp fearlessly provides a performance that seems nourished by deep wells of nuttiness.' Similarly, Lou Lumenick concluded in *The New York Post*: 'Trimming half an hour from this bloated, 143-minute blockbuster would have highlighted the film's treasures, not the least of which is Johnny Depp's endearingly eccentric performance.' Elvis Mitchell in *The New York Times* called Depp's comic performance a 'balm, an antidote to the raucous battles and swashbuckling.' Geoff Pevere in *The Toronto Star* concluded that 'it says something about the sheer perversity of Depp's counterclockwise turn that he's the movie's only unsinkable treasure.' Ann Hornaday in *The Washington Post* agreed: 'Depp is the single best reason to see *Pirates of the Caribbean* if you're past the age of ten.'

Several weeks before the release of *Pirates of the Caribbean*, Johnny Depp celebrated his fortieth birthday on 9 June 2003, with 'a couple bottles of wine – very calm. By the time you're in your late thirties, you're ready for it.'

The locals in the little French town where Depp lives know him as a doting 'papa poule' (father hen), which is just the way he likes it. 'Kiddies should grow up in a very simple, calm environment, where everything is not about the next movie,' he told ABC's Elizabeth Vargas.

Now he could even look ahead another ten years and contemplate turning 50, something that might not have seemed feasible to his twentysomething, hotel-trashing self. 'You know, it might be nice to sort of drop off [the radar] at some point and just go and write a book or paint,' he said, suggesting that acting might

recede into the background for him. 'I'm not totally sure that in ten or fifteen years I'll still be acting. Maybe I'd rather sit at home and be daddy, and make paintings with my daughter. I'll do anything to make my family's life good. If this all evaporates and I gotta go back to work pumping gas, I'll do it. I'll be OK.'

But there was little prospect of hitting the gas stations yet. Award givers were lining up to bestow nominations on Depp for his exuberant turn as Jack Sparrow. Depp won the Screen Actor's Guild Best Actor Award 2004, following a shock nomination for him as Captain Jack Sparrow. That was followed by an Academy Award nomination for Best Actor in a Motion Picture, a BAFTA nomination for Best Actor, a Golden Globes nomination for Best Actor in a Musical/Comedy, a Golden Satellite nomination for Best Actor in a Comedy/Musical, and the Online Film Critics Society nomination for Best Actor.

Depp also found himself the recipient of *People Magazine*'s Sexiest Man of 2003 award. Julie Jordan of *People Magazine* said: 'Johnny Depp was the perfect guy. He's often chosen obscure roles over the years. *Pirates of the Caribbean* put him right back into the mainstream's embrace, sexier than ever.'

The most important of all the awards and nominations that came Depp's way was his Oscar nomination for Best Actor. Johnny Depp and the Oscars seemed like an unlikely combination, not least in the eyes of the actor himself. 'I don't think I'm a particular favourite in the eyes of the Academy,' he'd said around the time of

Johnny and Vanessa arriving at the 76th Annual Academy Awards, where Depp was nominated for Best Actor in his role as Jack Sparrow in the Pirates of the Caribbean.

Chocolat's five Oscar nominations, including for Best Picture. 'I think there are guarantees for getting nominations. You have to take the most tragic Hallmark card, adapt it into a screenplay, bawl your eyes out constantly, do a bunch of clichéd turns and bing, you're in. I don't want to demean anybody. People are out there doing great work, and they get nominated and they win these awards based on the work that they've done. It's great for someone to be recognised for their work. But this whole award thing is really weird. When I did *Donnie Brasco*, I thought Pacino was as good or greater than he'd ever been. I was blown away by his performance, his subtleties, and his work in general. And he didn't get an Academy Award nomination.'

Nonetheless, come February 2004, there was Johnny Depp, nominee for Best Actor for the role of Jack Sparrow. Depp had been to the Oscars once before and it had not been a pleasant experience. 'They'd been asking me for a couple of years to come and present. I was really uncomfortable with the idea. I'm not very good at public speaking and I didn't want to make a complete fool of myself. But somehow I agreed because I was going to be introducing Neil Young.' Depp, however, wasn't prepared for how weird the Oscars could be. 'Really, really famous people were coming up and saying, "Hi, Johnny, how you doing? How've you been?" I'd never met them before. It was so weird. And then they wanted me to read this endless speech about the importance of music in film, and I thought, they don't want to hear this shit from me. They're waiting for Neil Young to sing his song. So I just said two sentences, and then I said, "Please welcome Neil Young." Then I left immediately. All in all, it was an awful experience.'

Several years later he was back, and in line to potentially pick up an Oscar himself. Depp had beaten friend and rival Sean Penn (the co-owner of the Man Ray restaurant in Paris) to the Golden Globe for Outstanding Male Actor. Others nominated included Peter Dinklage (*The Station Agent*), Ben Kingsley (*The House of Sand and Fog*) and Bill Murray (*Lost in Translation*). The Oscar list was very similar, with Depp up against Penn (again for *Mystic River*), Ben Kingsley (*The House of Sand and Fog*), Jude Law (*Cold Mountain*) and Bill Murray (*Lost in Translation*). This time around it was Penn who walked off with the golden statue, but Depp was as happy to have been nominated and recognised, as he would have been to receive the statuette itself.

When all the fuss was over, Depp credited those he really thought were responsible for his performance as Jack Sparrow: his kids, who'd inspired him to take the role in the first place. 'I could never have gotten the character right if I didn't have children of my own,' said Depp of four-year-old Lily-Rose and Jack, then nearly two. 'For a good four years, my daughter and I have been watching every single Disney animated film and after ten times, twenty times, 50 times, as an actor, I'm thinking, "What freedom these characters have." Because they're animated, we don't question it. So, going into *Pirates,* I thought, "Why not?" The goal was to create a character that five-year-olds could get into as well as the most jaded, hard-core intellectual. Keep it in that arena of the cartoon, but be believable in the arena of film.' It's clear from the reaction of the critics and the audiences worldwide who fuelled the box office that Depp had succeeded admirably in his goal.

CHAPTER NINE

Unfinished Business

Johnny Depp's low-key movie *Secret Window* began life as a Stephen King novella entitled 'Secret Window, Secret Garden' – part of King's collection of four spooky novellas called *Four Past Midnight*. Writer and director David Koepp (who'd written the blockbuster *Spider-Man* and David Fincher's *Panic Room*) had previously directed supernatural thriller *Stir of Echoes*, and he saw elements of that haunting tale in King's work. 'I like "guy-in-a-house-going-crazy" movies,' admitted Koepp. 'I enjoy the challenge of working out a story that takes place in a confined space. Even though there are some outdoor scenes, the story is really about Mort Rainey's [Depp's] living space. It's about somebody who's in a really bad place in his life where he is just spending way too much time alone at home. I wanted to explore the confinement and paranoia themes. Confinement can be really scary, and having bad things happen in your living space can be truly unsettling.'

It took a special film project to coax Depp away from his French family idyll. 'What I remember most was reading the screenplay,' said Depp of first encountering *Secret Window*. 'I got ten-to-fifteen pages into it and thought, "Wow, this is incredibly well-written. The dialogue is real and not forced, with an interesting train-of-thought quality to it." The situations felt true. As I kept reading, I got to the point where I was totally invested emotionally in Mort and his dilemma. And then, when I got to the ingenious plot twist, I was completely shocked. I really didn't see it coming, which is very satisfying for a reader and I knew it would be for audiences as well.'

Koepp was keen that Depp take the role of Mort Rainey, a successful author undergoing a divorce and suffering from writer's block who's confronted by John Shooter who claims Rainey has stolen his work. It's every writer's nightmare and one that King had explored several times before, notably in *Misery*. Koepp wrote the screenplay with Depp in mind with no guarantee that the actor would be interested in the role. 'Johnny sort of popped into my head midway through the first draft, and he wouldn't leave,' said Koepp, 'but the more I thought about him, the more it made sense.'

To woo Depp for the part, Koepp wrote him a letter and even trekked to the location filming for *Pirates of the Caribbean* to persuade the actor personally. 'I wrote that I was hoping to cast him in *Secret Window*, that he was the guy I thought about when creating this character. He's one of our great actors, so inventive and so different every time.'

For his part, Depp was impressed that Koepp would go to the lengths of travelling to see him. 'He is very meticulous and he draws us in by finding little moments of truth and behaviour that people recognise and identify with,' said Koepp of Depp. 'Therefore, they ultimately identify with the character. His choices are spontaneous and often unconventional, but they always work. He is also a completely fearless actor. In terms of this character, it's rare to find a movie star who is as unafraid as Johnny is to play fear. Needless to say, I was thrilled when he agreed to take the part.'

Depp was prepared for playing the part of a tortured author, having already essayed Hunter S. Thompson and researched J. M. Barrie for his role in *Neverland*. Hanging out with Thompson had also given him some insight into the creative process of writing. 'I think for anyone in the creative arts, but especially for a writer, your imagination is your best friend,' said Depp. 'It can also be your worst enemy if you are plagued by too much thought, an overload of information in your head. That's Mort's problem. He's definitely a recluse. He's uncomfortable around people and just wants to be left alone. Unfortunately, he can't leave himself alone.' Depp made sure that a volume of Hunter S. Thompson's work appeared among Rainey's books in the cabin to which he'd retreated.

'It's always great to get in the ring with actors you respect,' Depp said, addressing the challenge of acting alone in much of *Secret Window*. 'But when you're in there by yourself, it's quite challenging. You're not reacting, which is mostly what acting is. Instead, you just have to "be". There are scenes where it's like two minutes of just scratching the tablecloth. That interests me.'

As with *Pirates of the Caribbean*, Depp was inspired by a rock star in his characterisation of Mort Rainey. 'I remember hearing famous stories, or maybe myths, about Brian Wilson in his very reclusive period where he didn't leave his house. That was the level of reclusiveness I was looking for.'

Cast as the menacing John Shooter was John Turturro, who'd played opposite Depp before in *The Man Who Cried*. In Turturro's case, it was his thirteen-year-old son, a huge Stephen King fan, who persuaded him to sign up to the movie. Working with Depp again was also a big plus point for Turturro. 'Johnny is very easy to work with and very generous,' he said of the film's star. 'There is a real ease to his performance style. David Koepp gave us a lot of room to do our thing, and anything you throw at Johnny, he quickly catches and tosses back at you. He's very intuitive and inventive. As a performer, it's a big advantage to enjoy a common comfort zone with a fellow actor. We definitely had that. Johnny also has a great sense of humour. We enjoy some common interests and we've worked with directors with similar sensibilities. I've always enjoyed his performances and was happy to have the chance to work with him again.'

Mort's estranged wife Amy was played by *ER*'s Maria Bello, who was also happy to be playing opposite an actor she'd admired from afar. 'I've always loved Johnny's choices as an actor. The layers he brought to Mort, the levels he achieved, were fascinating and inspiring.' Rounding out the main cast was Oscar-winner Timothy

Hutton as Amy's new love, Ted, and Charles S. Dutton as doomed New York Detective Ken Karsch.

As was now usual for Depp on every movie, he came armed with a host of character suggestions, some of which would prove useful, others which would be discarded pretty quickly. However, it was an approach Koepp appreciated, even if every idea wasn't always used. 'He comes to the set with great ideas,' said Koepp of Depp, 'and they're not what you expect. At first, you think he's kidding. Then you say, "Let me think about it." That's what makes his characters accessible.' On *Secret Window*, Depp suggested that Mort wear teeth braces throughout the movie. Koepp thought that would be too much, but used the idea in the film's final sequences after Mort appears to have escaped the consequences of his actions.

'Here's my favourite,' Koepp said. 'The script has fourteen pages of phone calls. That's dull. You have to find new ways to do it. There's a phone call with Charles Dutton [the detective], and I was out of ideas. Depp said, "Well, my character has just driven up from New York. I've been in the car a long time, I've got to pee."' In the finished scene, Depp grabs the phone, takes it into the bathroom and does his business as the camera cuts back and forth between him and Dutton, relaxing in a motel room half dressed.

During the making of the movie, Koepp was determined to have his actors play their roles and reactions to events as 'real' as possible, even to the extent of isolating Bello and Hutton in a motel room set and having Depp unexpectedly burst in on them with a blast of out-of-context music. Shooting the movie's opening sequence, which recurs as flashback throughout the film, Bello recalled: 'We weren't sure when Johnny was going to come through the door. So, when the door burst open and this crazy loud music came on, we freaked. It was so real we couldn't help but react. David gave us so much to work with. He really let us play and explore. He and Johnny really set such a nice tone on the set.'

Depp has worked on some chaotic film sets and several films that were so badly organised they failed to be completed. In David Koepp he had a director who was meticulous in his preparation and planning. Koepp storyboarded every scene in great detail and like Stanley Kubrick; he had all the storyboards for each day's work pinned to a large board on the studio floor so everyone had a clear idea of what was being shot. As each shot was completed, the storyboard was struck through. Koepp and his cinematographer Fred Murphy watched some classic suspense thrillers in preparation including Roman Polanski's *Rosemary's Baby* and *The Tenant* and John Boorman's *Deliverance*. Taking a cue from the latter film, Murphy opted to shoot *Secret Window* in the wide screen Super 35 format, an interesting choice for a movie that is about confined spaces and the inner workings of the mind. 'Much of the movie is very interior, but Fred opened it up by including multiple reflections,' said Koepp. 'This is really a mirror movie. Fred said he's never had as many mirrors in a film. Because it is about reflection – looking at yourself and seeing things you may not like – mirrors are a major element, particularly the large one over Mort's fireplace. A mirror also makes the set look bigger, providing for some interesting shots.' Another approach was to bathe Mort's memories of his previous life with Amy in a sunshine glow with brighter, more cheerful colours in bold contrast to the drab hues that pervade his life after their break-up.

Costume designer Odette Gadoury found Depp to be a willing collaborator in her plans to bring out Mort Rainey's character. 'We tried to keep Mort's colours mid-tone, the kind of range that was very strong at some point, but faded down as if it had been exposed to the sun. We took colours like burgundy, brown and blue and aged the wardrobe to make them appear almost smoky. For me, Mort is lost – he's a kind of shadow. He's in a kind of Twilight Zone and we wanted his wardrobe to reflect that. Everything he wears is loose and wrinkled and washed out – not too bright, not too dark. By comparison, his character in flashback is dressed in more colourful, brighter apparel. The overall effect is to make him seem even more vulnerable in the present.' Her conversations with Depp resulted in Mort's signature costume: a tattered, striped bathrobe. 'That was Johnny's idea. I had long talks with both David and Johnny about it. At the first fitting in New York, I had a real one from a costume shop that Johnny fell in love with.'

Secret Window was shot from July to November 2003. The cast and crew spent three weeks shooting interior and exterior scenes at a tranquil, rustic resort in Quebec known as Sacacomie, where Mort's cabin is situated on the banks of the fictitious Tashmore Lake. Nestled amidst a rambling forest of pine and maple trees, abutting the majestic Lake Sacacomie, the resort offered the appropriate topography for Mort's lakeside retreat and a pastoral lodge in which to house the crew and ad-hoc production office. What it lacked, however, was Mort's cabin, which was designed and constructed by production designer Howard Cummings and his team. The production also filmed in several Quebec locations, including the town of North Hatley, which provided a view of Lake Massawippi from the small police station set that Cummings sandwiched in between the town's quaint restaurant, gift shop and clapboard drugstore. Lake Massawippi, along with Lake Sacacomie and Lake Gale – a green lagoon full of frogs in the village of Bromont – were merged for the production to become Stephen King's Tashmore Lake.

Depp played both Mort and 'the inner Mort', which meant that he had to separately film both parts, essentially acting opposite himself, a dramatic first for the actor. A wall of green screen enveloped the entire set and the camera, serving as Mort's inner voice, circled Depp as he reacted to 'himself'. Later, Depp replaced the camera, taking on the other part of Mort's secret self. 'First you see him talking to his dog,' explained Koepp, 'then you hear his thoughts and then you literally see him talking to himself. I think it's when he starts answering himself [in the car] that you're thinking that maybe something's not quite right here.'

Mort's inner voice bedevils him from various points around the cabin. Those points were marked by orange circles placed at the edge of poles for Depp's eyeline. Depp brought character to his marks by drawing smiley faces on them. 'In those kinds of situations, the level of absurdity is so high that it becomes a challenge – a grown man standing in the middle of a circle screaming at an orange face. It doesn't get much weirder than that. It's bizarre, but also a fun obstacle. You just put yourself in his situation and go with it. The idea is that this pushes Mort to a place where a light goes out for him and that part of him is completely in the dark,' Depp sums up. 'When he blacks out, though, another light comes on somewhere else.'

Koepp depicted the extent of Mort's dissociation in what came to be known as 'The Magritte Shot', inspired by a painting by the famous Surrealist artist. In the

As Mort Rainey in Secret Window, Depp tackled the role of a blocked writer who battles his inner demons.

painting, the viewer sees a man looking into a mirror, but instead of his reflection, the viewer sees the back of his head. Executing the shot with Depp required the intricate timing of two cameras filming him in front of the mirror – with the glass replaced by a green screen. One camera was devoted to Depp and the other served as the 'reflection camera'. The latter had to be bigger and faster to compensate for movement and perspective.

Secret Window recalls movies like A Beautiful Mind and Fight Club, especially with the climatic revelations about the true nature of John Shooter and the unmasking of Depp's Rainey as the real villain of the piece. Call your main character 'Mort' [French for death] and you're giving the game away. Living on a diet of Doritos and Mountain Dew, and seemingly sporting Tim Burton's birdnest hair, Depp's Rainey is an engaging, sympathetic character with echoes of his roles in Edward Scissorhands and Benny & Joon in his scatty performance. The twist ending should be obvious to any regular cinemagoer and Secret Window has little to add to the split-personality movie, but it is engaging nonetheless, succeeding almost solely on the basis of Johnny Depp's performance.

After the success of Pirates of the Caribbean and Depp's Oscar nomination, the release date of Secret Window was brought forward from April 23rd to March 12th 2004 in order to ride the wave of Depp's new-found popularity. The actor received strong notices for his role, continuing the critical acclaim he now seemed to receive, no matter what the film. 'Johnny Depp has emerged as the world's coolest actor,' commented John Anderson in Newsday. Roger Ebert in The Chicago Sun-Times wrote, 'he brings a musing eccentricity to an otherwise straightforward role…' Megan Lehmann in The New York Post called his performance 'witty and inventive' and noted that the movie 'leaned heavily on Depp's eccentric charm, as the actor is alone on-screen for much of the film.' The film itself received mixed notices. Elvis Mitchell in The New York Times commented that Depp's performance was 'the highlight of the underwhelming Secret Window… a suspense thriller whose only suspense comes from an audience wondering if the picture will hit its promised 97-minute running time.'

Despite these mixed responses, Secret Window opened at the number two slot with a take of $18.2 million, second only to the phenomenon of Mel Gibson's The Passion of the Christ which on its third week of release took a whopping $32 million.

Around the time Secret Window was released in the US, regulars in a Welsh pub were surprised to spot Johnny Depp in their midst. Despite trying to blend in on his evening visit to the bar in the Bear Hotel in the village of Crickhowell, Wales, Depp was instantly recognised and then surprised everyone by picking up the drinks tab for the entire bar.

Depp had been filming The Libertine in Britain since February 2004, starring opposite John Malkovich and Samantha Morton (Minority Report). The Libertine was a seventeenth century-set tale based on the true story of John Wilmot, the Earl of Rochester: poet, courtier and notorious rake. Naturally, that was the role Depp was playing. Adapted by Stephen Jeffreys from his own play, The Libertine marked the movie debut of British commercials director Laurence Dunmore. After a couple of high profile, high budget movies, Depp was returning once again to independent

film-making. The entire $20 million budget of *The Libertine* was close to Depp's personal asking price for a Hollywood blockbuster like the *Pirates of the Caribbean* sequel to which he was by now committed.

Samuel Johnson described the real-life Earl of Rochester as having 'contempt of decency and order, a total disregard to every moral and a resolute denial of every religious observation. He lived worthless and useless and blazed out his youth and health in lavish voluptuousness.' The Earl was a confidant of King Charles II (Malkovich) and his undoing, as well as his death at 33, came after he found himself smitten with failing actress Elizabeth Barry (Morton). Malkovich himself had previously portrayed the Earl when his Steppenwolf Theater Co. in Chicago staged the play in 1996. When his producing partners Russell Smith and Lianne Halfon highlighted the big screen potential of the play, Malkovich earmarked Depp as the ideal Earl of Rochester. According to *Variety*, Depp was keen to take on the part, but the project got tied up in eight years of struggles to attract solid financing. 'It was one of those rare occurrences where you read a script and you think, "This is great!",' Depp told *Empire* magazine. 'Three sentences into the opening monologue and I was in. I knew it was one of those things, the kind of material that you see just once. *Edward Scissorhands* was like that for me.' Not only was *The Libertine* a period piece, always an expensive prospect, but the draft script didn't soft-peddle the Earl's prodigious sexual appetites. *The Libertine* faced a restrictive

Depp treated Mort Rainey's dressing gown as a major prop in Secret Window, one which allowed him to get a handle on his character.

NC-17 rating in the US if the script was fully realised. Producer Russell Smith told *Daily Variety*: 'It's clearly something that will be a question. No doubt about it.'

Depp was sanguine about tackling such a role. 'It's very easy for the take on Rochester to be that he was a pig, a drunk, a randy, psychotic madman. But there are a million things to like about him and that's the beauty of it. You know, I'm amazed that the majority [of people] don't know who he is. If people do know him, they go, "Oh, yeah, he wrote the bits about 'pussy' and 'cocks'," or "He made fun of the King with these witty little satires." But man, he was very profound, it's amazing stuff. I'm amazed the Marquis de Sade got more action, you know? This guy has been kept in the dark too long. Rochester was like the first punk!'

Of course, Depp himself had known something of the lifestyle which was attributed to Rochester. Perhaps not the sexual excess, but drink and drugs were prominent in the actor's past, giving him some insight into the role he was playing in *The Libertine*. 'Back in those days, I'd go to functions and I literally had to be drunk to be able to speak and get through it,' Depp candidly admitted to *Empire*. 'I guess I was trying not to feel anything. My drug of choice back then was alcohol more than anything. Hard liquor, spirits. And yeah, I had a keen idea that it was not good. But you get liquored up and once you are in that spiral you don't even get hangovers any more. You wake up and have a drink again…'

The film's financing was thrown into doubt when in the 2004 national budget the UK Government unexpectedly closed tax loopholes which the production was intending to take advantage of. By April, the production was forced to relocate off-shore to the Isle of Man which offered a 25 per cent tax break for productions filming there, making up for the loss as a result of the Government's action. Locations there doubled for Hampton Court in the story. 'With a bit of smoke swirling all around us, hopefully you'll never know the difference,' hoped Depp. 'It's all smoke and mirrors.'

'We were in trouble for those ten or twelve days,' Malkovich recalled. 'We were trying everything. At one stage someone at the Inland Revenue said they were still discussing things. It was a big blow because we've been working on this film for seven years. To get someone like Johnny to do it takes a long time, for example, and it's not an easy film to get financed because, to be blunt about it, it's not retarded. As the French say, this fell like a hair in our soup.'

The only problem for the film's stars arriving in the Isle of Man to continue the filming was that luxury hotel rooms were scarce, as the island had no five-star hotels and the best four-star room had already been claimed by Malkovich. He was already in the capital, Douglas, shooting *Colour Me Kubrick*. Depp arrived to find Malkovich already ensconced in the Hilton's King Suite.

Depp's surprise appearance in that Welsh pub, when he was filming on location for *The Libertine*, wasn't the actor's only encounter with the public on his latest trip to Britain. Earlier, while filming in the Oceana Nightclub in Kingston-Upon-Thames, he attracted the attention of a pair of particularly devoted fans who tried to gain entry to the closed set. According to Britain's *Daily Star* tabloid, quoting 'an insider': 'These two girls were very persistent and desperate to get near Johnny. We told them that he wasn't there – but they wouldn't take no for an answer. We had to remove them twice from the set and once we were even forced to chase them from make-up. Security eventually had to corner them in the Venetian ballroom section of the club and forcibly remove them. You can't have a star of Johnny's size being bothered by crazy women running around the set.'

While filming in Wales, Depp and Vanessa Paradis had stayed at the Llangoed Hall Hotel, near Brecon. Bernard Ashley, the husband of the late fashion designer Laura, said Depp, his wife, their security and the film's co-star John Malkovich, all stayed at Llangoed Hall. He described them all as 'charming', adding that they worked a 'heavy' schedule, often returning late after a hectic day's filming. 'They sometimes didn't return until 10 at night so we kept our chef on to cook for them,' said Ian Miles, general manager. 'Mr. Depp and his family were with us for about eight days. They were model guests and had a great rapport with our staff – they were great communicators.'

That didn't stop more persistent fans tracking down Depp, even out in deepest Wales. Emily Hinshelwood, 37, travelled from Ammanford to see Depp on set at Tretower, near Crickhowell, Powys. 'I'd been there from 10.30am,' the mother-of-two told *The Western Mail*. 'The locals had been told that Johnny would sign autographs as a way of saying thanks for their hospitality. We waited while he removed his costume and then at about 8pm we saw him emerge from his trailer. Some women who had come to see him screamed.' Ms Hinshelwood, a self-described poet, added, 'I'd written him a poem and I passed it to him and he kissed me. He said "hello" and signed an autograph for me. He seemed so gentle and calm and quite relaxed. It was absolutely freezing outside, but we were all so desperate to see Johnny.' *Pirates of the Caribbean* had a lot to answer for...

As well as working once again with Jack Davenport, from *Pirates of the Caribbean*, Depp encountered one of his most unlikely co-stars to date, in the rotund form of British comedian Johnny Vegas. Known for his drunken slob image, it's easy to see how Vegas would fit into *The Libertine*. But Johnny Vegas, from St Helens in Lancashire, claimed to be disappointed when he met the more famous Johnny from Kentucky: 'I wanted him to open his mouth and talk with some huge speech impediment or something,' joked Vegas. 'It's frustrating – he's as cool and genuine as he comes across.'

Despite the problems encountered in making *The Libertine*, and the fact that the low-budget film would be of limited appeal to a mass audience, producer and co-star John Malkovich remained upbeat, yet realistic about the film's chances when Miramax eventually decide to release it: 'I think it's an awfully good script, and we have a lot of very talented people involved. But will it be successful? That you never know. You just hope for the best.'

Following a September 2004 screening in Canada at the Toronto Film Festival, *The Libertine* opened in the UK on 17 November 2005, cashing in on the recent Johnny Depp publicity from *Charlie and the Chocolate Factory* and *Corpse Bride*. *The Libertine* took an opening weekend gross of £278,482 on just 203 screens across the country. Three weeks later the film had grossed in excess of £630,000, far less than most Johnny Depp-starring films would earn, but not bad for a low budget art house movie. Following limited engagements (in the hope of some Oscar attention for the film and star) in New York and Los Angeles from 25 November, *The Libertine* was finally granted a wider US release in March 2006. Against expectations, the film enjoyed an opening weekend gross of $2.2 million, reaching $4.8 million within a month. Hardly blockbuster business but not bad for such a controversial art movie.

In *Sight & Sound*, Kevin Maher called *The Libertine* 'Restoration-era intrigue... with Depp playing a role that boldly announces from the outset, "I do not want you to like me." Depp has difficulty fulfilling this remit, and instead tackles Rochester's disparate dramas with galumphing rock-star swagger.... The actor's off-screen legend bleeds neatly into the character.... Director Laurence Dunmore has an admirable sense of style.' Other British reviews were not so kind. Peter Bradshaw in *The Guardian* called the film an 'overripe, over-long study of Rochester in his grisly pomp,' and dubbed Depp's portrayal as 'an essentially humourless character. All the cliches – alehouses, cackling whores and their sweaty, candlelit embonpoints, are present and correct.'

US reviews were also mixed, proving that *The Libertine* was a love-it or hate-it prospect, with little middle ground. Peter Travers, in *Rolling Stone*, wrote: 'You have to admire an actor who finds time between the family franchises of *Charlie and the Chocolate Factory* and *Pirates of the Caribbean* to sandwich in the role of the dazzlingly debauched John Wilmot. This one-of-a-kind spellbinder from first-time director Laurence Dunmore is not afraid to shock. Depp is a raunchy wonder, especially in a time-capsule-worthy opening monologue.' Michael Atkinson, in the *Village Voice*, described *The Libertine* as 'the cheesed-up life and times of the Second Earl of Rochester... Depp hardly seems motivated [and] despite the sniffly closure, his fate registers as less than a tragedy.' Showbiz 'bible' *Variety* had *The Libertine* pegged as 'starting out seductive but ending up tiresome. The onus [is] on Depp to keep viewers on his character's side. Depp's solution is to camp it up royally, playing the part with a satanic twinkle in his eye and a swagger in his step, like some Restoration rock star. [His] performance is almost a Mick Jagger-ish companion piece to his Keith Richards-like one in *Pirates of the Caribbean*. As usual, Depp gets the accent note-perfect and has star wattage to burn, but the character remains a cipher right up to the sordid, drawn-out ending.'

Before returning as Jack Sparrow for the first *Pirates of the Caribbean* sequel, Johnny Depp found the time to make his fourth film with Tim Burton: *Charlie and the Chocolate Factory*. This non-musical adaptation of the Roald Dahl children's novel was to be the first project produced by Plan B, a company set up by Brad Pitt and Jennifer Aniston. The colourful 1971 film version of the novel had starred Gene Wilder as the flamboyant Willy Wonka, into whose multi-coloured attire Depp was to step. 'You'll never escape that memory that's seared into your consciousness of Gene Wilder as Willy Wonka,' admitted Depp. 'It was really amazing to watch as a kid growing up, and I've watched it with my kids. So it's just, "Okay, where do I go from there?" Gene Wilder did something very beautiful and it's time to take it somewhere else.'

John August, screenwriter of Burton's *Big Fish*, scripted the new version of *Chocolate Factory*. Burton chose Depp over other actors he'd also worked with several times, like Michael Keaton (*Beetlejuice, Batman, Batman Returns*), because 'he's always surprising and funny and right now he's a big star.' The

director also knew that remaking such a well-loved film was going to be a tricky proposition, no matter who starred. 'I don't want to crush people's childhood dreams,' he told the *Chicago Sun-Times*, 'but the original film is sappy. It's sappy when it shouldn't be sappy and it's weird. Let's just say it's not one of my personal favourites. I'd rate *Chitty Chitty Bang Bang* much higher. I responded to the book because it respected that children can be adults, and I think adults forget that. There can be darkness and foreboding. Very sinister things are very much a part of childhood. I like that sort of humour and emotion put together.'

Depp was clear about his role in the film. 'I have big shoes to fill,' he told MTV. 'Gene Wilder did such an awesome job in that film in the early 1970s. Taking that character of Willy Wonka and going somewhere completely different is infinitely more difficult for me.'

Burton was relying on his star to give his version of *Chocolate Factory* a unique sensibility. 'I think just having Johnny in the film gives it a different spin, but I've got a few ideas up my sleeve, too. I love working with him…. He always surprises me. I like these kind of actors who don't care how they look. They're just willing, and there's a freedom to that and an excitement that I get from that. Some people are like, "Wait, my light's not right," or "I'm not coming out of my trailer until this happens or that." People like Depp are people ready to go.'

Depp was certainly ready to go on *Chocolate Factory* – but only once he

*Johnny Depp's role as Willy Wonka in Charlie and the Chocolate Factory marks his
fourth collaboration with director Tim Burton.*

considered his trailer up to scratch, ironically. The actor already had the largest trailer on the lot, but he found his surroundings rather too antiseptic. So he requested that all the fixtures and fittings be replaced with silk and satin drapes, according to a report in *The Sun*. Set designers at Pinewood were enlisted to make-over the star's trailer into a '$450,000 Bedouin tent', complete with huge cushions, colourful giant rugs and incense burners. (According to 'an insider', Depp is 'a real hippy at heart'.) The final flourish was the Jolly Roger – the pirate's skull-and-crossbones flag – flying from the roof of his trailer, according to *Empire*.

The original novel *Charlie and the Chocolate Factory* tells the story of Charlie Bucket (*Finding Neverland*'s Freddie Highmore in Burton's movie), who, along with four spoiled children (played by Annasophia Robb, Julia Winter, Philip Wiegratz and Jordan Fry), wins a Golden Ticket allowing access to Willy Wonka's mysterious chocolate factory. What no one realises is that Wonka (Depp) is looking for a worthy successor to run his factory, and, by a literal process of elimination, each of the badly-behaved kids is removed from the competition – learning an important (if fatal) life-lesson from the factory workers, the Oompa-Loompas (all played by a digitally manipulated four-foot-four actor, Deep Roy). In the end, only Charlie is left to replace Wonka.

Screenwriter John August purposely avoided watching the 1971 movie until two weeks after handing in the first draft of his screenplay, freshly adapted from Dahl's novel. He saw Charlie and Wonka as characters who needed each other in their lives: 'Wonka is lacking the things that Charlie has, a family. He has all the chocolate in the world, but he doesn't have somebody to love him. Charlie is the person who pushes him far enough that he actually changes…'

It resulted in Burton and August developing a new backstory for Willy Wonka, lacking from both the source novel and the first film. The role of Wonka's domineering dentist father, who loathes candy, was ideal for veteran screen villain Christopher Lee, who had previously featured in Burton's *Sleepy Hollow*. To Burton, this departure offered 'some possibility of why he is the way he is, without delving too deeply into it. Why is he behaving this way and what's behind it?'

Shooting started in June 2004 in the UK, utilising between five and seven soundstages at any one time, including the giant James Bond soundstage at Pinewood Studios. From the beginning, there was a determination to keep the by-now film-industry standard computer-generated imagery (CGI) to a minimum. This meant production designer Alex McDowell had to build traditional giant sets instead of working with huge bluescreens. McDowell even resorted to classic cinematic stand-bys like over-sized props for some of the Oompa Loompa scenes. To Depp – never a fan of CG trickery – this came as a great relief. 'Being in the real place gives you things to play off of,' he said. 'In a way, we have the opportunity to do what they did all those years ago on *The Wizard of Oz*, to be really in that world.'

The result was a chocolate river that dominated Pinewood's largest soundstage, with its 200,000 gallons of 'chocolate' actually made from a thickening agent used in toothpaste and baked beans mixed with food dye. The river was 270 feet long, six feet deep and led to a waterfall which used a further 30,000 gallons of the brown gloop. 'We had a huge flowing chocolate river,' said executive producer Richard Zanuck, 'and an 80-foot waterfall – all for real.' The rest of the movie's design aesthetic was, according to McDowell, 'a visual collision between psychedelic, inflatable pop art and the 1960s Russian-American space race.' Additional sets included the fake jungle in which Wonka discovers the Oompa Loompas (in a flashback), and the Bucket family's hometown, including their own rundown house. 'The movie goes for the surreal,' acknowledged McDowell.

The unique visual style extended to Depp's Willy Wonka. He was keen that his Wonka be very different to that of Gene Wilder, admitting that his own take on the character was 'creepy'. Annasophia Robb, aged eleven, who played Violet in the movie, was impressed with Depp's friendliness on set: 'Johnny's such a normal guy, he treats everyone with the same amount of respect. He invites us to his trailer to make us feel more comfortable with him.' But she admitted that his Marilyn Manson-inspired performance was terrifying, once the cameras started rolling.

Depp's Wonka, attired in thick, bug-eyed sunglasses and purple rubber gloves, carrying a transparent cane filled with candy, is just the latest in his long line of eccentric characters. 'We always thought of Willy Wonka as the Citizen Kane or Howard Hughes of candy,' claimed Burton of his and Depp's approach to the character. '[He's] somebody who has problems connecting with people. [He's] sad and slightly sinister, but not bad…'

Depp's own take on Wonka made further allusion to paranoid multi-millionaire Howard Hughes: 'I think that Wonka puts on his game face in front of people, but underneath he has an anxiety about contact or closeness. I believe he's a germophobe, which is why he wears gloves, and in addition to the gloves it's as if he's wearing a mask.' As an actor who hides behind character masks, this characterisation of Wonka as a sad, scared man acting out a role appealed to Depp. 'There are moments during the tour [of the factory] when we catch Wonka acting, and acting badly, literally reading off cue cards. I think he's struggling to put on an act and keep a smile…'

In designing a visual look for Wonka, Depp had some precise ideas in mind that related directly to the character. 'The hair was one of those elements I saw clearly very early on,' he explained. 'The top hat was easy, because that came right from the Quentin Blake drawings, but the hair I imagined as a kind of Prince Valiant "do" – high bangs and a bob, extreme and very unflattering, but something that Wonka probably thinks is cool because he's been locked away for such a long time and doesn't know any better, like the outdated slang he uses.'

'Johnny is bizarre and great as Willy,' said executive producer Zanuck. 'He plays it and gives it as much spin, but in an entirely different way from *Pirates*. It's a bizarre performance, but appropriately bizarre.'

But the original movie Wonka, Gene Wilder, was critical of the idea of remaking the film that contained what many regard as his signature role. 'It's all about money,' claimed Wilder of the Hollywood trend for updated remakes of classic films. 'It's just some people sitting around thinking, "How can we make some more money?" Why else would you remake *Willy Wonka*? I don't see the point of going back and doing it all over again. I like Johnny Depp, and I appreciate that he has said on record that my shoes will be hard to fill. But I don't know how it will all turn out.'

Despite the new film being a faithful adaptation of the book, rather than a remake of the Wilder film, the veteran actor's reservations were widely reported.

When the movie was released, however, he retracted his criticism and actually praised Depp's turn as Wonka, declaring the actor to be the perfect choice. 'If I were going to cast the movie,' Wilder declared magnanimously, 'I would cast Johnny Depp as Willy Wonka because I think he is wonderful. Mysterious – always – and magical.'

Wilder's initial criticism wasn't the only controversy to dog the movie. Depp felt compelled to deny basing his Wonka on the mannerisms and speech patterns of troubled pop star Michael Jackson, then recently acquitted on child abuse charges.

'It never entered my mind,' claimed Depp. 'Michael Jackson loves children, but Willy Wonka doesn't.' Instead, he said his true inspirations were US children's TV hosts Captain Kangaroo, Mr. Rogers and Uncle Al, who had mesmerised him as a child. 'There were memories I have as a little kid watching children's shows and children show hosts. I distinctly remember thinking their speech pattern was strange.'

Depp also credited his own children with the development of Wonka's unusual voice, which he came up with while playing with his daughter, Lily-Rose Melody. He emphasised how he always auditions his child-friendly characters in front of his own kids.

'A lot of times what happens is you come up with these ideas and you never get to try them until a read through,' he explained. 'I often play Barbies with Lily-Rose. Sometimes I will put on an accent and she'll say, "Daddy don't use that voice." Then, we were playing one day and I started to use my Wonka voice, and she kinda lit up a bit, like, "Where's that coming from?" I thought, "All right, I think I'm on the right

Depp claimed his true inspirations for the role of Willy Wonka were US children's TV hosts Captain Kangaroo, Mr. Rogers and Uncle Al, who had mesmerised him as a child.

track here." Children are always the most honest audience you'll get.'

However, there was one other piece of Wonka-related feedback that he really didn't require. 'Whenever Lily-Rose and Jack would watch the Gene Wilder film on DVD, I would immediately run out of the room because I didn't want to be influenced by his performance one way or the other.'

Released to US cinemas at the same time that another children's favourite, the latest Harry Potter novel, hit the nation's bookshelves, *Charlie and the Chocolate Factory* grossed $56 million on its 15 July 2005 opening weekend. As with so many remakes, or 're-imaginings', of classic films, it was greeted by mixed reviews.

Joe Morgenstern, in the *Wall Street Journal*, was one of many critics who concluded that the undoubted charm of Burton's movie 'gradually gives way to a peculiar state that I can only describe as engagement without enjoyment.' Similarly, Ann Hornaday of the *Washington Post* commented, 'The film's strenuous efforts at becoming a camp classic eventually begin to wear thin.' However, Jami Bernard in the *New York Daily News* confidently predicted the movie would 'delight children, annoy fans of the 1971 version . . . and perplex everyone else.'

A. O. Scott of the *New York Times* called this second adaptation of Roald Dahl's novel 'wondrous and flawed'. Veteran critic Kenneth Turan, in the *Los Angeles Times*, opened his review by remarking, 'When it comes to confections, Tim Burton has confessed, his preference is "dark, bitter chocolate". Which is not exactly a surprise. The director's visionary, phantasmagorical version of *Charlie and the Chocolate Factory* is equally dark and, if not exactly bitter, unapologetically, relentlessly strange. Burton's gifts ensure you won't be able to take your eyes off the screen, but that doesn't necessarily mean you'll be happy with what you're seeing.'

Charlie and the Chocolate Factory made the biggest July opening for a Warner Bros. film ever, surpassing *Terminator 3: Rise of the Machines'* $44 million in 2003, and the biggest opening for any movie starring Johnny Depp, surpassing his *Pirates of the Caribbean: The Curse of the Black Pearl*, which debuted in 2003 with $46.6 million.

It also fuelled a seven per cent, year-on-year increase in box-office takings, to the delight of movie executives who had been facing a terrible year at the box office. By the end of 2005, it had grossed in excess of $206 million in the US and an additional £37 million in the UK.

In the autumn of 2005, Johnny Depp narrated a BBC Radio 2 documentary on the life of James Dean, one of his acting idols. It was made to mark the 50th anniversary of Dean's untimely death in a car crash in California.

Over a year earlier, during the shooting of *Charlie and the Chocolate Factory*, he narrowly avoided his own James Dean moment when he crashed his brand new Mercedes into the gates of his French villa. According to reports, Depp sped the $28,000 sports car up to the electric gates outside his hideaway home in Plan De La Tour on the Cote D'Azur. Then, as an eyewitness described: 'We saw Johnny pull up outside his house going at quite a speed. He put the car in reverse but can't have been paying attention because he drove straight into the side of the gate. He knocked the gates' electric motor straight off the wall and left an almighty dent in the back of the car. Judging by the look on his face he got quite a fright.' The actor faced an $18,000 repair bill to fix both the car and the damaged electric gates.

In this first decade of the 21st century, Johnny Depp was taking stock of his life. Ever since the 1993 death of River Phoenix at his co-owned LA nightclub, the Viper Room, he had been reducing his involvement in the running of the venue. His partner in the venture, Anthony Fox, had sued Depp in 2001, accusing him of manipulating the Viper Room's financial records and pocketing the profits – an odd accusation against an actor who could command up to $20 million per film.

The attorney who represented Fox in his lawsuit, one David Eskevius, asserted, 'Anthony Fox is saying that Johnny Depp took advantage of him and basically stole the business from him.' Around Christmas 2001, Fox mysteriously disappeared, yet the case against Depp proceeded. According to the Celebrity Justice section of the Warner Bros. web site, the judge in the case eventually ruled that 'Defendant Depp… breached his fiduciary duties to the corporation and to Fox as a minority shareholder. The facts establish persistent and pervasive fraud and mismanagement and abuse of authority.'

Curiously, this outcome was not widely reported. Meanwhile, the court case and the disappearance of Fox just added to Depp's worries that the venue – which, in the 1940s, had been a gambling and drug den called the Melody Room, controlled by Bugsy Siegel and his associates – might be cursed. After all, this was the place where River Phoenix had met his tragic and untimely end . . .

Another of Fox's lawyers, Jay Stein, suspected that his client may have been murdered or kidnapped, or had committed suicide, and there was even a suggestion that the Mafia may have been involved. As Stein explained, 'There has been no trace of him, no financial or other activity to say whether he's alive.'

By late 2004, two years after Fox vanished, Depp quietly signed over his interest in the club to Fox's nineteen-year-old daughter, Amanda, who had plans to sell the venue.

Following these events, the unexpected suicide of Hunter S. Thompson in February 2005 delivered a further shock to Depp – who'd portrayed the controversial writer's alter ego, Raoul Duke, in the movie of *Fear and Loathing in Las Vegas*. He'd become a close friend of Thompson, hanging out at the writer's remote home in Woody Creek, Aspen, Colorado.

Thompson's body was discovered by his son, Juan. The 67-year-old author had died as the result of a single self-inflicted shotgun wound. Depp was one of many friends who attended what was described as a 'private memorial party' shortly after his death. Also in attendance was John Cusack, who'd appeared with Depp and Hunter in a 2003 documentary on the writer called *Breakfast with Hunter*.

The idea of a follow-up to *Fear and Loathing in Las Vegas* had been around for a while, but Thompson's death focused Depp's mind on the project. His *Fear and Loathing* co-star Benicio Del Toro had been lined up to co-star in and direct *The Rum Diary*, taken from another semi-autobiographical Thompson novel, written in 1959. It recounted the tale of how the 22-year-old Thompson was fired for kicking a candy machine at a small-town newspaper, fled to Puerto Rico, and took up a vagrant journalist lifestyle. However, by mid-2006 the project was set to be written and directed by *Withnail and I*'s Bruce Robinson instead.

During his time in Puerto Rico, Thompson covered cockfights, worked as a male model for Bacardi rum and wrote freelance articles. He lived in a wooden beach shack in Loiza, a community of mostly Yoruba slave descendants, a 25-minute drive from the capital. Depp was to play Paul Kemp, the Thompson character in the novel who winds up in Puerto Rico. He joins *The San Juan Daily News* in the midst of financial problems, on an island aflame with political turmoil. Not published until 1998, *The Rum Diary* features a period in Thompson's life before the infamy that followed the publication of *Fear and Loathing in Las Vegas*. Thompson had been planning his first visit back to Puerto Rico when the cast and crew assembled, to act as consultant. 'We're going to come down and take over the island,' he'd promised. Now, when the film went ahead, it would have to be without him.

Depp's personal affection for Hunter S. Thompson led to him spending $2.5 million of his own money, to give the author a suitably fiery send-off. He fulfilled Thompson's wish that his ashes should be fired into the air above his Woody Creek compound. 'We had talked a couple of times about his last wishes to be shot out of a cannon of his own design,' Depp explained to the Associated Press. 'All I'm doing is trying to make sure his last wish comes true. I just want to send my pal out the way he wants to go out.'

Depp hired a Hollywood party planner to put together the memorial event, but he took charge of the funding and construction of the cannon project. 'We're gonna give it our best shot, as it were,' he said at the time. 'Hunter's last wish was to have his remains fired out of a 150 foot cannon. That's the weird thing, you have to build the cannon. You have to actually design and engineer and build a cannon for Hunter.'

According to *The New York Post*, the memorial cannon, unveiled on 21 August, six months after the author's suicide, had been modelled on Thompson's Gonzo logo: a clenched fist, made symmetrical by the addition of a second thumb perched over a dagger. A star-studded party was held instead of a wake, once again fulfilling the author's wishes. Around 250 guests attended, including Depp, his Oscar rival Sean Penn, Bill Murray (who also played Thompson in a movie, *Where the Buffalo Roam*), country singer Lyle Lovett and the Nitty Gritty Dirt Band. Depp would appear along with Penn, Murray and others in a documentary tribute to Thompson entitled, *Buy The Ticket, Take The Ride*.

Thompson's widow, Anita, insisted that the upbeat celebration was exactly what her husband would have wanted. 'No crying, no tears, only celebration. He wanted people to celebrate. He envisioned it to be a beautiful party. The most amazing people would be there. His friends would celebrate his life. And he was even specific that there would be clinking of ice and whisky.'

As Thompson's ashes were fired from a 150-foot tower, Depp briefly addressed the crowd: 'It's nice to be able to give a little something back. Hunter, this is for you.' Later, he played his guitar and sang 'My Old Kentucky Home' with Lyle Lovett and Jimmy Ibbotson of the Nitty Gritty Dirt Band. As Anita Thompson watched her husband's ashes join the fireworks in the sky, she observed, 'He loved explosions.'

The phenomenal success of *Pirates of the Caribbean* meant that a sequel was inevitable. Depp, however, was surprised to find himself fronting a bona fide franchise as producer Jerry Bruckheimer began to talk of filming not one, but two *Pirates* sequels back-to-back in 2005. This would follow the successful example set by the *Matrix* and *Lord of the Rings* trilogies. Signed up for the sequels, with the working subtitles *Dead Man's Chest* and *Uncharted Waters*, were producer Jerry Bruckheimer, director Gore Verbinski, writers Terry Rossio and Ted Elliott, and on-screen talent Depp, Orlando Bloom and Keira Knightley.

'I went through a decompression period after the first film. If you're really connected with a character to some degree you miss the guy,' said Depp, welcoming a return to Jack Sparrow. 'You miss being that person. The only thing that was in the back of my mind was the hope that there would be a sequel some day, so that I could meet him again.'

Despite being wary of popular acclaim, Depp had come to appreciate the effect Sparrow had on audiences. 'I'm very thankful,' he said of the positive feedback. 'I'm very grateful for this past year, and certainly the things that have happened, I had no expectations at all. Certainly not nominations of any sort. So I'm very touched, very moved.'

This time round, Brit actor Bill Nighy was cast as Davy Jones, the villain of *Dead Man's Chest*, augmented by CG additions such as an octopus-like head, a lobster's claw and tentacles, while *Uncharted Waters*, would see Hong Kong action star Chow Yun Fat take the role of notorious pirate captain Sao Feng.

Shooting on the first *Pirates* sequel was not trouble free, however. In April 2005, the *Los Angeles Times* reported that a controversy on the Caribbean island of Bataka, Dominica was causing headaches for the production. Members of the 3,500-strong native Carib tribe called on fellow members to boycott the production because of a scene in which Depp's character, Captain Sparrow, was to be captured and tied to a skewer with fruits and vegetables 'like a shish kebab'. Chief Charles Williams told the *L.A. Times* that the film perpetuated the myth that the Caribs were cannibals. 'Today, that myth, that stigma is still alive… Disney wants to popularise that stigma one more time, this time through film, and film is a powerful tool of propaganda.'

Disney had hired about 400 Dominican locals to work on the sequel, many as extras at $95 a day. 'Shame on us that for a few dollars we are betraying our flesh and blood,' Williams told the *L.A. Times*. Disney executives attempted to downplay the uproar by insisting the scene was intended to be light-hearted, and in no way reflected the history of Bataka.

Still, *Pirates of the Caribbean 2* and *3* were set to be the hit movies of the summers of 2006 and 2007, making an even bigger star of Johnny Depp. 'Some people could look at it and say, "Ah-ha, Depp's sold out!"' said the star of his commitment to a commercial franchise. 'I don't believe that I have. I wanted to play Captain Jack again because he's so much fun to play and there's so much to explore. I'd keep going. If they want to do *Pirates 6* and *7*, I'm there!'

At halfway through the first decade of the 21st Century, Johnny Depp remained as busy as ever. He provided the voice of Victor in *Tim Burton's Corpse Bride*, the stop-motion animated follow-up to *The Nightmare Before Christmas*, the puppet character's looks clearly modelled on the actor's distinctive visage. Caroline Thompson, who wrote the screenplay for *Edward Scissorhands*, scripted *Corpse Bride* for Burton, while other vocal performers included Depp's *Charlie and the Chocolate Factory* co-stars Helena Bonham-Carter and Christopher Lee, alongside

Albert Finney and Emily Watson.

Corpse Bride was co-directed by Burton and Mike Johnson. For Burton, old-fashioned stop-motion animation was the ideal medium for his new gothic tale. 'I remember a few years ago [Dreamworks Animation CEO Jeffrey] Katzenberg declared cell animation dead,' he confided to *Dreamwatch* magazine. 'I think it's unfortunate when people declare any artform dead . . . with stop-motion there is that hand-made feel that's just kind of subconscious and visceral about people moving an inanimate object and bringing life to it. There is something special about that.'

There was something special about Johnny Depp, too, according to Burton. 'Johnny and I have this process where we sort of speak in the abstract to each other and yet can still understand each other,' the director explained. 'But we never like to use one reference. Like, I never say to Johnny, "Make it like this . . ." We like the same kinds of things. He's a character actor in a leading man's body. He's ready to do anything. He's probably more like Lon Chaney (the silent cinema's 'man of a thousand faces') than a leading man. He wants to transform. He likes to be different characters in different movies, so you know, he's an actor that you would think about, perhaps even for female roles. He could do it all. He's very versatile that way.'

Released on 23 September 2005 in the US, and 21 October 2005 in the UK, *Corpse Bride* had grossed over $52.5 million (more than *The Nightmare Before Christmas*) in the US by November 2005, with a further £4.1 million from the UK.

The stop-motion film drew almost uniformly rave reviews. Wesley Morris of *The Boston Globe* noted that Burton 'has rarely been in brisker, friskier form. This picture is 77 minutes, and while not all of them whiz by, they don't feel laden, either . . . The picture's industrious expressionism alone makes you forget the time.'

Bruce Westbrook of *The Houston Chronicle* called *Corpse Bride* 'the best-looking stop-motion animation film ever'. High praise indeed. Roger Ebert, in *The*

In Tim Burton's Corpse Bride, the puppet character Victor Van Dort, vocalised by Depp, was clearly modelled on the actor's distinctive visage.

Chicago Sun-Times, observed that *Corpse Bride* was 'not the macabre horror story the title suggests, but a sweet and visually lovely tale of love lost.' Eleanor Ringel Gillespie wrote in the *Atlanta Journal-Constitution*, 'The movie is a bit betwixt and between – whimsical but eerie, funny but melancholy. That said, *Corpse Bride* truly is like nothing else at the movies these days.'

October 2005 also saw the release on DVD of *Happily Ever After*, a French movie originally titled *Ils se marièrent et eurent beaucoup d'enfants* (literally, 'They Married and Had Many Children'). It saw Depp playing a cheeky brief cameo as Charlotte Gainsbourg's perfect fantasy man, for director Yvan Attal. His *Ninth Gate* co-star Emmanuelle Seigner also featured in the film.

Universal also called on Depp's much-in-demand services for a very different, challenging role, in an adaptation of Jean-Dominique Bauby's autobiography *The Diving Bell and the Butterfly* for director Julian Schnabel (*Before Night Falls*). Bauby, the editor of *Elle France*, suffered a stroke in 1995, at the age of 43, that left his body completely paralysed except for his left eye, while his mind remained unaffected ('locked-in syndrome'). Despite his affliction, Bauby used his eye to blink out a memoir, letter by letter, then tragically died two days after it was published. The book describes his pre-stroke life, what it was like to be a prisoner inside his now useless body, and imagined journeys to exotic places he'd never visited.

Depp was also connected with Gregory David Roberts' autobiographical script for *Shantaram*. It tells the tale of Lindsay, a heroin addict incarcerated for robbery who escapes prison in Australia and reinvents himself as a doctor in the slums of Mumbai/Bombay. His underworld connections eventually lead him to fight alongside the Mujaheddin rebels in Afghanistan against the Russians. 'He became known as the Gentleman Bandit in Australia because he never killed anyone, at least not in bank robberies,' Depp said of Roberts to Australia's *Sunday Herald Sun*. 'He's written this absolutely beautiful, poetic, allegorical, super thick, 1000 page novel that tore the top of my head off when I read it. It's an intense read. I was astounded. We just got our first draft of the screenplay and it's very, very exciting. It's going to be great.'

Another part mooted for Depp was that of eccentric shock-rocker Ozzy Osbourne, now famous for the reality TV sitcom *The Osbournes*. It's easy to see how Depp's portrayal of Ozzy could be a riff on his Jack Sparrow, but the idea for him to play the part had come from Osbourne's kids, Jack and Kelly. Ozzy himself admitted, 'We're talking to Johnny but it's not 100 per cent...', though Depp reportedly claimed Ozzy Osbourne is 'a deeply fascinating human being', and that he was 'desperate' to star in any biopic. The movie project was being developed by Sharon Osbourne, the former Black Sabbath frontman's wife. Depp was also talked of as a possible Michael Hutchence in a biopic of the tragic INXS frontman.

Equally unlikely sounding was a revival of Terry Gilliam's *The Man Who Killed Don Quixote*. The director was hoping his fantasy movie *The Brothers Grimm* would bring him enough Hollywood success to revive the project. 'I'm always trying to go back and do my Don Quixote film,' admitted Gilliam, while remaining realistic about the hurdles he faced. 'I can't get my script back,' he lamented. 'The German investors in the original film are suing the French investors who are holding the script ransom!'

With Depp's increasing fame, Gilliam felt he could use the actor's name to get the film back on track. 'I emailed Johnny to tell him I would soon be lying to the

world that he's back on board for the film. Suddenly people want to put money into a Johnny Depp film.' He insisted that Depp 'wants to do Sancho Panza,' the deluded Don Quixote's bemused sidekick. 'The part was written for him. Johnny is a huge fan of *Monty Python*. He told me he always wanted to be a Python and that was how he planned to do his Sancho.'

Gilliam had another project starring Depp in development. International financiers were willing to plough $45 million into his proposed film of Neil Gaiman and Terry Pratchett's bestseller *Good Omens*, starring Depp as a demon and Robin Williams as an angel. However, the American side of the financing, the final $15 million, could not be found. Gilliam told *US* magazine: 'I couldn't get $15 million with Johnny and Robin . . . These two guys, who would have been brilliant, were not worth $15 million in America. That was the moment where I went, "I don't understand this game. I don't understand this town [Hollywood]. I don't understand any of the rules. All I know is I don't like it."'

But Johnny Depp's work rate has certainly increased in recent years, with an inevitably higher visibility factor as the downside for the reluctant star. Tim Burton went so far as to credit *Pirates* with having 'saved' his quirky career. Recalling how he'd had to fight with fearful studio bosses to get Depp into *Edward Scissorhands*,

Johnny Depp was delighted to return to Pirates of the Caribbean: Dead Man's Chest.
'I wanted to play Captain Jack again because he's so much fun to play.'

he told *Empire*: 'Depp's always been known as a good actor, but you know, Hollywood is a very safe community, and it's like their attitude towards me: they think he is a good actor but they are also a little bit worried because he likes to transform himself. I hope and I think that they see an integrity to him and, except in my movies, they like the way he looks. Of course ever since the *Pirates* movie made money it's been different, because they see that as meaningful.'

In fact, Johnny Depp's star had risen so high, he made the Top Ten list in *Forbes* magazine's 2005 Celebrity 100 list, topped by TV chat show host Oprah Winfrey. Depp found himself at number seven, sandwiched between director Steven Spielberg at six and pop superstar Madonna at eight. The only other actors in the Top Ten were Mel Gibson at number three, following the success of his movie *The Passion of the Christ*, and Tom Cruise at number ten.

With his workload mounting, Depp was far more concerned with maintaining his home life. 'I'm more relaxed since I met Vanessa,' he admitted. 'I have more distance and because I have more distance I have more perspective. Before, I just felt as if I couldn't quite figure out my place. When you're living in Hollywood all the time you're constantly in that game, and you're susceptible to the pressures of success and the box office. I couldn't stand it because I had no interest in that.'

Depp had been tagged in the past as an actor who didn't care about commercial

*With no wedding in sight, Depp and Vanessa Paradis are content to be parents to
Lily-Rose and Jack and to continue with their respective careers...*

success. That wasn't strictly true. He was clearly not afraid of playing the Hollywood blockbuster game when it suited him. 'It wasn't that I was rejecting Hollywood; I was rejecting the idea of being a product. Then there's that great big question mark: What's it all about? What's it all for? You start thinking, "Am I just an actor? A puppet? Am I one of those ambitious cretins who's just looking for accolades and applause and recognition?" I'm happy to say I found out that I'm not.'

'I'd always wanted a film to do well but not at the cost of creative compromise,' he elaborated. 'I think that my kids have grounded me to the degree that I can step back and watch it all from afar. It feels really good.'

But he could never feel good about the paparazzi's interest in his family. He'd warned photographers before that, while he was fair game, his kids were strictly off limits. However, Depp felt he had to reinforce that warning in his inimitable wild-man style: 'I'm warning the paparazzi, if you're going to get me have a long lens and make sure you're really far away because if I get my hands on you it could get ugly. I don't care if they take my photo – although I don't know why anyone needs another picture of me. I don't care if they take Vanessa's photo, but when they take my kids, that I can't support. If I catch them I'll bite their noses off and swallow it.'

Depp attacked the press again in November 2005, after Kate Moss was dropped by major fashion chains Chanel, Burberry and H&M, following her exposure for abusing cocaine. 'It was unbelievably unfair the way she was treated,' said Depp of the press campaign against Moss. 'She was dragged through the mud. She's not running for office and she ain't looking to be the next Messiah. I think Kate should live her life how she wants to. She's no dummy, man.' Depp even admitted he still had feelings for his former partner. 'She's a great girl and I care about her a great deal.'

Whether Vanessa Paradis and Johnny Depp will marry has often been speculated upon, but a ceremony and a piece of legal paperwork didn't seem uppermost in Depp's mind. 'I consider Vanessa and I already married,' he said. 'We just haven't gone through the formalities, signing papers and all that, but to me and to her, we're husband and wife. The thing is, Vanessa has a great last name and I'd hate to ruin it. Paradis-Depp? It just doesn't have a ring to it. However, when the kids are old enough, we'd like to have a three day gypsy wedding.'

Johnny Depp has often been the best thing in middling films (*Nick of Time, The Astronaut's Wife, Secret Window*), the star turn in independent art-house movies (*The Man Who Cried, Before Night Falls, The Libertine*), the star of quirky cult movies (*Sleepy Hollow, From Hell, Once Upon a Time in Mexico*) or the acclaimed front man of family-friendly blockbusters (*Pirates of the Caribbean, Charlie and the Chocolate Factory*). Whatever the film, he has maintained the secret of always managing to do things his own way.

'I was in it for the long haul,' says Depp of the strategy that has made him not only one of the best actors of his generation, but one of the big screen's all-time unique talents. 'I decided early on to be patient and wait for the roles that interested me, not the roles that would advance my career. I never wanted to be remembered for being a star.'

Filmography

Nightmare on Elm Street (1984)
USA 1984 91 minutes. Directed by Wes Craven.
Screenplay by Wes Craven. Production Company: New
Line Cinema/Media Home Entertainment/Smart Egg
Picture for The Elm Street Venture.
Cast: John Saxon (Lieutenant Thompson), Ronee
Blakley (Marge Thompson), Heather Langenkamp
(Nancy Thompson), Amanda Wyss (Tina Gray), Nick
Corri (Rod Lane), Johnny Depp (Glen Lantz), Robert
Englund (Freddy Krueger).

Private Resort (1985)
USA 1985 79 minutes. Directed by George Bowers.
Screenplay by Gordon Mitchell. Story by Ken Segull and
Alann Wenkus and Gordon Mitchell.
Production Company: Tri Star Pictures.
Cast: Rob Morrow (Ben), Johnny Depp (Jack), Emily
Longstreth (Patti), Karyn O'Bryan (Dana), Hector
Elizondon (The Maestro), Dody Goodman (Mrs
Rawlings), Tony Azito (Reeves), Hilary Shapiro (Shirley),
Leslie Easterbrook (Bobbie Sue).

Slow Burn (TV, 1986)
USA 1986 94 minutes. Directed by Matthew Chapman.
Screenplay by Matthew Chapman.
Production Company: Castles Burning Productions in
association with MCA Pay TV Programming, Inc.
Cast: Eric Roberts (Jacob Asch), Beverly D'Angelo (Laine
Fleischer), Dennis Lipscomb (Ron McDonald),
Raymond J. Barry (Gerald McMurtry), Ann Schedeen
(Mona), Emily Longstreth (Pam Draper), Johnny Depp
(Donnie Fleischer), Henry Gibson (Robert).

Platoon (1986)
USA 1986 120 minutes. Directed by Oliver Stone.
Screenplay by Oliver Stone. Production Company:
Hemdale Film Corporation.
Cast: Tom Berenger (Sergeant Barnes), Willem Dafoe
(Sergeant Elias), Charlie Sheen (Chris Taylor), Forest
Whitaker (Big Harold), Francesco Quinn (Rhah), John
C. McGinley (Sergeant O'Neill), Richard Edson (Sal),
Kevin Dillon (Bunny), Reggie Johnson (Junior), Keith
David (King), Johnny Depp (Lerner).

21 Jump Street (TV, 4 series, 1987-90)
Pilot: "21 Jump Street"
USA 1987 120 minutes. Directed by Kim Manners.
Screenplay by Patrick Hasburgh.
Series created by Patrick Hasburgh & Stephen J.
Cannell. Production Company: Stephen J. Cannell
Productions Inc.
Cast: Johnny Depp (Tom Hanson), Frederic Forrest
(Captain Jenko), Holly Robinson (Judy Hoffs), Peter
DeLuise (Doug Penhall), Dustin Nguyen (H. T. Ioki).
Series: "21 Jump Street", 1987-1991, 50 minute
episodes, 103 episodes, 5 seasons.
Regular Cast: Johnny Depp (Officer Tom Hanson
[seasons 1-4]), Holly Robinson (Detective Judy Hoffs),
Peter DeLuise (Officer Doug Penhall).

Cry Baby (1990)
USA 1990 85 minutes. Directed by John Waters.
Screenplay by John Waters. Production Company:
Imagine Entertainment.
Cast: Johnny Depp (Cry Baby), Amy Locane (Allison),
Susan Tyrell (Ramona), Polly Bergen (Mrs Vernon-
Williams), Iggy Pop (Belverdere), Ricki Lake (Pepper),
Traci Lords (Wanda), Troy Donahue (Hatchet's Father),
Mink Stole (Hatchet's Mother), Joe Dallesandro
(Milton's Father), Patricia Hearst (Wanda's Mother),
Willem Dafoe (Hateful Guard).

Edward Scissorhands (1990)
USA 1990 90 minutes. Directed by Tim Burton.
Screenplay by Caroline Thompson, based on a story by
Tim Burton and Caroline Thompson.
Production Company: Twentieth Century Fox.
Cast: Johnny Depp (Edward Scissorhands), Winona
Ryder (Kim Boggs), Dianne Wiest (Peg Boggs), Anthony
Michael Hall (Jim), Kathy Baker (Joyce Monroe), Robert
Oliveri (Kevin Boggs), Vincent Price (The Inventor).

Freddy's Dead: The Final Nightmare (1991, cameo)
USA 1991 89 minutes. 3D Sequence. Directed by
Rachael Talalay. Screenplay by Michael DeLuca, based
on a story by Rachael Talalay. Production Company:
New Line Cinema.
Cast: Robert Englund (Freddy Krueger), Lisa Zane
(Maggie Burroughs), Shon Greenblatt (John), Yaphet
Kotto (Doc), Tom Arnold (Childless Man), Mrs Tom
Arnold aka Roseanne Barr (Childless Woman), Oprah
Noodlemantra [aka Johnny Depp] (Teenager on TV).

Arizona Dream (1991)
USA/France 1991 141 minutes. Directed by Emir
Kusturica. Screenplay by David Atkins, based on a story
by David Atkins and Emir Kusturica.
Production Company: Constellation/UGC/Hachette
Première. With the participation of Ministére de la
Culture et de la Communication (Centre National de la
Cinématographie).
Cast: Johnny Depp (Axel Blakmar), Jerry Lewis (Leo
Sweetie), Faye Dunaway (Elaine), Lili Taylor (Grace),
Vincent Gallo (Paul Blakmar), Michael J. Pollard
(Fabian), Sal Jenco (Man at Phone), Iggy Pop (Man with
Pumpkin).

Benny & Joon (1993)
USA 1993 99 minutes. Directed by Jeremiah Chechik.
Screenplay by Barry Berman, based on a story by Barry
Berman and Leslie McNeil. Production Company: MGM.
Cast: Johnny Depp (Sam), Mary Stuart Masterson (Joon
Pearl), Aidan Quinn (Benny Pearl), Julianne Moore
(Ruthie), Oliver Platt (Eric), Dan Hedaya (Thomas),
William H. Macy (Randy Burch).

What's Eating Gilbert Grape? (1993)
USA 1993 118 minutes. Directed by Lasse Hallestrom.
Screenplay by Peter Hedges, based on his novel.

Production Company: Paramount.
Cast: Johnny Depp (Gilbert Grape), Juliette Lewis (Becy), Mary Steenburgen (Betty Carver), Leonardo DiCaprio (Arnie Grape), John C. Reilly (Tucker Van Dyke), Darlene Cates (Bonnie Grape), Laura Harrington (Amy Grape), Mary Kate Schellhardt (Ellen Grape).

Ed Wood (1994)
USA 1994 127 minutes. Black and white. Directed by Tim Burton. Screenplay by Scott Alexander and Larry Karaszewski, based on the book *Nightmare of Ecstasy* by Rudolph Grey.
Production Company: Buena Vista.
Cast: Johnny Depp (Ed Wood), Martin Landau (Bela Lugosi), Sarah Jessica Parker (Dolores Fuller), Patricia Arquette (Kathy O'Hara), Jeffrey Jones (Criswell), G. D. Spradlin (Reverend Lemon), Vincent D'Onofrio (Orson Welles), Bill Murray (Bunny Breckinridge), Lisa Marie (Vampira), George "The Animal" Steele (Tor Johnson), Juliet Landau (Loretta King).

Don Juan DeMarco (1994)
USA 1994 97 minutes. Directed by Jeremy Leven.
Screenplay by Jeremy Leven. Production Company: New Line Productions for American Zoetrope.
Cast: Johnny Depp (Don Juan DeMarco), Marlon Brando (Jack Mickler), Faye Dunaway (Marilyn Mickler), Bob Dishy (Dr Paul Showalter), Geraldine Pailhas (Dona Ana), Talisa Soto (Dona Julia).

Nick of Time (1995)
USA 1995. 95 minutes.
Directed by John Badham.
Screenplay by Patrick Sheane and Ebbe Roe Smith.
Production Company: Paramount Pictures.
Cast: Johnny Depp (Gene Watson), Christopher Walken (Mr Smith), Roma Maffia (Ms Jones), Charles Dutton (Huey), Marsha Mason (Eleanor Grant), Peter Strauss (Mr Grant), Gloria Reuben (Krista Brooks), Courtney Chase (Lynn Watson).

Divine Rapture (1995, uncompleted)
USA 1995. 20 minutes of footage shot. Directed by Thom Eberhardt. Screenplay by Thom Eberhardt.
Production Company: Cinefin.
Cast: Johnny Depp, Marlon Brando, Debra Winger, John Hurt.

Dead Man (1996)
USA 1996 134 minutes. Black and white. Directed by Jim Jarmusch. Screenplay by Jim Jarmusch.
Production Company: A 12 Gauge Production with Pandora Film, JVC, Newmarket Capital Group and LP.
Cast: Johnny Depp (William Blake), Crispin Glover (The Fireman), John Hurt (John Scholfield), Robert Mitchum (John Dickson), Gabriel Byrne (Charlie Dickson), Iggy Pop (Salvatore "Sally" Jenko).

Donnie Brasco
USA 1997 127 minutes
Directed by Mike Newell
Screenplay by Paul Attanasio, based upon the book Donnie Brasco: My Undercover Life in the Mafia by Joseph D. Pistone and Richard Woodley
Cast: Al Pacino (Lefty), Johnny Depp (Donnie), Michael Madsen (Sonny), Bruno Kirby (Nicky), James Russo (Paulie), Anne Heche (Maggie).

The Brave
USA 1997 120 minutes
Directed by Johnny Depp
Screenplay by Paul McCudden, Johnny Depp & D.P. Depp, based upon the novel Raphael Final Days by Gregory MacDonald
Cast: Johnny Depp (Raphael), Marlon Brando (McCarthy), Marshall Bell (Larry), Elpidia Carrillo (Rita).

Fear and Loathing In Las Vegas
USA 1998 118 minutes
Directed by Terry Gilliam
Screenplay by Terry Gilliam & Tony Grisoni, Tod Davies & Alex Cox, based upon the book by Hunter S. Thompson
Cast: Johnny Depp (Raoul Duke), Benicio Del Toro (Dr. Gonzo), Tobey Maguire (Hitchhiker), Ellen Barkin (Waitress at North Star Café), Christina Ricci (Lucy), Cameron Diaz (Blonde TV Reporter).

The Ninth Gate
USA 1999 133 minutes
Directed by Roman Polanski
Screenplay by John Brownjohn & Enrique Urbizu and Roman Polanski, based upon the novel El Club Dumas by Arturo Pérez-Reverte
Cast Johnny Depp (Dean Corso), Frank Langella (Boris Balkan), Lena Olin (Liana Telfer), Emmanuelle Seigner (The Girl).

The Astronaut's Wife
USA 1999 109 minutes
Directed by Rand Ravich
Screenplay by Rand Ravich
Cast: Johnny Depp (Commander Spencer Armacost), Charlize Theron (Jillian Armacost), Joe Morton (Sherman Reese, NASA Representative).

Sleepy Hollow
USA 1999 105 minutes
Directed by Tim Burton
Screenplay by Andrew Kevin Walker, screen story by Kevin Yagher and Andrew Kevin Walker, based upon the short story by Washington Irvin
Cast: Johnny Depp (Constable Ichabod Crane), Christina Ricci (Katrina Anne Van Tassel), Miranda Richardson (Lady Mary Van Tassel/The Western Woods Crone), Michael Gambon (Baltus Van Tassel), Christopher Lee (Burgomaster).

The Man Who Cried
USA 2000 100 minutes
Directed by Sally Potter
Screenplay by Sally Potter
Cast: Christina Ricci (Suzie), Cate Blanchett (Lola), John Turturro (Dante Dominio), Johnny Depp (Cesar), Harry Dean Stanton (Felix Perlman).

Before Night Falls
USA 2000 133 minutes
Directed by Julian Schnabel
Screenplay by Cunningham O'Keefe & Lázaro Gómez Carriles & Julian Schnabel, based upon the memoir of Reynaldo Arenas
Cast: Javier Bardem (Reinaldo Arenas), Olivier Martinez (Lázaro Gómez Carriles), Andrea Di Stefano (Pepe Malas), Johnny Depp (Bon Bon/Lieutenant Victor), Michael Wincott (Herberto Zorrilla Ochoa).

Chocolat
USA 2000 121 minutes
Directed by Lasse Hallström
Screenplay by Robert Nelson Jacobs, based upon the novel by Joanne Harris
Cast: Juliette Binoche (Vianne Rocher), Alfred Molina (Comte De Reynaud), Carrie-Anne Moss (Caroline Clairmont), John Wood (Guillaume Blerot), Lena Olin (Josephine Muscat), Peter Stormare (Serge Muscat), Leslie Caron (Madame Audel), Victoire Thivisol (Anouk), Judi Dench (Armande Voizin), Johnny Depp (Roux).

Blow
USA 2001 124 minutes
Directed by Ted Demme
Screenplay by David McKenna, Nick Cassavetes, based upon the book by Bruce Porter
Cast: Johnny Depp (George Jung), Penélope Cruz (Mirtha Jung), Franka Potente (Barbara Buckley), Rachel Griffiths (Ermine Jung), Paul Reubens (Derek Foreal), Ray Liotta (Fred Jung).

From Hell
USA 2001 122 minutes
Directed by Albert Hughes, Allen Hughes
Screenplay by Terry Hayes and Rafael Yglesias, based upon the graphic novel by Alan Moore (words) and Eddie Campbell (art)
Cast: Johnny Depp (Inspector Fred Abberline), Heather Graham (Mary Kelly), Ian Holm (Sir William Gull), Robbie Coltrane (Sergeant Peter Godley), Ian Richardson (Sir Charles Warren).

Pirates of the Caribbean: Curse of the Black Pearl
USA 2003 143 minutes
Directed by Gore Verbinski
Screenplay by Ted Elliott & Terry Rossio, screen story by Ted Elliott & Terry Rossio and Stuart Beattie and Jay Wolpert
Cast: Johnny Depp (Jack Sparrow), Geoffrey Rush (Barbossa), Orlando Bloom (Will Turner), Keira Knightley (Elizabeth Swann), Jack Davenport (Norrington), Jonathan Pryce (Governor Weatherby Swann).

Once Upon A Time In Mexico
USA 2003 101 minutes
Directed by Robert Rodriguez
Screenplay by Robert Rodriguez
Cast: Antonio Banderas (El Mariachi), Salma Hayek (Carolina), Johnny Depp (Sands), Mickey Rourke (Billy), Eva Mendes (Ajedrez), Danny Trejo (Cucuy), Enrique Iglesias (Lorenzo), Cheech Marin (Belini), Rubén Blades (Jorge FBI), Willem Dafoe (Barillo).

Secret Window
USA 2004 96 minutes
Directed by David Koepp
Screenplay by David Koepp, based on the short story Secret Window, Secret Garden by Stephen King
Cast: Johnny Depp (Mort Rainey), John Turturro (John Shooter), Maria Bello (Amy Rainey), Timothy Hutton (Ted), Charles S. Dutton (Ken Karsch).

Finding Neverland
USA 2004 106 minutes
Directed by Marc Forster
Screenplay by David Magee, based upon the play by

Allan Knee
Cast: Johnny Depp (J.M. Barrie), Kate Winslet (Sylvia Llewelyn Davies), Julie Christie (Mrs. du Maurier), Nick Roud (George Llewelyn Davies), Radha Mitchell (Mary Barrie), Joe Prospero (Jack Llewelyn Davies), Freddie Highmore (Peter Llewelyn Davies), Dustin Hoffman (Charles Frohman), Kelly Macdonald (Peter Pan).

Happily Ever After/Ils se marièrent et eurent beaucoup d'enfants
France 2004 100 minutes
Directed by Yvan Attal
Screenplay by Yvan Attal
Cast: Charlotte Gainsbourg (Gabrielle), Yvan Attal (Vincent), Alain Chabat (Georges), Emmanuelle Seigner (Nathalie), Anouk Aimée, Claude Berri, Jérôme Bertin, Alain Cohen, Johnny Depp.

The Libertine
USA 2004 114 minutes (130 minutes USA)
Directed by Laurence Dunmore
Screenplay by Stephen Jeffreys, based upon his play
Cast: Johnny Depp (Rochester), Tom Hollander (George Etherege), John Malkovich (King Charles II), Samantha Morton (Elizabeth Barry).

Charlie and the Chocolate Factory
USA 2005 115 minutes
Directed by Tim Burton
Screenplay by John August, based upon the book by Roald Dahl
Cast: Johnny Depp (Willy Wonka), Freddie Highmore (Charlie Bucket).

Tim Burton's Corpse Bride
USA 2005 76 minutes
Directed by Tim Burton, Mike Johnson
Screenplay by John August, Pamela Pettler and Caroline Thompson
Voice Cast: Johnny Depp (Victor Van Dort), Helena Bonham Carter (Corpse Bride).

Pirates of the Caribbean 2: Dead Man's Chest
USA 2006
Directed by Gore Verbinski
Screenplay by Ted Elliott & Terry Rossio
Cast: Johnny Depp (Captain Jack Sparrow), Orlando Bloom (Will Turner), Keira Knightley (Elizabeth Swann).

Pirates of the Caribbean: 3
USA 2007
Directed by Gore Verbinski
Screenplay by Ted Elliott & Terry Rossio
Cast: Johnny Depp (Captain Jack Sparrow), Orlando Bloom (Will Turner), Keira Knightley (Elizabeth Swann).

Shantaram
USA 2007
Directed by Peter Weir
Screenplay by Gregory David Roberts based upon his novel
Cast: Johnny Depp, Emily Watson, Helena Bonham Carter.

The Rum Diary
USA 2008
Directed by Bruce Robinson
Screenplay by Michael Thomas, based upon the book by Hunter S. Thompson
Cast: Johnny Depp (Paul Kemp).